BREMNER

THE COMPLETE BIOGRAPHY

BY
RICHARD SUTCLIFFE

GREAT NORTHERN

For Annie

Great Northern Books
PO Box 213, Ilkley, LS29 9WS
www.greatnorthernbooks.co.uk

ISBN: 978-1905080-91-5

Design and layout: David Burrill

Printed and bound by CPI Group (UK) Ltd, Croydon, CR0 4YY

CIP Data
A catalogue for this book is available from the British Library

CONTENTS

	Foreword, by Simon Grayson	7
	Introduction	10
Chapter 1	Where It All Began	14
Chapter 2	A Foreign Land	17
Chapter 3	The Boss	25
Chapter 4	Small In Stature, Huge In Standing	29
Chapter 5	'World Champions'	38
Chapter 6	Captain Of The Crew	43
Chapter 7	Success With A Smile	52
Chapter 8	Champions, Champions, Champions…	59
Chapter 9	Heartache For Club And Country	68
Chapter 10	Bridesmaid Revisited	81
Chapter 11	It's Almost Cruel	88
	Illustrations I	97
Chapter 12	Stokoe And Salonika	116
Chapter 13	Back To The Summit	126
Chapter 14	The World Stage	137
Chapter 15	Doomed United	151
Chapter 16	Enter, Gentleman Jim	158
Chapter 17	The Hull Truth	169
Chapter 18	Calling Time	175
	Illustrations II	177
Chapter 19	Donny	200
Chapter 20	A Special Bond	208
Chapter 21	Bouncing Back	219
Chapter 22	Going Home	232
Chapter 23	So Near…	244
Chapter 24	A Boy Named Diego	261
Chapter 25	Rovers Return	270
	Epilogue	276
	Statistics	279
	Acknowledgments	284
	Bibliography	285

Foreword

by Simon Grayson

Every time I drive to Elland Road, I pass the statue of Billy Bremner and smile to myself. I smile because it was Billy who gave me my Leeds United debut at the age of 17. I smile because I remember all the happy times I had when Billy was my manager. And I smile because I am now in the fortunate position of following in Billy's footsteps as Leeds United manager. It is a tremendous honour and responsibility, and one I fully appreciate having been a supporter of the club all my life. To me, Billy symbolises everything that is good about Leeds United and his statue that sits outside the stadium is a daily reminder of that. He would have died for the cause and was so passionate about making Leeds United a success. I want every one of my players to feel the same.

I have been fortunate in my career as a manager to have been in charge of two clubs with such a rich heritage and tradition. At Blackpool, I tried to use that history as a motivation. I would tell the players: "Be the next Stan Mortensen, be the next Stanley Matthews, be the next legend in your own right." When I was appointed Leeds manager shortly before Christmas, 2008, I soon found myself saying the same to the squad about Billy and all those other great players who made Leeds United the special club it is today. There has been success since then, of course, such as the League Championship win of 1992 under Howard Wilkinson and the run to the Champions League semi-finals nine years later. But nothing compares to that team built by Don Revie. It is a group of players, with Billy as captain, that will live forever in the history of this club. I continually challenge my players to leave the sort of legacy that those great players of the past did all those years ago.

The Leeds team that Billy captained was a wonderful team. They may not have been loved outside the city but they were universally respected. Don Revie had so many great players - Peter Lorimer, Eddie Gray and Johnny Giles to name just three. But if any fans from that era were asked to name the player who made it all work, I would expect most would reply 'Billy Bremner'. I was never fortunate enough to see him play for Leeds United. But I was extremely lucky to have been a young player coming through at Elland Road when Billy was manager. He was a huge influence on me and all the young lads who came through during that time. A footballer never forgets his debut and I am no different. It came at Huddersfield Town's old Leeds Road ground on a Tuesday night and we drew 0-0. I wasn't told I was in the side until the lunchtime on the day of the game. A huge range of emotions suddenly ran through me but Billy was great. He pulled me to one side and said, 'You have earned this right so go out and enjoy yourself'. He made it clear he believed in me and knowing that someone like Billy Bremner felt like that made me feel ten feet tall.

Billy was also an amazing character around the club, with his story-telling being something else. As an apprentice, it was my job to clean the dressing room, sweep the terraces and polish the boots. It meant I was often in and around the first-team as they got changed and I would make sure I hung around just that little bit longer so I could listen to Billy talking to the senior lads such as Ian Baird or Ian Snodin. I was totally engrossed.

Billy was the sort of manager who would spend that bit of extra time with his players. He loved David Batty, probably because 'Batts' was his sort of player. So, they would spend a lot of time together. But, to be fair to Billy, he was like that with all the young lads he felt had a chance of making it in the game – whether that was going to be at Leeds United or not. He spent a lot of time with me and Gary Speed, for instance. We signed for Leeds on the same day at the age of 14 and both know the debt we owe to Billy. He would tell us ways we could improve our game and point out things that we could and should have done differently in the previous week's reserve or youth team game. People may not remember Billy too much for his management career but if you asked any of the lads who played for him then I bet they would all be full of praise for the role he played in their careers. Billy also had this amazing aura. Even now, my first team-coach at Leeds, Glynn Snodin, still calls Billy 'Gaffer' when he is reminiscing about the old days. Glynn played for Billy at both Doncaster Rovers and Leeds during the Eighties. Yet, despite those days being a long time ago now, I can't recall Glynn describing Billy as anything but 'Gaffer' since we both returned to Elland Road. That is an indication of the respect Billy continues to hold in the eyes of his players. It is something I have only come across once before in my career and that was at Leicester City when Martin O'Neill was manager and John Robertson his assistant. One day, Brian Clough came into the training ground and both Martin and John called him 'Boss' or 'Gaffer' throughout the visit. It was an illustration of the tremendous esteem and respect they held Brian Clough in and Billy's former players invariably feel the same. I feel privileged to have played under two managers who I view as great football men.

As a manager, I obviously use lessons that I picked up as a player. From time to time, I will spot certain things that I say or do and think afterwards, 'Billy would probably have done that'. Since Billy left Elland Road in 1988, there have been plenty of managers who have been and gone at the club. But I still regard him as the gaffer. There are also times when I have to pinch myself that I am the manager of the club where I started as a 14-year-old. Above all, though, I hope I can leave a lasting legacy, just like Billy did, both as a player and a manager, because his story is one that continues to inspire us all today.

Simon Grayson,
Leeds United manager

Introduction

When Billy Bremner died just two days short of what would have been his 55th birthday, football lost one of its greatest warriors. That the next game for Leeds United, the club where the Scot had spent all but two seasons of a hugely distinguished playing career, should be against Chelsea was an irony lost on no-one. Not only had Bremner's debut for Leeds come at Stamford Bridge nearly four decades earlier. But the rivalry between the two clubs that simmered throughout his time at Elland Road and exploded most memorably in the 1970 FA Cup final replay, had long since come to symbolise the combative nature of the United side that Bremner had captained. Perhaps inevitably, given that history and the raw emotions felt by many at Elland Road so soon after the death of the club's greatest captain, the 90 minutes that followed in west London turned out to be a throwback to the time when trousers were flared and shirts had huge collars. Ten players were booked that day in the capital, the first of whom was Leeds right-back Gary Kelly after less than a minute had been played. By full-time, no goals had been scored but both Kelly and United team-mate Alf-Inge Haaland had been sent off. The media, understandably, lapped it up, long-time critics of the club pointing out how fitting that the 'Dirty Leeds' persona should resurface in a game where the players were wearing black armbands in honour of the club's most famous captain. Of course, Bremner, one of football's renowned competitors, would have relished such a set-to. But the point overlooked by the vast majority during the inquest into the 'Battle of Stamford Bridge' was that he would have been much more selective and cute in picking and choosing when to leave his mark. The hotheads who soured that battling goalless draw for George Graham's side with their lack of discipline had none of Bremner's cunning, nor intelligence. Few, if any, did.

In the decade from the mid-Sixties that saw Don Revie's side become the benchmark for English football, Leeds were blessed with many great players. None, though, came to symbolise the club more than Bremner. He was at the heart of everything, leading by example to ensure every last drop of sweat and effort had been spent come the final whistle. If Leeds were ever beaten, it was not through lack of effort. And while few outside the West Riding liked Bremner, they all respected him as a symbol of courage, dynamism and industry – the sort of footballer, in fact, that the vast majority of supporters and managers want leading their own team. Not for nothing did the late John Arlott once write in *The Guardian*: 'If every manager in Britain were given his choice of any one player to add to his team some, no doubt, would toy with the idea of George Best; but the realists, to a man, would have Bremner.' It was a similar story among a media that were often hostile to Revie's Leeds, as illustrated by his polling of 95 per cent of the votes when named the Football Writers' Footballer of the Year in 1970 – an award that, until the advent of the Professional Footballers Association's own prize four years later, was the most prestigious in the game.

As captain, Bremner led Leeds to two League Championships, an FA Cup and a League Cup. In Europe, the Yorkshire club also lifted the Inter-Cities Fairs Cup twice. There would have been a lot more success had Revie not set out each season wanting to win every trophy available, a consequence being the sort of fixture pile-up that would today leave Sir Alex Ferguson and Arsene Wenger apoplectic. On the international stage, Bremner also shone. The very epitome of a Scottish footballer with his red hair and fiery temper, he won 54 caps and captained his country 39 times. In the 1974 World Cup, he was one of the players of the tournament as the Scots bowed out after the first group stage despite being the only one of the 16 competing nations not to lose a game. That and Scotland's 3-2 win at Wembley less than a year on from England lifting the World Cup – after which the patriotic Bremner only half-jokingly proclaimed Bobby Brown's side to be 'world champions' - were the clear highlights of an international career that ended just one appearance short of what would then have been a new record.

Once his playing days were over in 1978, Bremner moved into management with Doncaster Rovers. The bottom of the old Fourth Division was not an easy place to serve an apprenticeship with the rundown state of Belle Vue serving as a vivid illustration of how lack of money had held the south Yorkshire club back for decades. By the time he left seven years later, however, Rovers had been turned into a vibrant club with genuine hopes of winning a return to the second tier of English football. The transformation had been achieved through hard work and an ability to develop promising young talent. An inevitable return to Elland Road followed but, despite coming within a few minutes of winning promotion to the top-flight in 1987 and reaching an FA Cup semi-final, success eluded Bremner, who was sacked after three years. A brief second spell at Doncaster followed before a move into the media and after-dinner circuit. It was after one of these speaking assignments at Burnley's Turf Moor ground that I was fortunate enough to meet Bremner. The invitation from my late father, a committed Clarets fan since the 1950s, and his brother to come along and listen to the Scot had been too good to turn down for someone who had spent many a winter's afternoon bouncing up and down at the back of the Gelderd End while chanting 'Billy Bremner's Barmy Army' over and over again. It was a wise choice as, along with hundreds of Burnley fans, I was able to enjoy a hugely enjoyable evening listening to hilarious anecdote after hilarious anecdote – all reeled off with no need to consult any notes, something friends and family long since resigned to his terrible memory must have found hard to believe. At the end, Bremner received a standing ovation and seemed genuinely moved by the response. I was determined to meet the former Leeds manager. Eventually, my chance came as he made his way across Turf Moor's Centre Spot Bar towards the exit. Now, meeting your heroes can be a dangerous thing, especially at a young age when a refusal to sign an autograph can lead to a shattering of dreams. I know this from personal experience after being brushed aside, autograph book in hand, by Bob Willis at Headingley in 1982 – a dismissal that saw the aping of the fast bowler's run-up from the boundary edge in our local Keighley park abandoned for good. When it came to meeting Bremner, however, there was to be no such disappointment as, despite clearly being keen to head back across the Pennines towards home, he stopped to chat for five minutes with this lone Leeds supporter in a room of Lancastrians. Not only that, he gave the impression of being genuinely pleased to do so – even agreeing at the end to pose for a photograph, begrudgingly taken by my Clarets-supporting Uncle who usually finds it impossible to say the word 'Leeds' without adding the prefix 'dirty'. I have been minded of that night many times since, not least on that terrible day of December 7, 1997, when confirmation came that Billy Bremner had passed away at the age of 54. Leeds, as a city and football club, was left in a state of shock. Soon, though, plans were in place to pay tribute to a man who, for more than three decades, had been synonymous with the West Riding city. That Bremner's tribute had been decided upon just a few months after his death underlined the Scot's tremendous standing in the area, as it is a peculiar oddity of football that great servants are only usually recognised long after they have passed away. At Leeds, for instance, the Gelderd End only became the Revie Stand when made all-seater more than five years after Don's death, while it would be another 15 before an appeal was launched to erect a statue of the former United manager outside the ground. Similarly, the West Stand was only recently dedicated to the late

John Charles, who died in 2004. For Bremner, however, the club decided very quickly to commemorate him with a statue that now gazes out imperiously from the corner of Elland Road and Lowfields Road. The statue, which immortalises the club's most decorated captain in celebratory pose, has since become a focal point for supporters, in both good times and bad. When, for instance, two of United's loyal fans, Kevin Speight and Christopher Loftus, were murdered in Istanbul ahead of a UEFA Cup semi-final in 2000, the mourning was centred around the life-size statue of Bremner with flowers and tributes being left at his feet within hours of the news filtering through. More recently, during the summer of 2007 that saw Leeds slide into administration, supporters chose the statue as the place to lay flowers in protest when it seemed their club may have played its last game. The upshot of all this is that Bremner, well over a decade on from his tragically premature death, is as much a symbol of Leeds United as he was in the days when he was the heart and soul of a club that were the dominant force in English football. And that really is a fitting tribute to the man who supporters recently voted as the club's greatest player. King Billy – gone, but never forgotten.

Chapter 1

Where It All Began

In the proud working class district of Raploch stands a stone engraving dedicated to Stirling's most famous son. The choice of material to pay tribute to William John Bremner is no accident, the Scot's ability to tackle head on whatever life threw at him was such that many believed he really had been honed from granite. Certainly, that was the impression countless vanquished opponents on the football field had of a man who even now remains one of the game's most renowned competitors. As a youngster, Bremner was small for his age so had to continually prove that size does not necessarily equate to stature. That he did so to earn total respect owed everything to his upbringing on the often unforgiving streets and playing fields of Raploch – or, as it is often referred to by residents from elsewhere in Stirling, 'Raptap' or rat block. Bremner – who became such an inspirational figure for club and country that not only does his statue today stand outside Leeds United but he was one of the first to be inducted into Scottish football's Hall of Fame – would later stress the value of those hard-learned lessons.

To those who had known Bremner as a youngster, his subsequent success did not come as a surprise. Born on December 9, 1942, he benefited from having a loving family. Dad James, who was more commonly known in the area as 'Pop', was a hard-working kindly man, while Mum Bridget (Bess) ran the family's home on Weir Street with warmth and compassion. Football was always a big part of life in the Bremner household with Pop passing on his own love of the sport to his son. Many an hour was passed with the youngster perfecting the basic skills of the game under the watchful gaze of dad, who enjoyed nothing more than passing on snippets of advice. Later in life, Bremner would be quick to pay tribute to the important role his dad played in the triumphs that followed. As a schoolboy, he enjoyed all manner of pastimes, including swimming, cycling and walking. But it was football that brought most pleasure, so being selected for St Mary's Primary School Under-11s at the age of just nine came as a big thrill. It set a precedent with Bremner being only 13 when he graduated to adult league football. Any fears that his size would make signing for Gowan Hill a step too far were soon dispelled by some impressive displays from the carrot-topped youngster, who had also started to shine for the Stirlingshire Schools team. Bremner's football education also included regularly watching the two local Scottish League teams, East Stirlingshire and Stirling Albion. Later, visits to Ibrox and Parkhead would follow as Bremner took advantage of the two Glasgow giants being at home on alternate Saturdays to watch his heroes live. Bremner may have been brought up a Catholic but religious intolerance was never for him.

Once in his teenage years and having moved to St Modan's Secondary School, Bremner's talents and seemingly endless energy levels were starting to attract a wider audience. By the time of his final year at school, he was a regular for Scotland Schoolboys. Again, Bremner's ability shone through and, soon, clubs from all over Britain were beating a path to Raploch. Arsenal and Chelsea were among the earliest to show interest, inviting Bremner down to London for trials. Joining him on the trip to the English capital was friend and Scotland Schoolboys team-mate Tommy Henderson. Both clubs were interested, even if Chelsea let it be known they considered Bremner to be on the small side – something he never forgot. London life, though, didn't appeal so he returned north to the news that both Celtic, the club he wanted to join more than any other, and Rangers had been in touch. Rangers, on hearing Bremner was Catholic, quickly lost interest but Celtic remained keen. Pop, however, was not overly enamoured by the thought of his son getting caught up in any religious controversy. Instead, Bremner senior insisted the better option would be a move to England where religion didn't matter and, more importantly, the football was of a higher standard. His son knew better than to argue so that left only the question of which club. By now, Sheffield Wednesday and Aston Villa had joined Arsenal, Chelsea and a host of other clubs in the race for Bremner's signature. There had also been an approach from Leeds United, which had drawn the initial response from the Yorkshire club's intended signing of, 'Who the hell are they?' Leeds persisted, however, and eventually Bremner and pal Henderson agreed to head to Elland Road for a trial. In truth, it was not a yearning to join United that brought the pair south but, instead, the fact they were starting to enjoy being ferried around the country at someone else's expense. A trip to Leeds was much preferable to the teenagers than staying at home.

United chairman Harry Reynolds and manager Bill Lambton had first travelled to Scotland to meet the pair after being impressed by their performance in the Schoolboys international against England. Now the two youngsters were in Yorkshire, Reynolds outlined, in typically no-nonsense style, his ambitions for the club. He made no idle boasts nor promised either boy the earth, something they both appreciated. Reynolds also stressed how family-orientated the club was and that their careers would be best served at a place where they really mattered. Bremner and Henderson, who had both warmed to Reynolds' down-to-earth manner, went away to ponder their options. Leeds may not have been on their football radar just a few weeks earlier but they were in the First Division and seemed genuinely interested in the two lads' development. Bremner's hoped-for move to Celtic was out of the question on Dad's orders, while he had not warmed to the English capital during his fortnight-long stays with Arsenal and Chelsea. In the end, they both opted for Leeds. For Reynolds and Lambert, it was a tremendous coup to have beaten some of the biggest names in British football to such a prized signature as Bremner. For the teenager himself, meanwhile, the course of his life had been changed forever.

Chapter 2

A Foreign Land

When Leeds United had first made a tentative approach to the parents of Billy Bremner, it was little wonder the teenage Scot had never heard of the club. The 1950s had started full of promise for United and seen the legendary John Charles emerge to break all manner of goalscoring records and inspire a successful promotion push. But, by the end of the decade, the rot had well and truly set in with managerial upheaval and the sale of Charles to Juventus for a British record transfer fee having led to Elland Road falling off the football radar. They were still a First Division club, but one who even in their own city were considered to be distinctly second best. Where Leeds Rugby League club boasted seven Challenge Cup victories and several appearances in Championship finals, United had finished in the top half of Division One just six times in the near 40 years since being formed. With Hunslet viewed by many to be superior to the football club, Leeds, which also boasted Bramley as a representative in the 13-a-side game, was considered to be a 'rugby city' – especially once Charles had left for Italy. This was a notion that was only truly banished during David O'Leary's time as manager around the turn of the Millennium when the 'sold out' signs were regularly posted at Elland Road. No wonder, therefore, that when a young Bremner was informed of United's interest his initial response had been to ask, 'Who the hell are they?' It was a fair question, and one that fellow Scots Eddie Gray and Peter Lorimer would also ask when approached in later years by Don Revie about a possible move to Yorkshire.

Leeds United had, in fact, been born out of the ashes of the old Leeds City, who were expelled from the Football League eight matches into the 1919-20 season for making illegal payments to players. By the following May, the new club had been accepted into the League to begin an existence that, for the next four decades, would be the very epitome of mediocrity. In the FA Cup, the furthest they had gone by the time Bremner signed on his 17th birthday was the quarter-finals – on one occasion. United's league record was a similar tale of woe with the club having won just one trophy, the Second Division title. It was not just on the field, either, where the club's malaise was evident as Bremner signed his first contract as a professional footballer with Elland Road having clearly seen better days. The West Stand, built a couple of years earlier at a cost of £180,000 after fire had destroyed its wooden predecessor, had admittedly brought a touch of grandeur to a ground that started life as home to Holbeck Rugby League club. Its entrance and modern façade would become an iconic symbol for many years until the construction of the Banqueting Suite that today juts into the club's main car park. But, as impressive a structure as the new stand was, its most tangible impact was to underline just how run-down the rest of Elland Road had become. Behind one end was a huge uncovered Spion Kop, which gazed directly at the forlorn-looking 'Scratching Shed' – a shallow terrace with a barrel-shaped roof that had been built in the 1920s. Opposite the new West Stand could be found the rather primitive Lowfields Road Stand, again a structure that was erected during United's first decade of existence. Jack Overfield, who played 163 times for Leeds in the five years from 1955, recalls: "Elland Road was not the best of grounds in those days. We'd had the fire in 1956 that destroyed everything the club had – including all the players' boots – and that made things difficult. They had to stage a public appeal to re-build it as the insurance wouldn't cover the cost. Money was always tight, something I always put down to Leeds being a rugby city. I have lived in Leeds all my life and have always thought that. We got into the First Division during my time as a player and got crowds of 30,000 or more. But I still always felt the city was more interested in rugby."

Bremner may not have been aware of the city's leanings towards the oval ball when he moved south from Stirling. But what could not escape him or anyone at Elland Road in December, 1959, was the precarious league position the club was in. Just four wins from the opening 20 games meant United, who the previous season had finished 15th after winning three and drawing one of their final four games, were sitting 21st in the table. Relegation was looming, thanks in the main to a porous defence that had conceded 50 goals in those 20 games. For Bremner, the first-team was still unchartered territory with his appearances in a Leeds shirt having been restricted to the youth and reserve teams. His debut for the second string had come against Preston, aged just 15. It had been a reward for his refusal to bow to homesickness. Tommy Henderson, his close pal from the Scotland Schoolboys team, had already returned home after failing to settle in Leeds. Bremner had been sorely tempted to join him, but felt going home would be admitting defeat. So, he stayed and soon become a regular in the reserves. Now 17, however, Bremner's yearning for home had returned with a vengeance and life in Scotland was looking more and more attractive with each passing week. It was, therefore, with perfect timing that manager Jack Taylor, who had succeeded Lambton, let it be known he felt the youngster was ready to make the step up to the first team. Fittingly, considering the heights both men would reach together in the future, it was Don Revie who broke the good news to the youngster. Then the club's senior pro, Revie told an excited Bremner in the Elland Road car park that, due to Chris Crowe doing his National Service and having to play for the army, he would start at outside-right against Chelsea the following Saturday. All notions of a return home were, for now at least, forgotten as the 17-year-old looked forward to the day he had dreamed about since childhood. His League debut. That it would come against Chelsea, one of the clubs who had rejected him for being 'too small' a couple of years earlier, only added to his sense of anticipation. Revie, by then 32 and coming towards the end of a career that had included being named 'Footballer of the Year' when at Manchester City, sensed the youngster might benefit from a relaxed build-up to the game at Stamford Bridge so arranged for the pair to room together on the Friday night. He then made sure Bremner had an early night so they could both go for a leisurely early morning stroll in the capital to settle any nerves. Revie also passed on nuggets of advice that he felt would serve his young team-mate well, including a warning to ignore any jibes from the Chelsea players who would try and unsettle him.

Once the game was under way, Revie ensured Bremner, United's then second youngest debutant at the age of 17 years and 47 days, got an early touch. It did the trick of settling nerves on a pitch made heavy by an incessant downpour that had begun during the morning. United won 3-1 and Bremner was overjoyed on the return trip north that Saturday evening. In the following Monday's *Yorkshire Evening Post*, football reporter Phil Brown wrote of the teenage debutant: 'His was no sensational debut with a miry pitch and rain all being against a lightweight youth shining. But all the main football qualities were there – enthusiasm, guts, intelligence, most accurate use of the ball and unselfishness.' Brown's assessment was an encouraging one and meant there was an air of curiosity among the Elland Road crowd when Leeds returned to action a fortnight later against West Bromwich Albion, the club having had a blank weekend following the win at Chelsea due to their by now traditional FA Cup third round exit at the start of the month. Any hopes, however, that the red-haired newcomer could help Leeds to another two points were dashed as Albion coasted to a 4-1 win. Bremner missed the next two games with Crowe again being available, only to return when his rival for the outside-right berth was unexpectedly sold to Blackburn Rovers for £25,000 in early March. Whether Leeds needed the money or manager Taylor felt in Bremner he had a ready-made replacement was never made clear. But the upshot of Crowe's departure was that the young Scot became a regular in the first-team. He also got on the scoresheet for the first time, following a strike against Birmingham City in front of just 8,557 fans at Elland Road with another as the visit of Manchester City attracted a crowd of 32,545 despite taking place just ten days later. The disparity in attendance figures could partly be explained by the City side featuring Denis Law for the first time, the Maine Road club having just paid Huddersfield Town £53,000 for his services. Law duly rewarded not only those who had been tempted through the turnstiles but also the *Pathe News* camera present to capture the action by netting City's second goal with a typically cool finish in front of the Scratching Shed. He also created the visitors' third goal of the afternoon with a neat pass for Colin Barlow but it was Leeds who prevailed 4-3 thanks to two late penalties by John McCole that followed earlier strikes from Bremner and Noel Peyton. Bremner's delight at netting his second goal in as many games was only heightened by the result being enough to lift Leeds over Birmingham City and out of the relegation zone. Manchester City, meanwhile, stood just a point in front of Taylor's side. Any hopes of a concerted push for survival were, though, to be dashed as the team's form again fell away and United were relegated along with Luton Town after having conceded 92 goals in 42 games.

A return to the Second Division came as a blow to everyone at Elland Road, not least the directors who from bitter experience knew crowds would slump once out of the top flight. It meant funds were limited, hence manager Jack Taylor being turned down by the board after asking to recruit the few experienced players he felt were needed to bounce back immediately. A handful of signings were made, including Eric Smith from Celtic and Sunderland outside-left Colin Grainger. Both men had enjoyed good careers, with Smith, a former Scotland international, having won a host of trophies at Parkhead. Grainger, meanwhile, had won seven England caps and was a former team-mate of Revie's at Roker Park. Having been born and brought up in the Wakefield area, Grainger saw a move to Leeds as a welcome opportunity to return to his roots. What he found once back in Yorkshire, however, was not overly impressive with United's approach being less than professional compared to the club he had just left. Grainger says: "As a club,

Leeds weren't the best. Everything was different to how it had been done at Sunderland when Don and I were players. I quickly realised I had been spoiled at Roker Park. Things like how we travelled were massively different. Where with Sunderland we would travel to London the day before by train and stay over, Leeds went there and back in the day. The lads at Sunderland had always enjoyed staying in London on the Saturday night as well, especially if we had won. But there was nothing like that at Leeds."

As much of a culture shock moving to Leeds had been, one player who Grainger was impressed by was 17-year-old Bremner. He adds: "I remember seeing Billy in my first training session and thinking, 'This lad is some player'. He was only a young lad and yet so mature on the ball. Once the season started, I could see he was just the same in a game. He fought for everything and put most of the team to shame with his will to win. I could see Billy was going to be a very good player." Grainger may insist Bremner's potential was apparent the moment he joined Leeds in August, 1960, but that did not prevent Jack Taylor from dropping the teenager in the wake of a 2-0 opening day defeat at Liverpool. Bremner, still pining for a return to Scotland, vowed to change his manager's mind. He put in countless extra hours after training and every ounce of effort into his performances for the reserves. All it earned, however, was a brief recall against Leyton Orient in a game Leeds lost 3-1 before he was again cast aside. Eventually, frustration got the better of Bremner, who marched in to see Taylor. By the following week, he was back in the team and destined to play in all the remaining 29 league games that season.

Being back in the side was welcome but, as Bremner soon realised, it did nothing to cure his homesickness. The Scot was not alone in that among the youngsters at Elland Road, with Norman Hunter, a couple of years younger but someone who shared digs with Bremner, admitting to eagerly looking forward to returning to the North East every six weeks or so. Bremner, though, would return to Stirling much more regularly thanks to his wages of £13 per week plus £5 appearance fee allowing him the funds to own a car. It was on one such trip home that Bremner had met a girl called Vicky Dick at The Plaza dance hall in Stirling. Love had quickly blossomed, making the footballer pine for a return home even more. Ray Oddy started covering United for Gosnay's Sports Agency in 1960 and readily recalls Bremner's homesickness. "There was a phone box opposite Elland Road that Billy must have visited every day," says the journalist who supplied the national newspapers with copy on the club for more than three decades. "I don't think he had a 'phone at his digs so this was the only way to speak to his girlfriend. The lads would all be saying, 'There he goes again, ringing his girlfriend in Scotland'. It was the only way he could cope with being apart from her." At one stage, Bremner was missing Vicky so much he even spoke about seeking a transfer to Stirling Albion before it was pointed out by friends that his career would be much better served at Leeds.

One aspect of life at Elland Road that Bremner did enjoy in his first full season was the training under Syd Owen and Les Cocker, two men who would, in later years, be integral members of Don Revie's backroom team at Leeds. They had both arrived at Elland Road during the summer of 1960 after being lured north from Luton Town by Taylor. Of the two, Owen had enjoyed the more illustrious playing career – making three appearances for England and being named 'Footballer of the Year' in 1959 when unfashionable Luton reached the FA Cup final. Cocker, meanwhile, had retired from playing a couple of years before joining Leeds after more than 300 league appearances for Accrington Stanley and Stockport County. Before joining United, he had been one of the first generation to take the FA Coaching Certificate. Between them, the pair endeavoured to try and make training interesting while also improving the players' fitness and skills. Colin Grainger recalls: "The one thing at Leeds that was thoroughly professional was the training. Les Cocker and Syd Owen did it all and they put a lot of thought into it. We trained on Fullerton Park behind the main stand at Elland Road and did our running in Roundhay Park. The lads all enjoyed working with Les and Syd, even if a few would take the mickey a bit at times."

Bremner marked his return to the first-team in late October with two goals but it was still not enough to prevent Norwich City triumphing 3-2 at Elland Road. The defensive problems that had brought relegation the previous season had not gone away, so much so that United would concede 83 goals on their return to the Second Division. Matters were not helped by the manager's apparent indecision; he would select 25 players before deciding in mid-March that managing United was not for him. Highlights were few and far between, though forward John McCole's tally of 20 goals in 35 league appearances was a notable return in a struggling side. Likewise, Bremner, once restored to the side, enjoyed a profitable campaign to finish as the club's second highest goalscorer in the league behind McCole with nine. The Scot also netted once in the League Cup, making its debut that season, as Leeds reached the fourth round before bowing out 5-4 to Southampton at The Dell. Grainger, who made 37 appearances that season, recalls: "Billy was one of the few positives for the club in what was a disappointing year. He might have been 17 or 18 but he was afraid of no-one. He could play anywhere and if someone kicked Billy, he would kick them back. The only problem was Billy being homesick and wanting to go back to Scotland. But, in football terms, he was already becoming a key player and one of the first names on the manager's team-sheet. What I also liked was that, off the field, he was a good lad. Me, Billy and Alan Humphreys would have a drink after an away game. We first did it after a game at Norwich when Billy had scored a couple of goals and then just carried on doing the same thing after every game. He was only a young lad but great company. He would always have half a bitter and a whisky chaser."

As favourable an impression as Bremner was making, the same could not be said for the team. United were stagnating and supporters becoming disillusioned, as witnessed by the 9,995 crowd at Elland Road to watch Luton Town inflict a fourth straight defeat on Taylor's men on March 8. Respite did come with a 1-0 win over Norwich three days later but Taylor had seen enough. He resigned the following Monday. Few were surprised, with even the United board seeming more preoccupied by the staging at Elland Road that weekend of the FA Cup semi-final clash between Leicester City and Sheffield United. The directors' prevarication was perhaps understandable considering the humiliation that had been heaped on the club two years earlier when searching for a new manager to replace Bill Lambton. Not only were United turned down by Charlie Mitten of Newcastle United, Norwich City's Archie Macauley and Bob Brocklebank of Hull City. But Arthur Turner of non-League Headington had also found the potential of a club who within a year would become known as Oxford United to be more enticing than the step-up to manage in the First Division with Leeds. Fate, however, was about to intervene in the form of a simple request from Revie to director Harry Reynolds. The 33-year-old had played just once for Leeds since the turn of the year and was keen to move into management. An offer to become player-coach of Chester had already been rejected along with interest from Tranmere Rovers and a club in Australia. But now a vacancy had arisen at Third Division Bournemouth and Revie wanted the job. He approached Reynolds to ask for a reference in support of his application. Reynolds, on the board since 1955 and destined to step up to chairman later that year, duly obliged only to later pause while writing. Here, he suddenly realised, was the very man Leeds needed as their own manager. Reynolds promptly ripped up the reference and threw it in the bin. In that moment,

Revie became the tenth manager of Leeds United. The legend is a romantic one, though it should also be noted that Bournemouth baulking at the £6,000 fee Leeds were asking for Revie may also have played a less than insignificant part in the turn of events. Either way, Reynolds' sudden realisation about Revie was destined to have a huge impact, not only on English football but also the career of Billy Bremner.

Chapter 3

The Boss

Making the transition from player to manager at the same club is considered one of the hardest moves in football. One day, you are one of the lads and able to share in all the dressing room banter. The next, you're the man in charge whose arrival among the players is met with wary eyes and hushed conversations. Some former team-mates may even be openly hostile, especially if they were also in the running to become manager. Don Revie, on taking over Leeds United, was acutely aware of the potential problems. 'Soccer's Happy Wanderer', as he called himself in the title of his 1955 autobiography, had passed through four different clubs before arriving at Elland Road three years earlier so knew the importance of laying a set of ground rules straight away. Chief among those was asserting his new-found authority. With that in mind, Revie called a meeting of the United squad to explain the situation as he saw it. He was no longer to be known as 'Don', nor did he want to hear the words 'Mr Revie'. Instead, all the players were to refer to him, simply, as 'Boss'. Only one player, John Charles a couple of years later, would forget the edict and was rewarded with an ice-cold stare from his one-time Leeds team-mate. The mistake, made when travelling on the team coach to an away game, was never repeated. Jack Charlton believes the transition being so comfortable was down to Revie himself. "He did it very easily. I have known in football for a player stepping up to become manager having trouble but Don never did. He put the players first and we all appreciated that, which is probably why the change happened so smoothly."

For Bremner, the appointment of the man he had roomed with on the eve of his Leeds debut was a surprise, if a welcome one. A bond had been forged that night in London, as Revie made sure any nerves on the part of his teenage team-mate were eased ahead of facing Chelsea the following day. Fifteen months on, Bremner had established a regular place in the first-team with 36 appearances to his name. He had also scored nine goals, a decent return playing for a club who since Bremner's debut had been relegated and now found themselves languishing in the lower half of Division Two. Despite such an encouraging start to his career, however, the flame-haired Scot was disillusioned with life in West Yorkshire. Homesickness had been a problem ever since he had left Scotland with fellow schoolboy international Tommy Henderson to sign for United. His friend had returned north within a few months to join, first, Celtic and then Hearts before returning to Elland Road in 1962 via a short stint with St Mirren. Bremner, as a result, was left feeling lonely and isolated during those first couple of years in England, with even the buzz of making his debut and becoming a first-team regular doing little to ease the desire to return north of the Border. Meeting and falling in love with Vicky, who, on November 14, 1961, would become his wife, only added to his longing to return home. Eddie Gray, like Bremner, moved from Scotland to Leeds in his early teens. He says: "Billy was really homesick. He missed Vicky hugely, they had met when both were still at school – whereas most of the boys at the club had met girls in Leeds, and that made it hard for Billy." It was a problem Revie inherited from predecessor Jack Taylor and one that, for a time, put a strain on a relationship that would be at the very heart of Leeds United's later success.

The first few weeks of Revie's reign were difficult, not least on the field as Leeds won just one of the nine games that rounded off the 1960-61 season to underline the size of his task in reviving the club's fortunes. Adding to Revie's on-field problems was Bremner's overwhelming desire to leave, the teenager rarely letting a day go by without asking for a move back to Scotland. Among those regular pleadings was a first transfer request. Hibernian, on hearing of how Bremner was unsettled in England, immediately bid £25,000, an offer that, much to Revie's annoyance, the Leeds board seemed willing to accept. The player also wanted the transfer to go through, leaving Revie in a difficult position. The teenager's unhappiness was clear and letting him go would be the kindest option. But Revie was desperate to keep hold of Bremner, someone who he felt had the potential to be the cornerstone of his new-look Leeds United. With that in mind, Revie insisted that Bremner could only leave if Hibs bid £30,000 and not a penny less. Revie's stance was influenced by contacts in Scottish football, who suggested the Edinburgh club had pushed their finances to the limit to make the original bid and another £5,000 would be beyond them. It was a huge gamble on Revie's part but one that, ultimately, paid off. As he had been led to believe, Hibs baulked at the increase and withdrew their interest. For Revie, it was a victory. To Bremner, however, it was tantamount to a betrayal. He was furious with the Leeds manager and wasted little time in telling him so. Revie, displaying the sensitive handling of players that would characterise his time at Elland Road, let Bremner have his say before calmly outlining his vision for United. Just as importantly, he underlined how central the Scot was to those plans. It may not have cured the homesickness, that would only truly happen later when Revie, unbeknown to his player, travelled to Scotland to explain to Bremner's fiancée Vicky how he would be doing a disservice to himself by leaving. But, crucially, the heartfelt appeal to Bremner bought Revie some much-needed time.

Revie, in truth, had a multitude of problems to sort out if his dream of turning Leeds into a major force was to be realised. Changing the team's kit from the traditional city colours of blue and gold to all-white in a clear statement of intent to emulate Real Madrid was one thing. As was changing the ethos of the club by insisting his players prepared for games by staying in the very best hotels and travelling in comfort. But, the bottom line for the fledgling manager was that the United squad was not good enough. For all the promise of Bremner and the, as yet, untapped ability of Jack Charlton, the playing staff was largely made up of journeymen pros. A malaise also hung over the club, something that Revie had recognised the moment he had joined from Sunderland. This sense of listlessness had only become more acute since relegation.

Money, as ever, was tight at Elland Road during Revie's first summer in charge. Developing the very best youngsters, therefore, was his best chance of building a side in the mould of Real Madrid. Along with Harry Reynolds, the director who would become chairman in December 1961, Revie would tour the country to speak to the boys he wanted to sign. A personable manner and ability to empathise with working class families were the two aces up Revie's sleeve as he persuaded a host of highly-promising youngsters to sign for Leeds. Eddie Gray, Peter Lorimer, Paul Reaney and Gary Sprake were just four of those persuaded to ignore offers from some of British football's biggest clubs to sign for Second Division Leeds, while Norman Hunter – already on the groundstaff when Revie was appointed – was another earmarked for a bright future by the new manager.

This determination to build a side around youth was an admirable – and, ultimately, successful - policy. But, by its very nature, it also meant progress would be slow and patience required. The priority, therefore, for Revie in his first full season was cobbling together a squad capable of keeping United ticking over until the youngsters blossomed. Derek Mayers, a winger who had started his career at Everton, was signed from Preston North End but, otherwise, the side that faced Charlton Athletic on the opening day of the 1961-62 season included only players who had been at the club the previous

May. Among those familiar faces was Bremner, who netted the only goal in front of 12,916 fans at Elland Road. The Scot was also on the scoresheet at Brighton & Hove Albion three days later as a 3-1 triumph ensured United started the campaign with back-to-back wins for the first time in six years. Any hopes this may herald a push for promotion, however, were soon dispelled when a 5-0 thrashing at Liverpool started a run of 14 games that would yield just two wins and seven points. Revie's response to the slump was to abandon plans to concentrate solely on management by making a return as a player, though with little success – as his brother-in-law David Duncan recalls: "Things were tough at Leeds so, against his better judgement, Don played a few games but he realised it just wasn't possible to fulfil both roles and soon went back to the dugout."

Amid the gloom surrounding Elland Road, Bremner's form was, at least, a beacon of light. By Christmas, he had netted nine goals from outside-right – making him comfortably the club's top scorer following the surprise departure of John McCole, who had netted 20 times the previous season, to Bradford City early in the Autumn. Despite such a healthy return from the teenager, United's league position was starting to look more precarious with every passing week. The club needed a lift. It came in the form of boardroom changes and a much-needed injection of capital as prominent Leeds businessmen Manny Cussins and Albert Morris became directors in return for an interest-free loan of £10,000 apiece. With Reynolds, on succeeding Sam Bolton as chairman, putting in £50,000 it meant Revie finally had some spending power in the transfer market. Bill McAdams, a one-time team-mate of the Leeds manager at Manchester City, was immediately signed from Bolton Wanderers to bolster a struggling attack.

The Belfast-born forward's home debut saw Bill Shankly's Liverpool, destined to be crowned Second Division champions a few months later, beaten courtesy of a Bremner goal but, again, any hopes of it sparking an upturn in form were soon dashed by a shocking post-Christmas run that brought one win from the next nine league games. United also made their customary third round exit from the FA Cup, Derby County prevailing 3-1 in a replay at the Baseball Ground. Revie made one last attempt to galvanise his side from on the field at Huddersfield Town in early March but it, too, ended in defeat to leave Leeds teetering on the precipice of a drop into the Third Division. Salvation was required and it duly arrived courtesy of a player who would not only lead United to safety but also instil the desire and will to win in Billy Bremner that would turn the Scot into one of football's all-time greats.

Chapter 4

Small In Stature, Huge In Standing

The maxim about 'one man not making a team' is generally accepted in football circles. In the case of Bobby Collins at Leeds United, however, few will argue against the assertion that the Scot came closer than most to being the exception to the rule. Pinpointed as the man to help United avoid what would, in terms of the club's ailing finances, be the disaster of relegation, Don Revie initially had to overcome reluctance on the board's part to spend £25,000 on a player who was 31 years old. Such a sum – around £400,000 in today's money – was seen by the directors as hugely excessive, especially as Everton had paid the same amount to sign Collins from Glasgow Celtic four years earlier. Revie, however, was adamant and the money was found in time for the former Scotland international to make a scoring debut in a 2-0 win over Swansea Town on March 10, 1962.

The transfer proved a masterstroke and a turning point in the history of both Leeds and Revie. Not only did Collins inspire the initial improvement in results that saw United to safety on the final day of the season courtesy of a 3-0 win at Newcastle United. But, in the longer-term, it was his tutelage and nurturing of a promising group of youngsters that provided the platform from which Leeds began their ascent towards the very top of English football. Collins set the tone for much of what followed at Elland Road, his irascible appetite for combat and overwhelming desire never to be beaten becoming so ingrained in the group of youngsters whom Revie worked so hard to bring to the club that it characterised their play for the next 13 years. All the crimes against football that would subsequently be levelled at Revie's Leeds, from being serial foulers to the mass manipulating of referees, can be traced back to the arrival of Collins.

Revie, determined to harness the hurt his new signing felt at being deemed surplus to requirements at Goodison Park, made Collins his on-field leader. His team-mates soon learned to take note of what the new signing said, not least Bremner who was particularly impressed by Collins' professionalism and the way in which he could coax, cajole and even bully a good performance out of his team-mates. Eddie Gray is in no doubt as to the influence Collins had on a young Bremner. He recalls: "I'll be perfectly honest, when I first came to Leeds and watched the team play, I was terrified. It was brutal stuff, and definitely win-at-all-costs. Bobby was at the heart of all that. He was the main man and someone who taught the whole club how to win. Bobby would never admit when he was beaten or that the odds were against him. There was one night when Bobby had an accident and cut his arm badly. I think he had been messing around with Big Jack. Don went ballistic but Bobby just turned round and said, 'I'll be playing tomorrow and I'll be the best player on the park'. And he was. Nothing ever fazed him, and the determination that Bobby brought to the team was definitely something he passed to Billy and Norman. It was almost like they had inherited their competitiveness from Bobby."

The upsurge in form inspired by Collins' arrival – Leeds lost just once in the final 11 games to finish 19th – meant Revie, with the threat of relegation banished, was able to think big during the summer of 1962. And in Leeds, there was no bigger figure than the Gentle Giant. John Charles, since leaving Elland Road five years earlier, had become an idol in Italian football thanks to winning three championships with Juventus and an Italian Cup. Charles, who Leeds had sold for £65,000, had also been handed the ultimate accolade when named Italy's Footballer of the Year to go with the 108 goals he had scored during five seasons sporting the colours of Juve. Revie, and particularly the directors who recalled an average crowd of 32,000 during Charles' last season at Elland Road, wanted to bring him 'home'. Leeds duly got their man, though not until after some often tortuous discussions and the agreeing of a £53,000 fee. With Charles playing through the centre, much was expected of Bremner and Albert Johanneson on either flank. However, despite scoring three goals in the opening five games of the 1961-62 campaign, the Charles that had returned from Italy was a very different attacking beast from the one that had left in 1957. By the October, he had gone - the sweetener for Leeds being a handsome profit thanks to Roma paying £70,000 for the forward. Revie was disappointed by Charles' failure to recapture his best form but this was tempered by what had happened a month before the Welshman's departure when four of United's promising band of youngsters made an impressive step-up to first-team duty. The venue was Swansea's Vetch Field, where Gary Sprake, Paul Reaney, Norman Hunter and Rod Johnson helped Leeds to a 2-0 win. Bremner, who had previously shared digs with Hunter in the city, had netted one of the goals to add to Revie's pleasure. John Reynolds had joined the Leeds groundstaff in 1957 after his promising playing career had been shattered by an injury sustained in an FA Youth Cup tie. He was in his native Wales that afternoon and remembers the feeling of optimism generated by the successful blooding of so many youngsters. "I travelled with the first-team in those days," recalls the Welshman who has worked at Elland Road for more than 50 years. "From that Swansea game onwards, I could see the way it was going. Most of the young lads who went on to be part of that great side played that day. You could see straight away that they were going to be something special."

What was less encouraging for Revie, however, was that Bremner was still feeling homesick. His pining for Scotland and fiancée Vicky was such that just three weeks after the win at Swansea he went AWOL to hand a future Leeds great an unexpected debut. Peter Lorimer, who remains the club's all-time record goalscorer with 238, was just 15 years and 289 days when he lined up against Southampton at Elland Road. He recalls: "The gaffer called me in and said, 'You are playing tomorrow because Billy won't come back from Scotland'. I didn't play again that season but, thanks to Billy, I still hold the record as the club's youngest-ever player."

Lorimer may have been destined not to become a first-team regular for another three years but Sprake, Reaney and Hunter had, by the end of the season, joined Bremner as mainstays of the side. With Collins and Jack Charlton missing just one and four games respectively, Revie was getting ever nearer the settled side he craved. Results responded accordingly and by Christmas Leeds seemed handily placed to launch a concerted challenge for promotion. That was, though, until one of the harshest winters on record stepped in. As temperatures plunged and the snow fell, English football went into hibernation. An FA Cup tie between Lincoln City and Coventry City had to be postponed 15 times. Leeds were as badly affected as most, not managing to play at all between December 22 and March 2. Not only did this impact on the club's finances but, once the temperature rose, it left United struggling to fit in their 19 remaining fixtures before the season's scheduled end in mid-May. Such was the gruelling schedule, in fact, that April brought a staggering nine games, while May saw Revie's side in action a further five times. Nevertheless, Leeds set about their task with relish and only really stumbled in the final straight when consecutive defeats in May against Middlesbrough, Huddersfield Town and Southampton ended any hopes of a return to the top-flight. Despite just missing out, it had been an encouraging season for Leeds. Several promising youngsters had made the step-up to the first team, Revie had hit upon a reasonably settled side and there was plenty to suggest the following year could be a successful one.

For Bremner, though, the season had been something of a mixed bag. He had netted 10 goals in 24 appearances to finish third in the club's goalscoring charts behind Jim Storrie (25) and Albert Johanneson (13). But, towards the end of the season, he had been left out of the side due to what his manager considered to be a dip in form. Revie felt Leeds were not getting the best out of Bremner and that a switch of position would be in both his and the team's interest. Eddie Gray, who signed for Leeds that summer, recalls: "Don had this ability to spot something others had missed and he thought Billy was more suited to central midfield. Bearing in mind the career Billy went on to have from that position, it shows just what a great judge Don was of a player."

Revie's decision to move Bremner into midfield created a vacancy at outside-right, one he filled with the signing of Manchester United's Johnny Giles. Less than three months earlier, 23-year-old Giles had been in the United side that had won the FA Cup at Wembley so his decision to step down a division took many in the game by surprise. Revie, for his part, was delighted by a £30,000 signing that he considered to be a huge coup and was confident that Leeds now had a squad capable of winning promotion. His optimism proved justified as the first 24 games brought just one defeat, a 3-2 loss at Manchester City, when, tellingly, the inspirational Collins missed his only game of the season. Losing a ferocious contest to promotion rivals Sunderland at Roker Park between Christmas and New Year was a setback but not one that unduly worried Revie, whose side responded by upping their performances to suffer just one more reverse en route to clinching the Second Division title. No-one, least of all Revie, would claim it was pretty as Leeds adopted a physical approach that some of their critics felt bordered on thuggery. They were also ruthless, particularly once ahead in a game that Collins, Bremner et al would subsequently play a huge role in closing out. But, after landing the club's first trophy in 40 years, the feeling in Leeds was that the end had justified the means.

First Division football was back at Elland Road, something that only Bremner and Jack Charlton had experienced. Giles with Manchester United and Collins for Everton had also played at the highest level but, otherwise, there was a distinct lack of top-flight know-how among the Leeds ranks that led many outside the club to write off their chances before a ball had been kicked in 1964-65. One man not worried, however, was Revie who decided not to move into the transfer market during the summer. Instead, he planned to give the lads who had won promotion a chance to prove themselves among the elite. A setback came when Alan Peacock, signed during the run-in to promotion from Middlesbrough, was injured in pre-season. The England international had netted eight goals in 14 games to help end United's four-year stay in Division Two and was seen as a perfect foil for Jim Storrie. Peacock remembers the frustration well. "It was really bad luck on my part," says the striker who did not return to action for Leeds until the spring of that first season in the top-flight. "We'd won promotion and everyone was looking forward to the season. Leeds were a hard side back then but what most people didn't realise until we came up was just how many tremendous players there were at Elland Road. Young lads like Norman Hunter and Peter Lorimer really came to the fore once Leeds were in the First Division and everyone at the club fancied our chances to do well, not least the manager. The potential of the younger lads was one of the things that Don had used to persuade me to move to Leeds the previous season. So, it was hugely disappointing to be ruled out for so long through injury."

Losing Peacock was a blow but Revie saw no need to move into the transfer market. His most pressing concern ahead of the new season, in fact, was whether an article that had appeared in the Football Association's summer edition of *FA News* would prejudice referees against his players. The article had labelled newly-promoted Leeds, 'The dirtiest in the Football League'. The tag left everyone at Elland Road puzzled, not least as during the previous season none of Revie's players had been sent off and only Bremner had served a suspension. Fears it could make the Leeds players marked men with the officials were not realised in the opening weeks of the season. But Revie would have cause to return to the offending article in early November after a 1-0 win at Everton was dubbed one of the most violent games the First Division had ever witnessed. The tone for what followed across 90 often chaotic minutes was set early on by a late tackle from Sandy Brown on Giles. The challenge, literally, kick-started a battle that became so ferocious referee Ken Stokes felt the need to take the players off the field to cool down 10 minutes before half-time. The game eventually resumed with Leeds 1-0 ahead through a Willie Bell goal, an advantage they retained until the final whistle. Condemnation rained down on United almost as quickly as had the missiles from the Everton fans when play was temporarily halted. What the critics chose to ignore, however, was the home side had committed the majority of the fouls – 19 to 12 by Leeds. Bremner, who had been confronted by a home fan when leaving the field, had been at the heart of several flare-ups, though the *Yorkshire Evening Post* football reporter Phil

Brown was at pains to point out the following Monday that the Scot had been more sinned against than sinner. He wrote: 'Bremner, hunted by Roy Vernon from the start, had a great game in both defence and attack, controlling his temper against heavy fouls both given and overlooked.'

Two days later, the Leeds board met to discuss the events at Goodison Park. A statement was then released, condemning the *FA News* article from the summer and pointing out that the club had 'only had two players sent off in 44 years'. The statement continued: 'We maintain that the 'Dirty Team' tag, which was blown up by the press, could prejudice not only the general public but the officials controlling the game.' The FA responded by revealing their 'regret' at correspondence between the game's governing body and the club being made public.

Eventually, the furore died down as Leeds maintained what had been a hugely encouraging start to life back in the top division. The 1-0 win over Everton had been United's tenth victory in the opening 16 games. Such an encouraging start was then followed by eight wins from their next 10 outings, the last of which was a 2-1 triumph over Sunderland on January 2 that took Leeds to the top of the Football League for the first time in the club's history. With champions Liverpool preoccupied with Europe, Revie's side were in a three-way chase for the title with Manchester United and Chelsea. With Peacock edging ever closer to a return, hopes were growing at Elland Road that a first major trophy could be theirs. Three consecutive draws in January, including a 2-2 stalemate with Chelsea, did little to dispel the optimism, especially as progress was also made in the FA Cup – a competition in which Leeds had a miserable recent record – as Southport were beaten 3-0 and Everton knocked out after a replay. Shrewsbury Town and Crystal Palace were then beaten to put Leeds into the semi-finals, where Revie's men would face Manchester United. Suddenly, the talk around West Yorkshire was not of one trophy being won but two. Matt Busby's side, who like Chelsea and Leeds had stayed the course in the league, did, however, represent a major obstacle. Nevertheless, Revie's side maintained their push for the double with league wins over Burnley and Everton in the two fixtures preceding the semi-final at Hillsborough.

Revie, ahead of the trip to Sheffield, recognised his side were in unchartered territory in the Cup. But any fears of United being overawed were soon dispelled as Revie's players belied their inexperience in a ragged, if at times violent, goalless draw. Once again the accusations about 'Dirty Leeds' were given an airing, even though both teams had contributed to the unsavoury nature of the tie. Four days later, battle was resumed at the City Ground, Nottingham, and, once again, the action was not overly pleasing on the eye. This time, though, there would be a winner as Bremner, displaying a habit that would continue throughout his career, delivered something special at a critical moment to head past Pat Dunne in the Manchester United goal with just three minutes remaining on the clock. Leeds, as a city, celebrated long into the night but there was to be no such privilege afforded a squad who had the prospect of a title run-in and eight games in just 23 days to tackle before thoughts could turn to Wembley.

Wins against West Ham United and Stoke City in the five days that followed the Cup semi-final maintained the momentum ahead of the crucial home meeting with Manchester United, who Leeds had now beaten twice after also winning 1-0 at Old Trafford back in December. A win for Revie's men would mean a five-point lead with just four games to play. Crucially, however, Bremner was missing through suspension and his absence was keenly felt as Busby's men exacted revenge for their FA Cup defeat by triumphing 1-0. Suddenly, the impetus had swung back the way of Old Trafford – a feeling that was only strengthened two days later when Sheffield Wednesday beat Leeds 3-0 at Hillsborough. A chance to make amends against the Owls came just 24 hours later, which Leeds duly did with a 2-0 win. Sheffield United were then beaten 3-0 at Bramall Lane, only for Manchester United to triumph by an identical scoreline the same night against Liverpool. It meant Leeds went into their final game of the season at Birmingham City one point ahead of their rivals from Old Trafford, but having played one game more and with Busby's side boasting a superior goal average. The equation was simple – Leeds had to win at St Andrews, while hoping their great rivals claimed just a point from their two remaining matches against Arsenal and Aston Villa. Already relegated Birmingham were not expected to put up too much of a fight but, instead, it was Leeds who froze as the home side raced into a 3-0 lead. A Giles penalty on 65 minutes reduced the arrears, which were cut further when Paul Reaney netted after a goalmouth scramble. Jack Charlton then equalised with four minutes to go but, even with eight players in the home penalty area during the closing stages, Leeds could not find a winner against a Blues side who had, in the days before substitutions, been reduced to ten men by a first-half injury to winger Alex Jackson. Manchester United, who as Leeds toiled in the Midlands were beating Arsenal 3-1, were able to celebrate winning the championship on goal average, their defeat at Villa Park two days later proving academic.

After the effort of the previous nine months, it was a heartbreaking way to lose the title. But, with the prospect of a Cup final against Liverpool just five days away, few at Elland Road dwelt on the disappointment. Cup fever had, since the semi-final triumph over Manchester United, taken a hold in Leeds with the *Yorkshire Evening Post* reporting how a ticket priced at 7s 6d was being sold on the black market for £25. The enticing prospect of a trip to Wembley, something supporters of Leeds and Hunslet Rugby League clubs had already enjoyed on several occasions, persuaded more than 15,000 football fans to head to the capital on May 1. Despite missing out on the league title by the slimmest of margins, those travelling south did so in optimistic mood. The two league games had finished with both United and Liverpool claiming a win apiece – the home side prevailing with a 4-2 triumph at Elland Road and 2-1 on Merseyside. However, with both meetings having taken place within the opening fortnight of the season, Leeds supporters reasoned that their team were much improved for the experience of a first full season of top-flight football.

Liverpool's route to Wembley had involved victories over West Brom, Fourth Division Stockport County, Bolton Wanderers and Chelsea. To the Leeds fans, it represented a less than arduous run of games with only the Blues, who Bill Shankly's side had beaten 2-0 at Villa Park in the semi-finals, having finished the season in the top half of the First Division. The Reds' place in the last four of the European Cup, where they would host Inter Milan in the first leg just four days after the Cup final, also gave the Yorkshire invaders hope.

At Anfield, however, confidence was equally high as forward Ian St John recalls: "Leeds were a good team with a lot of good players. They also had Billy Bremner, who had already shown he had the knack of being able to get Leeds out of a tight spot by popping up to score a late goal. He did it in the semi-finals and it was something he carried on doing throughout his career. We were wary of him. Leeds had also had a good season in the league but we still felt, deep down, this was going to be our year in the Cup."

The final was a disappointment, both as a spectacle and in terms of Leeds' performance. Liverpool, whose full-back Gerry Byrne suffered a broken collarbone in the third minute but bravely played on, produced the few instances of quality play and, but for the agility of Gary Sprake, the Cup would have been won in normal time. Peter Thompson was denied three times and Geoff Strong twice, while Leeds, with Johanneson below par out wide and Jim Storrie troubled by a pulled muscle, offered little in terms of attacking threat. So much so, there was no denying who was the more relieved side to see a final go to extra-time for the first time since Charlton Athletic had beaten Burnley 18 years earlier. Afterwards, Shankly likened proceedings at the end of normal time to, 'A game of chess that had reached stalemate'. It was difficult to argue with the Liverpool manager's view, with some newspapers neatly summing up the lack of action by naming the final, 'The bore of the roses'.

Either way, there was little doubt as the additional 30 minutes got under way that things needed livening up. Liverpool did just that when, three minutes in, Roger Hunt connected with a cross from Byrne to finally break Sprake's resistance. Leeds, forced to abandon their cautious approach, responded by moving Bremner upfield and the switch brought reward four minutes before the interval when he was picked out by a cross field pass from Hunter. The ball landed perfectly at the feet of Bremner, who connected beautifully on the half-volley to beat goalkeeper Tommy Lawrence from 20 yards. There was, however, to be no fairytale ending for United whose hopes of forcing what would have been an undeserved replay were ended when Ian St John met Ian Callaghan's cross with a flying header to ensure the Cup was on its way to Anfield for the first time. St John recalls: "We were the best team on the day. I watched a recording of the final only recently and that much was clear. It was a very competitive game played in the pouring rain. Billy's was a fantastic goal but my winner meant justice was done. No-one could claim it was the best game, which was a shame as both ourselves and Leeds had had good seasons. But we weren't bothered about that at the final whistle."

As the Liverpool players celebrated, their devastated United counterparts slumped to the turf. Bremner, in tears, was inconsolable, though Revie tried his best by pointing out there would be plenty more chances of claiming silverware. Leeds, Revie reasoned to his future captain, were only just beginning their adventure and that defeats like the one at Wembley would only make success in the future all the sweeter.

Chapter 5

'World Champions'

No-one at Elland Road was ever in any doubt as to what Scotland meant to Billy Bremner. Long before making his full international debut a week after Leeds United had lost the 1965 FA Cup final to Liverpool, he had made it clear the pride and honour he felt at being a Scot. His yearnings for a return home to Stirling had been apparent from the very start. Homesickness was, however, not a trait felt exclusively by Bremner with a young Norman Hunter equally missing the comforts of his native County Durham during those early days in Yorkshire. What did, though, set apart a youngster who would become Don Revie's flame-haired midfield enforcer was his attitude to the Scotland v England five-a-side games in training. Taking his lead from equally proud Scot, Bobby Collins, Bremner never let the fact he was up against players he would defend to the hilt come match day temper his own competitive instinct. He had to win for Scotland and, as Eddie Gray recalls, it led to some almighty tussles on the Fullerton Park training pitch that used to stand behind the West Stand at Leeds. "Those five-a-side games could be brutal," says the Scot who was a little over five years younger than Bremner. "I came to Leeds in 1963 and, at times, would be left terrified by what went on during first team games. But, if anything, what went on in those Scotland v England games in training was even worse. They were all out-war, even though everyone played for the same club. It didn't matter that Norman Hunter, Jack Charlton, Paul Madeley and Paul Reaney were Leeds team-mates, only that they were English. Bobby Collins was the main instigator but Billy played his part. Billy was usually not the best trainer, he never used to like any of the physical stuff. But once the ball came out and it was Scotland v England, it was like a switch had been flicked inside Billy. He became totally different. It was as if he was representing his country and winning was everything. The games eventually got so bad that Don had to stop them. He was worried someone would be seriously injured."

For Bremner, this determination to see Scotland prevail was omnipresent throughout his life. It had been honed as a boy, his first international call-up having come when still a pupil at St Modan's Secondary School. During his final year, Bremner made four appearances for Scotland Schoolboys –

including one never-to-be forgotten visit to Wembley in 1958 and a game against an English side that included Terry Venables. Further representative honours came his way after moving south to England, including an appearance for a Scotland XI to take on the Scottish League in 1963. Three Under-23s caps followed against France, Wales and England before the moment Bremner had dreamed of since boyhood arrived with his debut for the senior side. Spain were the visitors to Hampden Park for a friendly as Bremner, fresh from scoring United's goal in the Cup final defeat a week earlier, lined up alongside Scottish greats such as Denis Law, Billy McNeill, John Greig and Bobby Collins. The 22-year-old Leeds midfielder was, along with fellow debutant John Hughes and Alan Gilzean, one of three changes from the side that had drawn 2-2 with England at Wembley a month earlier. Ian St John was one of those to drop out of the side, destined never to add to his 21 caps and nine goals due to a fall-out with the Scotland management. It remains a major regret that he never got the chance to play alongside Bremner for his country. "I retired from international football just before Billy made the breakthrough," says the former Liverpool forward who went on to form one half of the hugely popular television double act *Saint & Greavsie* after retiring from the game. "I'd had a row with the selectors and decided enough was enough, which was a shame as it meant I never got the chance to play alongside wee Billy. I would have liked to because I knew from the many tussles we had between Liverpool and Leeds what a tremendous player he was. Billy always gave 100 per cent and never threw in the towel. I wasn't surprised at all that Billy later went on to become one of the great players for Scotland."

Bremner's international career began with a goalless draw against Spain in front of 60,146 fans. Coming just a week after playing and scoring in front of 100,000 at Wembley, he could have been forgiven for being blasé at running out before another big crowd. Not Bremner, though, who if anything was even more excited at making his international debut, even if the subsequent game became best remembered for the farcical events that saw one of the Spanish players being sent off but then allowed to stay on the field by a confused referee. The chaos began when, after punching Denis Law, the soon-to-be dismissed Spaniard had thrown himself to the ground as if injured. He was, nevertheless, still sent off – only to win a reprieve after spending so long on the ground during the ensuing bedlam that saw players from either side square up to each other that the referee forgot the Spaniard had been dismissed and the game resumed with 11 players a side. It was not the most auspicious of starts to an international career and Bremner had to wait another five months for his next appearance. Hampen Park was again the venue as Poland came to Glasgow for a World Cup qualifier that ended in a 2-1 victory for the visitors. Defeat was a major blow to the Scots, who before facing the Poles had claimed five points from a possible six – including a creditable draw in Warsaw. That both of Poland's goals at Hampden had come in the final six minutes only added to the frustration. Scotland's hopes of qualifying for the 1966 World Cup were still alive, but it meant not even taking four points off Italy in the forthcoming double-header would be enough if Poland managed to claim a point in Rome. In the end, the Italians thrashed Poland 6-1 en route to claiming top spot with a 3-0 win over Scotland on home soil in the final group game. The Scots, courtesy of beating Italy 1-0 in Glasgow, did finish second but it was scant consolation.

Italy's triumph in topping the group meant Scotland's only involvement in the following year's World Cup was as warm-up opponents for Portugal and Brazil. It was in the second of those games at Hampden Park on June 25 that Bremner learned a very important lesson from the world's greatest footballer, as he revealed two years later in the tenth edition of the *International Football Book*: 'There are some players you just cannot afford not to worry about. Give them an inch and they take a yard. Let your attention wander for a solitary second and you find yourself right up the creek. Such a gentleman is Pele, the idol of all Brazilian soccer fans and true lovers of the game throughout the world. When I think of him I automatically think of the juiciest black eye I ever had in my life. It was Mr Pele who dished it out when I was a member of the Scottish side which played Brazil at Hampden just before they took part in the World Cup. My orders that day were to stick to him like glue. If he went off the field for attention, I virtually had to stand with him on the touchline to pick him up again the second he stepped back on to the field. Looking back on the game, I still get a certain amount of satisfaction about the way I did the job. The first chance I had, I let him know I was on the park with as hard a tackle for the ball as I have ever mustered. After that, I have found most of the so-called 'greats' just do not want to know. But not Pele. He's not much bigger or heavier than myself but the next time we clashed I knew all about it. We both went all-out for a high ball together and I must admit I was expecting him to draw back in the last split second. But the next thing I knew I was on the ground nursing as good a shiner as you will see in many a long day. It was entirely accidental, of course, but he proved to me once and for all times, that he has the courage and guts which, in my book, are just as much a part of greatness as fantastic ability.'

The Tartan Army's initial disappointment at missing out on the 1966 World Cup in England was nothing compared to the utter dejection felt when Geoff Hurst's hat-trick at Wembley ensured the hosts lifted the trophy. England's success meant the next meeting between the two countries assumed even more importance than usual in the Scottish dressing room. By the time of the annual clash with the Auld Enemy, Sir Alf Ramsey's side had not been beaten in the eight or so months since lifting the World Cup. They were a prized scalp for the Scots. Not only that, but two European Championship qualification points were at stake due to UEFA deeming Group 8 should be decided by the results of the Home Internationals of 1966-67 and 1967-68. Scotland, with Bremner now a constant presence in the midfield, made a solid start with a draw against Wales in Cardiff and a 2-1 home win over Northern Ireland. England, meanwhile, won both their opening games – 2-0 in Belfast and a 5-1 thrashing of the Welsh at Wembley – to top the group ahead of the Anglo-Scots rivalry being resumed in London on April 15, 1967.

The hosts, who had not been beaten in 19 games, were the favourites. Scotland, though, could not be discounted with the team that started at Wembley featuring four Celtic players who a month later would win the European Cup in Lisbon and two Rangers players who, during the same week, would be beaten by Bayern Munich in the European Cup Winners' Cup final. Add in Denis Law, Jim Baxter and Bremner - three names who would surely walk into any all-time great Scotland XI – and it was clear England were in for an almighty battle. Such a strong line-up meant the 30,000 fans who headed south to the English capital did so in confident mood. For once, the Tartan Army's optimism would not prove misplaced as Scotland stunned the world champions with a 3-2 victory. Law, who had refused to watch the 1966 final on television, opened the scoring in the first half before Bobby Lennox added a second 15 minutes from time. England halved the Scots' advantage through Jack Charlton only for Jim McCalliog to restore their two-goal lead. Geoff Hurst then pulled another goal back for the hosts with 90 seconds remaining but there was to be no denying the Scots their magical moment. The blowing of the final whistle by West German referee Gerhard Schulenberg was the cue for unrestrained celebrations among the players and supporters who had flocked to the English capital.

Scotland hadn't just beaten England, they had beaten the world champions. And they hadn't just beaten the World Cup holders, they had humiliated them with Jim Baxter even finding time late on to flick the ball over a helpless Nobby Stiles in a style more reminiscent of a matador taunting a bull. It was a day when Scotland showed the Auld Enemy how the game should be played, while as far as the Tartan Army were concerned it was also the day their team had been crowned world champions. Unfortunately for Scotland, that win at Wembley was as good as it got for the next few years. Not only did dropped points later in the qualifying campaign – a 1-0 defeat to Northern Ireland being particularly costly – mean Scotland finished second in Group 8 as England went through to win a third-place play-off against the Soviet Union in the 1968 European Championship finals. But further disappointment came courtesy of the Scots failing to reach the finals of either of the next two major tournaments. Even so, Bremner never forgot the elation of being the first team to beat Sir Alf Ramsey's World Cup winners. Eddie Gray, whose own Scottish debut came two years after that victory at Wembley, recalls: "Beating England in 1967 was, undoubtedly, one of the highlights of Billy's career. Billy had an amazing pride in playing for his country. If anything, it brought that little bit of extra fire out of him. At Leeds, Don Revie would sometimes ask the international lads to miss the next game to ensure they remained fresh for an important Cup tie or big league match. He would say things like, 'We've a big league match coming up at the weekend, I think it would be best if you gave the international on Wednesday a miss'. A lot of the time, the lads would agree but not Billy. He wouldn't pull out of a squad. Billy took so much pride in representing his country that he always joined up when fit. He loved playing for Scotland and took great delight in us winning, particularly if it was against England. I think it is a Scottish trait and probably something to do with how we were all brought up at school when the English were painted as the enemy. Billy took that feeling out on to the pitch, so you can imagine how proud it made him feel to have been part of the team that beat England, the World Cup winners, at Wembley. Billy always used to say, 'That was the day we became the world champions'. And he meant it."

Chapter 6

Captain Of The Crew

The matchday programme for the first Leeds United home game after Billy Bremner's death in December, 1997, was unequivocal. He was the greatest captain in the club's history. Due mention was given to Bobby Collins and Gordon Strachan, two Scots who had played significant roles in transforming United's fortunes almost three decades apart. But neither man could, or indeed would, claim to rival a captain whose statue today stands proudly outside Elland Road as a permanent reminder of just what Billy Bremner did for Leeds United. What is often lost amid the memories of vital goals, the energy, the indefatigable spirit and the total commitment he brought to a United shirt was that the captaincy was thrust upon Bremner before Don Revie had originally planned. The Leeds manager, having cured the initial homesickness and fended off several would-be footballing suitors from north of the border, had always viewed Bremner as his future captain. He just didn't plan for it to happen quite so early.

The first step towards Bremner becoming Revie's on-field leader came in early October, 1965. After finishing the previous First Division season as runners-up, Leeds had secured a first foray into Europe via a place in the Inter-Cities Fairs Cup. Originally starting life as a vehicle to promote international trade fairs – only cities that had hosted one could compete – the Fairs Cup had evolved into a respected competition by the time of United's debut in Europe. It meant there was great excitement in both the city and dressing room ahead of the draw for the first round, which would be a two-legged knockout affair. In time, the continent – and particularly the unforgiving football fields of Eastern and Mediterranean Europe – would be where the finer arts of gamesmanship that Revie's Leeds are still renowned for would be honed. But, after being paired with Torino, the initial feeling in Leeds was one of anticipation, mixed in with a little trepidation about stepping into the unknown. Revie, for his part, knew the Italians would be unfamiliar with his players so decided to try and use this to United's advantage in the first leg at Elland Road by sending them out wearing unfamiliar numbers. The plan was to disrupt Torino's rigid man-marking system. It might have been the oldest trick in the book but, initially, the tactic worked as goals from Bremner, the club's first in Europe, and Alan Peacock gave United a 2-0 lead. Torino, once they had got to grips with who should be playing where, then claimed a late strike of their own to set up the return leg a week later. Turin would be where Leeds came of age in Europe as they refused to be intimidated by the physical approach of their hosts to claim a goalless draw on a night when Bobby Collins suffered a broken thigh and the English side had to play the final 40 minutes with ten men. Losing Collins, destined to play only a handful of games at Elland Road once recovered from an horrific injury, was a major blow. But, for Bremner, it ultimately proved his making due to the need to fill the huge void left by the diminutive Scot. Collins, voted Footballer of the Year just a few months earlier, had been a huge influence on Bremner, particularly since the youngster had moved into the centre of midfield alongside his fellow countryman ahead of the 1963-64 promotion-winning season. Now, Bremner had to somehow – along with Johnny Giles, who was moved inside from the right by Revie following Collins' injury – make light of losing a player many at Elland Road considered irreplaceable. For the time being, this would not involve becoming captain – that honour would initially be bestowed upon Jack Charlton, who in the absence of Collins was now the senior pro at the club. But, to all intents and purposes, Revie wanted Bremner to assume the mantle of his on-field leader. It was a responsibility he relished.

To fill the gap on the right caused by Giles' switch into midfield, Revie made what, by now, had become a rare foray into the transfer marker by paying Huddersfield Town £30,000 for Mike O'Grady, who until then had played exclusively on the left flank. Born in Leeds, the 23-year-old had been overlooked at Elland Road as a junior – hence his subsequent move to Leeds Road, where he worked his way up through the ranks to the first-team. An England call-up duly followed, which he marked by netting twice as Northern Ireland were beaten 3-1 at Windsor Park in October, 1962. Since then, however, O'Grady's career had stalled so the chance to move across West Yorkshire was hugely appealing. His debut came at home to Northampton Town in what was only United's second game without Collins. Straight away, he could see how vital Bremner was to Leeds. "I had first met Billy when we were both 15," recalls O'Grady, who went on to become a regular under Revie for much of the next four years. "I was playing for Huddersfield's juniors and Billy was in the Leeds team. I could see he was a decent player, but by the time I signed for Leeds a few years later he had developed into a great player. Billy seemed to have this inner confidence and belief that whatever happened, we were going to win." United did, indeed, mark O'Grady's debut with a win, Northampton having no answer to the home side as they crashed to a resounding 6-1 defeat. A week later, a 2-1 triumph at Stoke City underlined that Leeds, with eight wins from the opening 13 games and just two defeats, were again in the running for the title. That good form would continue for much of the rest of the season, both at home and abroad. In the league, Leeds would again finish runners-up – though without the dramatic finale of the previous year as Liverpool sealed a deserved title in mid-April. Revie's men finished six points adrift of the Reds, another commendable effort by a young team still learning. That maturing process was further aided by a stirring run in the Fairs Cup that took Leeds to the semi-finals. Along the way, Revie's side picked up all manner of tips as to how to cope with hostile crowds and referees who often leaned towards the home team. In Leipzig, for instance, a foot of snow had fallen on the eve of United's second round first leg tie so Revie ordered his players to shave off the bottom of their studs so the nails came through. That way, he reasoned, they would be able to get some sort of grip on the by now icy surface. Knowing the referee would inspect everyone's boots ahead of kick-off, cardboard was then used to cover the studs. Once on the field and with the officials happy following their inspection of everyone's footwear, the cardboard was kicked off and within minutes the Leipzig players, with blood pouring down their shins, were complaining bitterly to the officials. The referee, happy with his earlier inspection, merely waved the East Germans away and United won 2-1. A goalless draw in the return at Elland Road earned Leeds a third round meeting with Valencia, which would prove to be another important step in the development of Bremner, Giles et al. O'Grady recalls: "We all had to grow up fast in Europe. Some of the things that went on in those early Fairs Cup games had to be seen to be believed. Against Valencia, one of their players asked me to help pull him up off the ground but as I did he lunged forward to try and head-butt me. I was also spat at and someone tried to poke me in the eye. Those games in Europe had a big impact on how Don Revie wanted us to play. In Italy, I was head-butted by this Napoli player, who then as the referee turned round threw himself to the ground. The referee fell for it and I was booked. Afterwards, Don came in the dressing room and said, 'This is what we're up against lads'. He knew we had to fight fire with fire."

United overcame Valencia 2-1 on aggregate after two stormy encounters, the first leg at Elland Road being most notable for the referee calling a halt to play for 11 minutes in an attempt to allow tempers to subside following a clash that saw Jack Charlton and Francisco Vidagny sent off. In the quarter-finals, Ujpesti Dozsa were comfortably dealt with as Leeds followed a 4-1 home win with a 1-1 draw in Hungary to set up a semi-final meeting with Real Zaragoza. A 1-0 deficit from the first leg in Spain was overturned at Elland Road to leave the tie level at 2-2 so, with the Fairs Cup not yet under the auspices of UEFA and no away goals rule in place, a replay was needed to decide who would face Barcelona in the final. Leeds captain Jack Charlton called correctly at the toss of a coin to decide the venue but it was Zaragoza who rose to the challenge in the Elland Road replay to win 3-1.

Any feelings of disappointment at failing to reach the final were soon eased by the undoubted progress Leeds had made for a second consecutive season. The youngsters Revie and his coaching staff had spent so long nurturing were maturing fast. They had also made light of Collins' extended absence thanks, in the main, to a formidable partnership struck up between Bremner and Giles. Peter Lorimer, who became a regular in the Leeds team for the first time during the 1965-66 campaign, says: "Billy and Johnny complemented each other perfectly. Johnny was our brains and organiser. He kept us together as a team. Billy, on the other hand, was totally different and undisciplined in the respect that he would tear about all over the pitch. He did that due to believing, 'There is only me who can get us out of trouble'. The thing with Billy was that he was a totally brilliant footballer and that meant him and Johnny were great for each other." Eddie Gray agrees. "Billy and Johnny were completely different," says the Scot whose first-team debut had come on New Year's Day, 1966. "But they were great together. Billy would play the game by tearing about all over the place, whereas Johnny would bring some order and discipline. He would calm things down by saying things like, 'Eddie, come and sit in here a bit and protect the defence'. He would know keeping it tight in the next 10 minutes would be vital. Billy was totally different, tearing here, there and everywhere. But what a player he was. Billy's record for scoring goals in big games was unbelievable. We won so many of them due to Billy's ability to pop up at the vital moment." The Bremner-Giles partnership would become one of the most admired in English football with even United's harshest critics admitting they were something special. Alan Hudson was at Chelsea when games against the Yorkshire club would invariably descend into no holds-barred battles due to an overwhelming desire among both sets of players to get one over the other, either by fair means or foul. But, even allowing for the ill-feeling that existed between Chelsea and Leeds, Hudson insists the Stamford Bridge players recognised Bremner and Giles as being something special. He says: "I played against Leeds many times and I have to say I looked forward to those games more than any other. People complain about the game being physical these days but it is nothing compared to what Leeds were like. I knew every time I walked out to face Leeds that I would be kicked all over. Bremner and Giles were the worst, a couple of pocket-sized assassins. You could never turn your back on them for a second or they would have you. The great thing about Bremner and Giles, though, was that they were great players - truly great players."

In the summer of 1966, English football enjoyed its finest two hours at Wembley. Jack Charlton was in the team that beat West Germany 4-2 in the final, so was given an extra couple of weeks off when the Leeds squad returned for pre-season training. Charlton was 31 and had been handed the club captaincy following the injury to Collins. The Scot, though, had returned to the United side for the final game of the campaign against Manchester United. He also started the first two of 1966-67 before again succumbing to injury. The upshot was Charlton again leading the side, only for the defender's superstitious side – a trait he shared with Revie – to bring about a change. "I always wanted to come out of the tunnel last, which was not possible as captain," he explains. Revie, therefore, was faced with having to find a new captain. He knew the very man. The United manager had, for several years, viewed Bremner as United's likely captain in the long term but, thanks to Collins' unfortunate break and Charlton's superstitions, the time had come to bestow the honour on the 23-year-old. An incident on the eve of United's Fairs Cup trip to Holland to face DWS Amsterdam had also played a part in the decision, Revie reasoning that the extra responsibility would be the making of Bremner after he had turned up at the airport without his passport. Revie was not best pleased, especially after a subsequent search could not find the missing document and Bremner had to get another issued before catching a later plane. Revie's son Duncan recalls: "Dad loved all the young lads but he had a special bond with Billy. It was very, very strong. They were both winners and he saw Billy as his leader. Dad knew Billy would go through a brick wall for him and vice-versa. There was an implicit trust between them. It was why he made Billy captain. Even though he knew how forgetful Billy could be, such as turning up at the airport without his passport. Dad confiscated it, in the end, as he felt it the only way to make sure Billy would have the passport for the European trips."

Bremner's forgetfulness was legendary at Elland Road, so much so that team-mates lost count over the years of the times he arrived late at a function, dinner or presentation. Once, he totally forgot a pre-match promise to give Norman Hunter a lift home from Hampden Park after a Scotland v England international – only remembering the arrangement the following morning when an irate Hunter burst into the Leeds dressing room. Another team-mate who discovered the Scot's absent-minded nature the hard way was Mike O'Grady. He recalls: "I lived close to Billy when I joined Leeds and he helped me settle. We would enjoy a few drinks in the tap room of our local. But he also was responsible for getting me in trouble in those early days. I didn't have a car so he offered to pick me up but, by the following day, he would have forgotten all about it. I was late three times in my first month at Leeds and they were all down to Billy. Once, he even drove straight past without seeing me. Billy was always very apologetic, not that this helped much when I was being told off for being late." What O'Grady also recognised along with the forgetfulness was just how important a figure Bremner was at Elland Road. And how, once made captain, his influence only grew. "He was a total inspiration," he says. "I remember a few games after he became captain where we were losing and I would just look at Billy and think, 'He'll pull something out of the fire here'. And a lot of the time he did. It might be a goal, a tackle or even this trick he had where he would look one way but chip the ball the other. Whenever he pulled that one off, it gave us all a lift and we stepped up a gear." Barry Foster, the *Yorkshire Post* football writer who covered United for 27 years from 1967, similarly recalls the influence Bremner had over his team-mates – and the value put upon that by Don Revie. He says: "Don and Billy were like father and son in so many ways. Don also knew Billy would run through a brick wall for him. I always remember a game at Elland Road when Billy was leading the line on his own due to injuries. He was getting kicked to death by the opposition defence and the pitch was a real mud-heap in those days so, in the end, Billy was totally exhausted. He had given absolutely everything to the team but wanted to do more and that was when he got sent off after lashing out. It was the first and only time I have seen a player get sent off for caring too much. Don recognised that and came on to the field, as Billy walked off, to put his arm round him. It was Don's way of showing that he understood what had just happened. There was this amazing bond between them. On another occasion, Billy was in the medical room and was bruised from his buttocks right down to the back of his knees. There was no way he could play on the

Saturday and yet, after chatting to Don, Billy suddenly declared himself fit. Things like that were why Don made such a good decision in making Billy captain. Billy was such a selfless player and the most inspirational captain I ever saw."

To his team-mates, the honour of being captain seemed to have added a dimension to Bremner's game. Winning had been everything before but now it became almost an obsession, as Peter Lorimer recalls. "I thought it was very clever on Don's part to make Billy captain," he says. "To me, Johnny was our main man on the field as he was the brains of the team. But Don had to make Billy feel he was the main man to get the best out of him. It was clever thinking on Don's behalf."

By the time Bremner had been named captain on a permanent basis, much of 1966 had been and gone. So had any genuine chance of Leeds going one better than the previous two seasons and winning the league title. A disappointing start that brought just four wins from the opening 13 games meant United were always playing catch-up with their rivals. In the end, Manchester United would be crowned champions – five points ahead of Leeds in fourth place. Any hopes the League Cup could provide Revie with the first trophy he craved were ended with a 7-0 thrashing at West Ham United in the fourth round, a defeat so resounding that *Yorkshire Evening Post* reporter Phil Brown wrote the following day: 'The seven goal blitz that hit them resembled something like the pounding that Tilbury Docks, a stone's throw away from the Hammers ground, received during the war.' Leaving aside the inordinate length Brown seemed, at least in his mind, able to throw a stone, the assessment of United's performance was wholly accurate. That it was so out of character only added to Bremner's frustration, which manifested itself in a late booking for the midfielder. The defeat, together with such a slow start in the league, meant if Leeds were to end their search for a trophy then it would have to be in either the FA Cup or Inter-Cities Fairs Cup. In the domestic competition, progress was made past Crystal Palace and West Bromwich Albion to set up a fifth round meeting with Sunderland. Just three years earlier, the two clubs had memorably slugged it out on their way to promotion so the tie generated huge interest both in Yorkshire and the North-East. A crowd of 55,763 packed into Roker Park saw Jack Charlton net for Leeds in a 1-1 draw that meant the two sides would meet again just four days later. Due to the short time scale, the game was not made all-ticket and such was the demand that the gates had to be shut almost half an hour before kick-off with 57,892 fans inside Elland Road.

The crowd remains a club record, some fans being so desperate to see the action they clambered on to the roof of the Scratching Shed. Disaster almost struck 10 minutes into the game when a 10ft crush barrier collapsed under the weight of the crowd and dozens had to be taken to hospital, causing referee Ray Tinkler to halt proceedings. An appeal over the PA system by Leeds chairman Harry Reynolds helped restore order and play resumed with fans sitting on the touchline. Leeds then fell behind to a goal by Scottish forward John O'Hare, who would later move to Elland Road during Brian Clough's ill-fated spell in charge, before Bremner netted another of his vital goals to force the tie to another replay. Staged at the neutral venue of Hull's Boothferry Park, Leeds won a stormy encounter 2-1 as Sunderland duo George Herd and George Mulhall were sent off. A 1-0 win over Manchester City in the quarter-finals then set up a last four meeting with Chelsea. Again, controversy reigned as a late 'goal' from Peter Lorimer was ruled out due to the defensive wall having not retreated the requisite 10 yards. The re-taken free-kick was subsequently cleared and referee Ken Burns blew the final whistle moments later to signal Chelsea were through to the final courtesy of a 1-0 win. That left Leeds with just the Fairs Cup to prevent a third consecutive season ending with no reward for their endeavours, Revie's side having knocked out DWS Amsterdam, Valencia and Bologna to book a semi-final meeting with Kilmarnock. The first leg was scheduled three weeks after the defeat to Chelsea in the FA Cup and Leeds wore the look of a side determined not to end the campaign empty-handed as Rod Belfitt scored a hat-trick in a 4-2 win. A goalless draw in the return at Rugby Park was, therefore, enough to clinch a first appearance in a European final. United's opponents would be Dinamo Zagreb, who had beaten Czech side Spartak Brno, Dunfermline Athletic, Dinamo Pitesti of Romania, Juventus and Eintrecht Frankfurt en route to the two-legged Fairs Cup decider. Due to fixture congestion, both ties were held over until the following season and it was the Yugoslavian side who took a decisive two-goal lead in Zagreb. Leeds' preparations had not been helped by Syd Owen, the compiler of the dossiers on the opposition that Revie put such store by, being unable to watch Dinamo in action beforehand due to a flight cancellation. Even so, United's performance in humid conditions was uncharacteristically poor as they conceded two goals on European soil for the first time. A week later, the return saw Bremner and Charlton have shots cleared off the line as Dinamo held on to claim a goalless draw and become the first Yugoslav side to lift a European trophy. It meant that, three years after winning promotion, Leeds had nothing tangible to show for their considerable efforts. The suggestion in the newspapers was that United were 'serial chokers', destined never to make the step-up following two runners-up spots and an FA Cup final defeat. Within six months, however, such talk had been banished forever.

Chapter 7

Success With A Smile

Despite the disappointment of Leeds United having once again fallen short in the hunt for that elusive first trophy, Elland Road was still a fun place to be. The dressing room, where many of its members had grown up together, was a strong one, thanks in no small part to the careful guiding hand of its father figure, Don Revie. The banter between team-mates, the one element that all retired former players miss once their careers are over, could be ferocious, not least if an unfortunate soul had turned up in a particularly unusual garment such as a flashy coat or new jumper. Practical jokes were also a permanent part of life at Elland Road, with Billy Bremner, as captain, often the leading protagonist. Eddie Gray recalls: "Billy was always up to something, a real character. No-one was safe from one of his wind-ups. One of his favourites was when we went over to Sheila's Café for lunch after training. It was just over the road from the ground and owned by Terry Yorath's in-laws. We had a ritual where we would toss a coin to decide who paid the bill for everyone's lunch. If, say, 12 of us had gone across and eight called 'heads', then the four who said tails would have to pay. Billy was not a big one for lunch and would usually just have a cup of tea and a Kit-Kat. But if a couple of the lads who were a bit tight ended up having called incorrectly, he would have the works. A full three-course lunch would be ordered and then he would also take a few Kit-Kats home for the kids. Often, he would leave the lunch untouched – and then get up to go home with a big smile on his face." It wasn't just Bremner's team-mates who could find themselves on the wrong end of a wind-up, either. Eddie again: "There was one morning when we were training down at Fullerton Park behind the West Stand and a supporter, who looked drunk even though it was around 11 o'clock, had come down to watch. We had drawn the previous weekend and this fan was determined to make his point, shouting things like, 'Bremner, you're useless – I'm a better player than you'. He also told us all that we were 'crap'. Billy had heard enough and marched over to where this supporter was stood and said, 'So, you're better than us are you? Prove it then'. With that, he walked off towards the little gymnasium that used to be under the main stand and the fan followed. We did the same, as we could clearly see Billy was up to something. Anyway, they got into the gym and Billy said, 'Come on then, show me what your heading ability is like'. Billy then tossed him the ball and this guy headed it as powerfully as he could. Unfortunately for him, Billy had deliberately picked up a medicine ball and it knocked the guy clean out. Eventually, the fan came round and as he did, Billy walked off with a smile and said, 'Well, you're crap at heading for a start'." Members of the press also found themselves in the firing line when Bremner was feeling at his most mischievous. Mike Morgan, who has covered the Yorkshire patch for several national newspapers since the 1960s, recalls: "There was one European trip where Bill Mallinson, who worked for the *Daily Mail*, was sitting in front of Billy on the flight. Nowadays, the press and team would be segregated on the plane but that was not the case back then. So, when Bill took his false teeth out in order to go to sleep, Billy waited until he had dropped off before swiping the teeth and putting them in his bag. Poor Bill woke up later and went ballistic, but still didn't know who had taken his false teeth. It wasn't until much later that Billy owned up and handed them back."

The strong team spirit engendered at Elland Road had been no accident, Revie having worked very hard to create an atmosphere he felt was conducive to producing a successful team. Whether it was the groundsman, the tea lady or Jack Charlton, everyone had to feel part of Leeds United. No-one, Revie insisted, was allowed to feel they were more important than anyone else, a trait Bremner adopted once captain. Mike Morgan, who started covering Yorkshire football for the *Daily Express* before moving to the *Daily Star* and then *The Sun*, says: "Before a big game, Don made it open house in terms of the press and told us we could interview who we wanted. But Billy wanted to make sure everyone was involved, not just the 'big' names. He didn't think it would be fair if, say, everyone spoke to Norman but not Mick Bates. So, he would quietly go round the press lads and ask if we would interview Batesy as well as, for example, Norman or Big Jack. Billy was a big one on the importance of everyone feeling part of the team."

As enjoyable as life was behind the scenes at Elland Road, United's start to the 1967-68 season provided little to smile about. A 1-1 draw at home to Sunderland on the opening day was followed by back-to-back defeats at Manchester United and Wolves. Add in a 2-0 defeat against Dinamo Zagreb in the first leg of the Inter-Cities Fairs Cup final held over from the previous season and it meant August was a pretty miserable month. A 2-0 win over Fulham on September 2 did lift the mood, though not sufficiently to spark a comeback in the Fairs Cup final second leg four days later when Dinamo claimed a goalless draw and the trophy. After that, however, Leeds' best form returned as three successive victories and a draw at West Ham was followed by a particularly sweet 7-0 thrashing of Chelsea at Elland Road. The winning run extended into the League Cup as light work was made of Luton Town and Bury, who included in their side Bobby Collins following his transfer from Leeds to Gigg Lane the previous February. In the Fairs Cup, the goals really flowed as Spora Luxembourg were thrashed 9-0 and 7-0 by a rampant United. Strangely, only one of the 16 goals put past the minnows was scored by the man whose £100,000 capture from Sheffield United had just smashed the club's transfer record. Mick Jones had twice played for England before his move to Elland Road and Revie saw him as the solution to the lack of goals that he felt was hindering the push for honours. In time, Jones would go on to net 111 times for Leeds – making him the club's seventh highest goalscorer. But, in those first few games after his transfer from Bramall Lane, what impressed fans and team-mates alike the most about the new signing was his tremendous appetite for work. In the seven-goal rout of Chelsea, Jones hadn't got on the scoresheet. But his unselfish and energetic display had underlined just why Revie had signed him.

In the league, a run of nine wins in 12 games through December and into the New Year kept Leeds among the front-runners. They maintained that position right until very late in the season when a four-game losing run ended any hopes of lifting the title, United having to settle for a second consecutive fourth place finish. The Cups proved to be much more to the liking of Revie's men in 1967-68 – their consistency in knockout football being such that they reached two finals and a semi-final. Most importantly of all, however, the United players finally got their hands on some silverware. The trophy that broke the club's duck was the League Cup, a competition that had gained credence the moment it had reverted to a one-off Wembley final a year earlier. Adding the incentive of European qualification for the winners had also proved an inspired move by the Football League. A 4-2 aggregate win over Brian Clough's Derby County was how Leeds booked their place in the March 2 final, which due to a lack of nous in the League's marketing department took place on a Saturday amid a full programme of First Division games. Live television coverage was also banned due to League secretary Alan Hardaker's long-held belief that live broadcasts drove down attendances.

United's opponents in the final were Arsenal, who since the appointment of Bertie Mee two years earlier had developed into a dangerous side. The Gunners had finished seventh the previous season and there was a growing feeling in north London that success was not too far away. Despite that, Leeds started as favourites and duly settled first in what turned out to be a scrappy affair punctuated by numerous flare-ups between two groups of players who clearly didn't care much for each other. The game was decided in the 18th minute when Eddie Gray's in-swinging corner was only cleared as far as Terry Cooper, who thundered a volley past Jim Furnell in the Arsenal goal. On each of the three nights leading up to the final, Cooper had dreamed about scoring in just such a way. Once ahead, Leeds opted to try and protect what they had. Such a negative approach led to the final being one of the worst seen at Wembley in a long time. But, bearing in mind how many times United had gone so agonisingly close to winning a trophy in recent years, such an approach was perhaps understandable. Jimmy Greenhoff, in the United starting line-up at Wembley, recalls: "The first trophy is always the most memorable and that League Cup win kick-started the success that followed. It made success that bit more special that a lot of the lads had come through together. Norman Hunter, Gary Sprake and Paul Reaney all played in the 1968 League Cup final after having made the breakthrough to the first-team at the same time. Myself, Peter Lorimer and Eddie Gray came through a year later, while Billy was a couple of years older. The squad had a really youthful feel to it. Despite that, we were geared towards playing well in the big games. It was something Don Revie had worked a lot on when we were 16 or 17. I am also sure it was why he opted for us to wear Real Madrid's colours, in an attempt to try and instil that big game mentality in us." On the accusations that Leeds turned the 1968 League Cup final into a dull affair, Greenhoff adds: "As a spectacle, it was a bit of a non-event. Us scoring so early was probably the worst thing that could have happened for the neutrals because we just shut up shop. Don Revie was a very cautious man and, once 1-0 ahead, he always wanted us to protect what we had. It happened every week and Wembley was no different. I was on one wing and Eddie Gray the other, but all we did once ahead was sit in front of the full-backs. I helped Paul Reaney out, while Eddie did the same for Terry Cooper. It was effective, but I doubt anyone outside Leeds enjoyed the 1968 final very much."

The celebrations that followed the final whistle, which saw Bremner do a forward roll before joining his overjoyed team-mates, were a mixture of elation and relief at finally getting their hands on a major trophy. The wait had been a long and frustrating one. Revie's son Duncan says: "Leeds had gone very close to winning a trophy several times so that day at Wembley was like a burden had been lifted. That much was evident in the celebrations that followed. Everyone knew the breakthrough has been made and that the team, which was still very young at the time, was capable of achieving sustained success."

Revie was hungry for more and determined his players would deliver on the pre-season target he had set of wanting to win 'any two' of the four available trophies. Jimmy Greenhoff says: "That was Don. He was never someone who would let the team rest on its laurels. He always wanted to drive the team forward. His message every year in pre-season would be, 'Last season has gone, you are only as good as how you do this season'. He was the same after the League Cup win, insisting we push on as a team and win another trophy that season."

For a time, the FA Cup looked like satisfying Revie's pre-season target of winning a second major honour as Derby County, Nottingham Forest, Bristol City and Sheffield United were all dumped out to earn a semi-final meeting with Everton at Old Trafford. With Alan Ball, who Revie had unsuccessfully tried to sign a couple of years earlier, suspended, Leeds were expected to edge what was likely to be a tight encounter. The semi-final did prove to be closely fought, but it was Everton who progressed after Jack Charlton had been forced to handle a goalbound shot from Jimmy Husband and Johnny Morrissey converted the penalty. Coming so soon after the League Cup win at Wembley that had suggested United's tendency to choke at the vital moment was at an end, the defeat was a major blow – though not one Revie was keen to dwell on. There was still the Fairs Cup to win. In a repeat of their exploits in the League and FA Cups, United's passage through the first few rounds had been relatively straight-forward. After putting 16 goals past Spora Luxembourg, further victories had followed over Partizan Belgrade and Hibernian to set up a quarter-final meeting with Rangers. Such was the interest in the tie at Ibrox that it was beamed back live to Elland Road – a first for the club, though Chelsea had done the same for a European tie in Barcelona a couple of years earlier. Those watching back in Yorkshire saw Revie's men claim a goalless draw en route to progressing 2-0 on aggregate. In the semi-final, Leeds were paired with another Scottish side, Dundee, and Paul Madeley's tenth goal of the season was enough to earn a 1-1 draw at Dens Park in the first leg. The return soon became enveloped in a row after Norman Hunter and Jack Charlton were called up for England's

European Championship quarter-final against Spain on May 8 – a date that clashed with the Dundee encounter. The Scots, unsurprisingly, wanted to stick to the original schedule but Leeds protested to the Fairs Cup Management Committee. Keen to avoid a repeat of the previous season when the Leeds v Dinamo final had to be held over until the following August, they initially tried to strike a compromise only to realise there was no alternative but to delay. As a result, the return leg against Dundee was set for May 15 with the final taking place at the start of the following season. It was not ideal, but Leeds at least made sure it was they who would have to wait all summer for a chance at lifting the Cup and not the Scots by triumphing 1-0 courtesy of an Eddie Gray goal.

The dates for the final, which would be against Ferencvaros of Hungary, were duly set for August. The timing of the first leg at Elland Road could not have been worse for United as it fell during traditional Leeds holidays – meaning many fans were away. The upshot was just 25,268 fans - more than 11,000 down on the league average crowd for the 1967-68 season – turning up to watch Mick Jones give United a precious 1-0 advantage to take to Hungary. The return was originally supposed to be played the following week only for politics to intervene in the form of the Warsaw Pact's invasion of Czechoslovakia, designed to halt Alexander Dubcek's Prague Spring political liberalisation reforms. For a time, it was suggested by the football authorities that the second leg could be declared void – something both Revie and the Hungarians were keen to avoid. Eventually, a compromise was reached that saw Leeds travel to the Nep Stadium on September 11 – almost five weeks after the first leg had been played. The unusually long gap was hardly ideal, though it did provide Jimmy Greenhoff, who had come off the bench in the 1-0 win in Leeds, with an unusual claim to fame. He says: "I joined Birmingham not long after the first leg. It means I was the first player to be transferred halfway through a Cup final. I can't even remember whether I got my winners' medal or not, though I at least played my part."

In Budapest, Ferencvaros predictably threw everything at the English visitors only for Leeds to produce one of their finest rearguard actions. Attacking intent was restricted to set-pieces and the occasional unsupported foray forward by Mick Jones or Peter Lorimer, meaning Gary Sprake came under intense pressure in the Leeds goal. He rose to the challenge admirably, pulling off a string of fine saves to earn the grateful thanks of his team-mates at the final whistle. Even on the rare occasion when Sprake was beaten a team-mate would come to the rescue, as happened in the first half when

Gyula Rakosi thundered a shot goalwards that Terry Cooper acrobatically cleared off the line. It saved a certain goal and underlined the determination and desire running through the entire team that night. United's display in Budapest is regularly cited as one of their finest under Revie and it was a clearly overjoyed Bremner who was presented with the Fairs Cup a few minutes after the final whistle had blown. The squad retired to their city centre hotel, where they were joined by club president, Earl Harewood, as an impromptu sing-song got underway. Mike O'Grady, whose usual attacking instincts had been curtailed earlier in the night, recalls: "Billy loved a drink and a sing, so nights after we had won something or even just got a good result were when he was in his element." After every player had sung his party-piece, Bremner turned his attention to the press lads who, somewhat reluctantly, had a go. Suddenly, Revie piped up, 'No exceptions, Billy – the president next'. As Bremner called for silence, the Earl stepped forward and brought the house down with his own tune. To Bremner, the sight of the Queen's cousin joining in with the fun showed the tremendous team spirit that ran through the heart of Leeds United. It also suggested that the sky really was the limit for this group of players in their push for honours, starting with the biggest prize in English football – the League Championship.

Chapter 8

Champions, Champions, Champions...

Timing, in football as in life, is everything. So, as Don Revie cast his eye across the First Division in the summer of 1968, the Leeds United manager sensed an opportunity. Buoyed by the League Cup triumph of the previous March and with the delayed Inter-Cities Fairs Cup final against Ferencvaros still to come, he believed the time had come for an all-out assault on the League Championship. After four seasons in the top-flight, Leeds had grown into an impressive team. Few, if any, opposing sides looked forward to facing United and Revie felt his players were certainly capable of landing the biggest prize in English football. But what really encouraged the 42-year-old was what he saw when analysing the strengths and weaknesses of Leeds' main rivals. Reigning champions Manchester City, according to Revie, didn't have the resilience to repeat their success – a feeling borne out by the next three seasons bringing 13th, 10th and 11th place finishes at Maine Road. He also felt Manchester United had peaked with the fulfilment of Matt Busby's dream of winning the European Cup when Benfica had been beaten 4-1 at Wembley in May. Arsenal and Everton would, Revie believed, win honours in the near future but were still not quite there in terms of the re-building work being undertaken by Bertie Mee and Harry Catterick respectively. Chelsea and Tottenham Hotspur also lacked the required consistency, leading Revie to believe a Liverpool side showing signs of being on the wane the most likely to pose a threat to his Leeds side. The stage was set for a concerted effort to bring the First Division title to Elland Road for the first time.

Assessing the resources at his own disposal only strengthened Revie's belief that Leeds could do it. The youngsters that he had worked so hard to bring to Elland Road had matured into a formidable unit. The signing of Mick Jones the previous autumn had also brought an extra dimension to the United attack, while after several seasons of making full use of his squad Revie had now settled upon a first choice XI. During the 1968-69 season, that thinking would manifest itself in four players – Billy Bremner, Gary Sprake, Paul Reaney and Norman Hunter - being ever-present, while Jack Charlton and Jones missed just one and two games respectively. In addition, another five would feature in 31 games or more.

The players, on returning for pre-season training, were left in no doubt as to the trophy their manager wanted. Usually, the aim was to win every competition entered – an approach that had cost Leeds since promotion as tired legs towards the end of a season made the last step seem insurmountable. But, ahead of the campaign, Revie made it clear no distractions would be allowed this time around – even if, as proved to be the case on August 24 at Nottingham Forest, such focused thinking could have near fatal consequences. Mike O'Grady recalls: "We were playing at Forest when, just before half-time, smoke started to appear in the main stand. We didn't think much of it as we left the field, we just presumed whatever the cause was would be dealt with quickly. We got to the dressing room and Don started his team-talk. Gary Sprake, who thought he could hear the fire crackling, then tried to speak, but Billy Bremner just said, 'Shut up, the boss is talking'. Don continued and it was only when one of the lads opened the door to go to the toilet that all the black smoke poured in. Don said, 'We need to find somewhere a bit quieter, lads'. He only wanted to carry on the team-talk, even though it was clear the stand was ablaze. Talk about being focused. Eventually, it was suggested we should get the hell out of there and that's what we did – though not before Norman Hunter had turned the wrong way out of the dressing room and almost been burnt alive." Happily, no-one was injured in the fire that left the £100,000 main stand destroyed and the match abandoned.

Blazing stands apart, the start to the season proved to be a profitable one as the United players responded admirably to their manager's pre-season assertion that the league title was winnable. Seven of the opening nine games ended in victory, with the other two – against Sunderland and Leicester City – drawn. The seventh of those wins, Arsenal slipping to a 2-1 defeat at Elland Road, was particularly sweet as it allowed Revie's men to leapfrog over the Gunners and claim top spot. Manchester City then inflicted United's first defeat of the season with a 3-1 victory at Maine Road. Worse was to follow three weeks later when Burnley thrashed Leeds 5-1 at Turf Moor. Revie remained undaunted, however, and his players responded admirably to embark on a long unbeaten run that included revenge over the Clarets in the form of a 6-1 victory at Elland Road shortly before Christmas. The reason for Revie's confidence was the unshakeable belief and faith he had in his players, and in particular his captain. Bremner and his manager had grown incredibly close over the years. Revie, on becoming manager, may have had some early struggles due to the Scot being homesick. But, once that had been sorted following a direct appeal from the Leeds manager to Bremner's fiancée, the pair had forged a strong bond that handing Bremner the captaincy had only served to strengthen. Eddie Gray recalls: "Billy and Don had an unbelievably close relationship, if at times it could be a bit volatile. That is something that can happen when two people are as passionate as Billy and Don. But there was also such a strong bond between them that they seemed inseparable." As Revie's on-field lieutenant, Bremner was the man entrusted with carrying out his manager's orders. That, however, did not prevent the two men having the odd fall-out – as Peter Lorimer remembers. "They were close and most of the time Don thought Billy was brilliant," he says. "But there were also times when they didn't get on. Billy could be a bit of a Jekyll and Hyde-type character, especially with a drink inside him. He could be aggressive and dish out some verbal abuse. Don knew what he could be like and, at times, had a difficult job handling him. My favourite story to illustrate the love-hate relationship that existed between Don and Billy involves the time we were due to play West Ham in London on a weekend. The idea was to meet at Leeds station on the Friday and get the train down. Billy's wife Vicky had gone home for a few days so Billy went out with his pals on the Thursday night and had a few beers. Come Friday morning, everyone was at the train station waiting to set off but there was no sign of Billy. We knew where he was, he had got pissed and stayed in the Griffin Hotel nearby. Don, who was such a powerful man in Leeds at that stage that he could order the station master to delay the train, sent Les Cocker off to get him. Ten minutes later, Les walked down the platform with Billy behind. Billy's tie was all over the place and he looked the worse for wear. All the lads were laughing but Don was not amused and sulked about it all the way to London. Normally, he would play cards with us but this time he refused and sat on his own instead. Billy tried to get him to play but Don wouldn't budge. Eventually, Billy shouted across the carriage, 'If I let you down tomorrow, you can fine me or do whatever you want – but I'll tell you now, I won't let you down'. Sure enough, Billy was outstanding and we won the game. Afterwards, Don and Billy had their arms around each other and there were big smiles across their faces. They were the best friends in the world and you would never have known anything had gone on the previous day. But that's how their relationship was – very close but also capable of being volatile."

The odd spat aside, little ever came between manager and captain at

Elland Road. There was an implicit trust between the two men that the occasional disagreement was not going to affect. John Helm, now a respected football commentator, got to know the two men well after starting to report on the club for the *Yorkshire Evening Post* in 1968. He says: "Billy was the first player I interviewed when covering the club as a reporter and I was very surprised at how erudite he was. He was one of the most competitive footballers you could wish to see on the pitch and a bit of a demon. But, off the field, he was very articulate. The masterstroke that I thought Don pulled off was making Billy captain. Until then, Billy had been a bit of a problem for the management with wanting to go back to Scotland and so on. But, for the rest of Don's time as manager, he behaved fine. It was only after Don left in 1974 that his disciplinary problems resurfaced with that Kevin Keegan clash at Wembley in the Charity Shield. Don just knew how to handle Billy, how to channel his competitive streak. I also thought that clever handling extended to off the pitch as well. In later years, I got to know Don really well and he would invite me over to his house. He was much more relaxed and we would chat about all sorts, all of it off-the-record. It gave me a real insight into Leeds United and the characters at the club. Don would often talk about Billy and Jack Charlton. They were not the bad boys of the team or anything like that but they would share a drink sometimes the night before a game. They would also go to their local on a Thursday for a game of dominoes and a drink. Don knew about this, even if the lads thought he didn't. But because Don trusted both Billy and Jack to perform on the Saturday, nothing was said. If it had been someone else such as Paul Reaney, Don said he would have made an issue out of it."

Revie's unshakeable faith in his players continued to be rewarded as United's good form extended into the New Year. Leeds had made the breakthrough in 1968 by winning two trophies but the coming months, Revie believed, could finally see Leeds promoted to the elite club of title winners. By now, the four-way scrap for the First Division championship had been reduced to two as Everton and Arsenal started to fade. They were destined to fight it out for third place, leaving Leeds and Liverpool as the two remaining title challengers. It meant cranking up even further a rivalry that had grown in importance since the mid-1960s. Ian St John, in his eighth season at Anfield as Liverpool and Leeds slugged it out for supremacy at the top of English football, recalls: "The Liverpool-Leeds rivalry was one of the biggest back then. It probably started around the time of the 1965 FA Cup final. We had played Leeds a few times before then, including in the

Second Division when I remember this little ginger lad called Billy Bremner on the wing. None of us knew anything about him but by full-time we did as he had scored. But, in terms of a proper rivalry, it didn't really get going until a couple of years later. We had probably been about a year or so ahead of Leeds in terms of our development thanks to Bill Shankly. He took us to the Second Division title in 1962 and then the League Championship a couple of years later. We did it again in 1966 and, by then, Leeds were established in the top division and we had already met in the Cup final. After that, we had some great tussles. Towards the end of the 1960s, it had become clear that Leeds had caught us up and it made for some cracking matches."

In the early weeks of 1969, United were still playing catch-up in the race for the title but, crucially, the substantial advantage once held by Bill Shankly's side had been whittled down to just a couple of points. Finally, on February 12 and courtesy of a 2-0 win at home to Ipswich Town, Leeds overhauled the Reds to return to the top of the table. By then, their involvement in the two domestic cup competitions had come to an end. In the League Cup, it was Second Division Crystal Palace who had knocked United out at Selhurst Park in the fourth round. Revie could not have been accused of taking the tie lightly, his starting XI containing only one change from the 2-0 league win over West Ham a few days earlier as Eddie Gray came in for the suspended Bremner. There were a couple more changes when Sheffield Wednesday triumphed in the FA Cup at Elland Road as Mick Bates and Albert Johanneson started. But, again, the team was still a strong one. Nevertheless, Revie was not unduly concerned about bowing out of both domestic Cup competitions. Nor was he overly fazed when Ujpesti Dozsa ended any hopes of retaining the Inter-Cities Fairs Cup with a 3-0 aggregate triumph in the quarter-finals. Instead, he reasoned, it would allow United to focus solely on their number one aim of clinching the title.

The fatigue that had been such a problem during previous seasons was nowhere to be seen as Leeds stayed clear of the field with a 5-1 victory at Stoke City on March 8, their tenth in 11 league outings. Goalless draws at Wolves and Sheffield Wednesday followed before a 1-0 victory over Manchester City avenged the early season loss to the reigning champions. Another draw on the road, this time at West Brom, meant Leeds travelled full of confidence to Highbury in mid-April. That optimism proved justified as Arsenal were beaten 2-1, though only after referee Ken Burns had decided not to send Gary Sprake off for thumping Bobby Gould in the face after the burly forward had clattered into the Leeds goalkeeper. It was a major let-off for Sprake and one several newspapers made much of the following day. United were not a popular side due to what many saw as their gamesmanship tactics, not least in terms of wasting time once ahead. Brian Glanville, the football correspondent of *The Sunday Times*, wrote after that win over Arsenal: 'Leeds would be deserving rather than popular champions. One has to admire them but it is still hard to like them.' Negativity continued to follow United, their approach proving hugely unpopular with supporters and pressmen alike. One rival who refuses to condemn Leeds, though, is Ian St John. "People say Leeds strayed over the line at times but every team had its hard players back then," says the former Liverpool forward. "We certainly did at Liverpool. There was a big rivalry between ourselves and Leeds but it never went too far. I remember once going to watch Leeds play Everton at Goodison Park and the referee had to take the players off because things had got so bad. It was an all-out kicking match. But we never had anything like that when playing Leeds. Maybe that was something to do with both our managers being such big pals. Shanks and Don Revie got on so well it probably filtered through to the players. What also probably helped is they both liked to take their teams to Blackpool for the bracing sea air. Often, it would be at the same time so we would bump into each other from time to time and have a few pints together."

The scathing assessment from such a respected scholar of the game as Glanville was the sort that usually stung Revie, who had an overwhelming desire for his team to be admired and liked by the wider football public. But to the players, it was neither here nor there. Leeds were chasing the league title and nothing was going to knock them off course. The triumph at Highbury was followed a week later by a win over Leicester City at Elland Road. With three games to go, Leeds were tantalisingly close – the only possible football equivalent to a banana skin being that their run-in included two trips to Merseyside, to take on Everton and the only side still capable of pipping them to top spot, Liverpool. The first of those two visits, to Goodison Park, ended in a goalless draw. On the same night, Liverpool had travelled to Highfield Road to take on relegation-threatened Coventry City but only been able to come away with a point. It meant, ahead of the two title rivals going head-to-head at Anfield on Monday April 28, that Leeds led the way with 64 points from 40 games. Liverpool were five points behind but had played one game fewer. A point, therefore, would be enough to bring the title to West Yorkshire for the first time since the last of Huddersfield Town's three back-to-back championship successes in 1926. A home win and Leeds would need to beat Nottingham Forest two days later or risk losing out altogether if Liverpool won their remaining games at Manchester City and Newcastle United.

Two days after Manchester City had lifted the FA Cup by beating Leicester City at Wembley, all eyes were on Anfield for a game that had originally been scheduled for March 22 only for a flu outbreak at Elland Road to cause a postponement. Understandably, nerves were jangling in both camps ahead of the rearranged game. Eddie Gray recalls: "There was a lot of tension among our lads, even Billy Bremner felt it. He was usually the Leeds player who worried the least ahead of a game but he found it almost impossible to sleep the night before we faced Liverpool."

Such was the interest generated by the game, the Anfield gates had to be locked five minutes before kick-off with a crowd of 53,750 inside. The famous Kop, that seething, surging mass of humanity, was packed to the rafters with excited Liverpudlians. Among them was at least one native of Yorkshire, John Helm having been sent by the *Yorkshire Evening Post* to cover the game from the spiritual home of the Liverpool support. He recalls: "I went on the Kop with a Liverpool fan called Nick Rizzo and the atmosphere was electric when we got in, even though kick-off was still some time away. Night games are always that bit extra special in my opinion but this was something else. There was a real air of expectancy on the Kop, all those around me certainly seemed to believe it would be Liverpool's night. I was nervous watching as the Leeds team came out so God only knows what the players must have been going through."

Bill Shankly had tried to crank up the pressure on the visitors during the build-up by telling the Press: 'If Leeds United do not win the First Division championship this year, they never will.' If it was an attempt to unsettle Leeds, it didn't work as they belied any pre-match nerves to produce an ice-cool performance amid the furious atmosphere of Anfield. Paul Madeley, selected in midfield, dropped deep to provide extra cover for the back four, while Liverpool's widemen, Ian Callaghan and Peter Thompson, were kept in check by Terry Cooper and Paul Reaney. As a result, chances were at a premium with Gary Sprake called into action just a couple of times to deal with an ambitious 35-yard effort from Callaghan before the break and a curling shot just after the hour from the same player. Young striker Alun Evans also wasted a couple of decent openings but, otherwise, a defence led superbly by Jack Charlton kept Liverpool in check. Leeds, who played with Mick Jones operating as a lone frontman, came closest to breaking the deadlock with a deflected Bremner effort that had goalkeeper Tommy Lawrence scrambling along his line. Eventually, and after much imploring from the Leeds fans who had made the trip to Merseyside, referee Arthur Dimond blew the final whistle to spark wild celebrations among the visiting players and coaching staff. The drama of the evening, however, was far from over as, amid the celebrations, Revie sought out Bremner and reminded his captain of what had been said between the two before kick-off. Namely, that, should Leeds get the point they required, Bremner must take the team to the Kop end. Now, Revie was reinforcing those words. Bremner looked at his manager warily, fearing it was a bad idea. But, in common with everyone else at Elland Road, the captain did what he was told by his manager.

Bremner, a little hesitantly at first, duly set off walking towards the giant terrace that once dominated Anfield as an eerie silence descended over the crowd. John Helm recalls: "I remember seeing the Leeds lads come towards us. Billy looked reluctant, to say the least. You could hear a pin drop as they got as far as the penalty area and I did wonder how it was going to end. Eventually, this chant of, 'Champions, Champions, Champions…' began, and within seconds, it seemed everyone around me was joining in. The Kop could see the Liverpool players had given everything but had lost out to the best team in the country. The reception was amazing and totally genuine. It was a magical moment and one I will never forget." The players, led by Bremner, continued to bask in the adulation for another 20 minutes before returning to the dressing room where the champagne corks were already popping. Afterwards on the team bus home, the United captain would lead an impromptu sing-song of the song he and his team-mates would sing together after special occasions - *It's a grand old team we play for…*

Even as the bus pulled back into Elland Road, few of the players could believe what they had just experienced, the amazing sportsmanship of the Liverpool football public being such that Phil Brown was moved sufficiently to write in the following day's *Yorkshire Evening Post*: 'It was nice to hear the greatest Kop in football giving generous tongue – like hounds cheering the fox that has just beaten them.' Ian St John, a member of the Liverpool attack that had been so well marshalled by Leeds that night, was equally appreciative of what the Yorkshire club had achieved. He says: "They came to Anfield needing a draw and were full value for their point. Leeds were so well organised that night and deserved it. The Liverpool supporters are very knowledgeable and recognised that for themselves. That is why they gave the Leeds lads such a fantastic reception after the final whistle. They knew

Leeds had proved themselves the best team in the country that season."

Almost ten years after making his Leeds debut, Bremner had reached the very top. Revie, too, had come a long way since the time as a player he had shared a room with Bremner the night before the Scot's bow at Chelsea's Stamford Bridge. He would be rewarded by being named Manager of the Year a few weeks later, typically dedicating the award to his players and coaching staff. What most pleased the United manager, however, was the accolade bestowed on his team by Bill Shankly in the Anfield dressing room. After having spoken to his own dejected players, Shankly went to congratulate the celebrating Leeds players. Revie's son Duncan says: "Shanks was a good friend of my Dad's and asked if he could say a few words. Dad called for quiet and, suddenly, the dressing room was silent. Shanks stepped forward and said, 'We have not lost the title, you have won it and you're the best team in the country'." Shankly's view was backed up by statistics as Leeds, who rounded off their season 48 hours later with a 1-0 win over Nottingham Forest, set a number of new records. Their 67-point haul was the highest of all-time, beating Tottenham's double-winning side of 1960-61 and Arsenal's 1930-31 champions who both claimed one point less. Leeds also won more games (27) than anyone else had managed in history, suffered the fewest defeats (two) and collected the most points at home (39). They also conceded just nine goals in remaining unbeaten through 21 games at Elland Road, while the club record of 12 straight home wins in the league – a run that began in November and ran throughout the rest of the season - still stands today. It meant United, despite the criticism that had come their way, were worthy champions and deserving of their crack at the big one, the European Cup.

Chapter 9

Heartache For Club And Country

Any hopes Billy Bremner may have harboured of rest following the exertions of a demanding title race had to be put on hold. Not, however, that someone who was as passionate a Scot as the Leeds captain really minded bidding farewell to his team-mates to join up with the international squad. Not only was there the traditional Home International series of games to play, but also an important World Cup qualifier against Cyprus. Scotland had been handed a tough group in the quest for a place at the 1970 finals in Mexico. With just 14 qualifying berths up for grabs – England, as holders, and hosts Mexico had automatically been handed a place at the finals – it meant a mad scramble for a host of countries. Of those 14 spots, only eight were available to teams from Europe so the draw was always going to be important. For Scotland, it could scarcely have been crueller as Bobby Brown's side were handed a daunting group containing West Germany, Austria and Cyprus. The Germans had been the losing finalists in 1966 so were strong favourites to claim the one qualifying place in Group 7 ahead of the Scots and Austria. Eddie Gray, who as qualifying got under way was hoping to make the step up from the Under-23s to the senior side, says: "It was a difficult group, there was no question about that. West Germany were a very good team so from the moment the draw was made no-one in Scotland was in any doubt as to the challenge that lay ahead."

The last major finals Scotland had qualified for had been the 1958 World Cup, when a team who would have been led by Matt Busby but for the injuries he sustained in the Munich air disaster drew with Yugoslavia but lost to Paraguay and France. Once handed a qualifying group including West Germany, hopes of a repeat of even that first round exit come the 1970 finals in Mexico appeared forlorn. By the midway point of the group, however, Scotland's indomitable spirit had shone through to leave Brown's men level on five points with the Germans. Qualification was very much up for grabs. Scotland had started their campaign with a 2-1 win over Austria at Hampden Park on a night made all the sweeter for Bremner by captaining the side. The honour of leading his country had first been bestowed on the Leeds midfielder a month earlier in a friendly against Denmark in Copenhagen.

But, with a crowd of just 12,000 present to watch the Danes win 1-0, the magnitude of being captain only really sank in when the Austrians visited Hampden on November 6, 1968. Gray says: "Billy was always terribly proud to pull on the Scottish shirt, we all were. I always put it down to the pride that was instilled in us as schoolboys. For Billy, playing for his country always brought that little bit of extra fire from him. So, you can imagine how being made captain left him feeling. I doubt much in football compared to leading Scotland out at Hampden Park for Billy." Perhaps inevitably considering his ability to pop up with a goal at the vital time as Leeds captain, Bremner marked leading out his country for the first time on home soil by netting the winner in front of 80,856 fans as the Scots came from behind to secure two precious points. That it was his first goal in international football just made the 76th minute decider all the sweeter. The following month, Cyprus – beaten 7-1 in their opening qualifier by Austria – were thrashed 5-0 as Bremner again led from the front in Nicosia. Four points from two games was a dream start but the visit of West Germany in April was always likely to provide a more accurate guide to the Scots' prospects. Bremner may have been in the midst of an ultimately successful, if draining, title challenge with Leeds but he still found the energy to drive Scotland forward in front of 115,000 fans. A point, earned when Bobby Murdoch cancelled out Gerd Muller's first half strike with just five minutes remaining, was a fair reflection of the home side's endeavours. It also meant a draw from the return in Hamburg six months later could, depending on the other results, be enough to claim top spot in the group. Before then, though, there was the annual battle for 'local' pride in the Home Internationals.

Wales were Scotland's first opponents on May 3, a 5-3 victory at Wrexham's Racecourse Ground again seeing Bremner's name feature on the scoresheet. Three days later Northern Ireland claimed a 1-1 draw at Hampden before the Home Internationals were rounded off with a trip to Wembley, the scene of such a memorable win for Scotland just two years earlier. Much to Bremner's disappointment, however, there was to be no repeat this time around as two goals apiece from West Ham duo Geoff Hurst and Martin Peters sealed a 4-1 win. Colin Stein netted for the visitors but it was a hugely disappointed Tartan Army that returned north of the border as England finished the Home Internationals with a maximum six points. Eddie Gray, who made his Scotland debut that day at Wembley, recalls: "Everyone was really down afterwards, none more so than Billy. He loved nothing more than beating the English, which was why our 1967 win at Wembley just 12 months after England had won the World Cup was one of the highlights of his career. The rivalry between Scotland and England was intense, probably much more than it is today. Back then, it didn't matter to those of us at Leeds that we played together for our club – all we wanted to do was beat our English team-mates. There was also plenty of banter in the Leeds dressing room afterwards, depending on who had won. It raised the stakes even more."

There was, though, no time to dwell on such a chastening defeat with Cyprus due at Hampden just a week after the loss to England. Victory would bring Scotland level on points again with West Germany, who since their draw in Glasgow had beaten Austria 1-0 thanks to an 88th minute strike by Muller in Nuremberg. More importantly, bearing in mind how woeful Cyprus had been so far in Group 7, the Scots needed to win convincingly to boost their goal difference. They did just that, Gray's 16th minute opener paving the way for a taking apart of the minnows with such venom that eight goals were scored with no reply as Scotland leapfrogged over the Germans to top the group. West Germany's subsequent 12-0 thrashing of Cyprus four days later took some of the gloss of the Scots' own efforts but, crucially, it meant Brown's men would be very much still in the race to qualify for Mexico when qualifying resumed in October with a trip to Hamburg.

After enjoying a much-needed summer holiday, Bremner returned to Leeds for pre-season training in buoyant mood. The glow of having been crowned champions the previous April together with what had been an inspired piece of transfer business in June by Don Revie meant hopes were high of another successful season. Allan Clarke had been a target of the United manager 12 months earlier but his interest had only become apparent after the then Fulham forward had promised to sign for Leicester City. Being a man of his word, Clarke, who was also wanted by Manchester United, felt it only right to join the Foxes, whose manager Matt Gillies he had taken a liking to. A year on, however, and Leicester had been relegated so Revie returned to Filbert Street to sign Clarke for a British record fee of £165,000. The Leeds players were familiar with Clarke, so knew all about the qualities that had made Revie so determined to get his man. He was a genuine 20-goals per season frontman, the sort of player that United would need to build on the success of the previous two seasons – especially in the European Cup. The signing also signalled to the wider football world that Leeds were intent not to rest on their laurels. What those outside Elland Road couldn't know, however, was just how intent Revie was in bringing unprecedented success to one club. Only the players, who he had called together in pre-season to outline his aims, knew that they were chasing something that had never been achieved before by an English team. Namely, the treble. Revie was clearly not fazed by the fact that only one team, Tottenham Hotspur in 1960-61, had managed to pull off the double since the turn of the century. No, he felt Leeds were capable of not only retaining the league title but also bringing the FA Cup and the European Cup to Elland Road. It was a mighty ask, though one his loyal players bought into immediately. If the Boss said it was possible, it was. Peter Lorimer says: "The boys had total faith in what Don said. If he said we were going for the treble, we were going for the treble."

After claiming the Charity Shield with a 2-1 win over FA Cup holders Manchester City at Elland Road, United started a season brought forward to accommodate the following summer's World Cup finals taking place in Mexico with a 3-1 home win over Tottenham. Clarke marked his league debut with a goal but, in those early weeks, it was clear that his arrival – and the resulting change of approach – would take a little getting used to. With Peter Lorimer also becoming a mainstay of the team for the first time – in the title-winning success the Scot had sat out 17 of the 42 games – United had much more attacking threat than in 1968-69 when Mick Jones had been the only player whose goal tally reached double figures. The upshot of Clarke joining Jones up front and Lorimer's permanent inclusion was that Bremner and Johnny Giles' own freedom to get forward had to be curtailed. These teething problems were why, come September 6 when Manchester United claimed a 2-2 draw at Elland Road, Leeds' record read two wins and five draws from the opening eight games. Their one defeat – United's first in 34 league outings – had come, ominously, against an Everton side strongly-fancied to challenge for the title. The week after the draw with the Red Devils, however, Leeds finally clicked into gear with the first of four straight wins in the league as Sheffield Wednesday were beaten at Hillsborough. Revie's plan to let his players 'off the leash' compared to the title-winning campaign that had been built on defensive solidity was reaping reward.

The upturn in form at club level meant Bremner flew off with the Scottish squad to West Germany in late October for their vital World Cup qualifier in buoyant mood. The Germans, two points ahead of Bobby Brown's side but having played one game more, remained favourites to qualify for the finals in Mexico. But there was a genuine feeling among the Scots heading to Hamburg that an upset could be on the cards. Eddie Gray, who collected his third cap in the qualifier against West Germany, recalls: "We knew they were a very good side but we also had a lot of good players. Our boys could play, no-one was in any doubt about that, and we travelled full of enthusiasm. We definitely didn't feel inferior, in fact if anything knowing we were due to play such a good team made us feel that bit more confident because players like Billy always relished playing against the best."

The confidence within the Scotland ranks seemed justified when, within just three minutes of the kick-off, Jimmy Johnstone put the visitors ahead with a predatory finish from close range after goalkeeper Sepp Maier had spilled the ball. As was to be expected of a side who had only lost the most recent World Cup final after extra-time, West Germany rallied and equalised through Klaus Fichtel. They then took the lead through Gerd Muller, a striker so prolific during his career that the Bayern Munich man netted more goals for his country than he played games – 68 from 62. Alan Gilzean then brought the scores level just after the hour to again raise hopes of a shock as Scotland, driven forward by Bremner, laid siege to the home goal. The Germans, though, stood firm as Maier produced a stunning display and were rewarded 11 minutes from time when Libuda capped a sweeping counter-attack by netting the winner. More than four decades on, the frustration of that night has not left Gray. "Losing after playing so well was awful," recalls the former Leeds manager. "We were the better team, no doubt about that. We battered them and created loads of chances. Franz Beckenbauer was in the middle of the park but we dominated them. I remember walking out and the atmosphere was sensational. Uwe Seeler was the West Germany captain and because he played for Hamburg, the home fans were really fired up. But it never fazed us, if anything we thrived on it. The most disappointing part was sitting in the dressing room afterwards and realising that we should have beaten West Germany. We got a couple of goals but should have had more, while we also gave away a couple of silly goals. It is a big regret even now that we didn't get the win we deserved. If we had won in Hamburg, I am sure we would have gone on and qualified."

Courtesy of the defeat in the Volksparkstadion, Scotland's qualification hopes were over. A 2-0 defeat to Austria in Vienna a month later proved academic with Germany having already gone through courtesy of their triumph against the Scots in Hamburg. It was a disappointing end to what had, at one stage, promised to be a memorable qualifying campaign. For Bremner and Eddie Gray, it also proved to be a taster of what, ultimately, lay ahead with Leeds later in the season.

Back at Elland Road, the pair initially put any frustration felt at missing out on a place at the World Cup finals behind them as Leeds maintained the push for honours. Following a 6-1 thrashing of Nottingham Forest with a 4-0 victory over Ipswich Town was a particular highlight, as was a 6-0 aggregate second round triumph over Ferencvaros in the European Cup after Norwegian amateurs, SK Lyn Oslo, had been dismissed 10-0 and 6-0 in the earlier stage. The band of brothers spirit that Revie had worked so hard to create in his early years as manager was evident not only on the pitch but also off it, as *Daily Mail* chief football writer Jeff Powell discovered on his first European assignment with Leeds in Budapest. He recalls: "Back then, the press guys socialised with the players and we went out to a nightclub after the game. We had a few drinks before asking for the bill. When it came, one of the lads thought the money they were asking was too much and then the bouncers got involved. It became heated very quickly and when Billy Bremner said, 'Everyone pick up a chair', I remember thinking, 'What have I got myself into?' We ended up having to fight our way out and a few of the lads suffered cuts and bruises. But it showed how much those players were willing to back each other up."

Bremner, displaying the 'attack is the best form of defence' mentality that characterised his playing career, also revealed the loyal streak that burned within him in the aftermath of that trip to Hungary after being left impressed by one particular member of the press corp. Powell again: "On the return home, we arrived at the airport in Budapest and a few of us wanted a hair of the Hungarian dog. Billy was one of those who fancied a drink and stationed himself in between Jack Charlton at the counter of this tiny bar and myself at the door. The plan was to pass the drinks out to those waiting outside. I took the orders and passed them on to Billy, who then told Jack. Eventually, we got to one particular member of the press, who asked for a double Barasch. As Billy handed over the drink, Hungary's national liqueur, he stopped to inhale the fumes and found it particularly pungent. The press man in question gulped it straight down and asked for another. Billy was impressed and asked, 'Who the hell is that?' The reply was, 'Geoffrey Green of *The Times*'. I found out later that from that day on, Billy ordered *The Times* to go with his normal tabloid. He continued to order the paper until the day after Geoffrey died, he had been so impressed by his drinking ability. Mind, I also found out once off Billy's wife Vicky that he never once read it."

If Bremner had cared to open *The Times* each morning in the early weeks of 1970, he would, no doubt, have enjoyed what he read. After ending the old year with a 2-1 victory over Everton that cut the leaders' advantage to just one point, they routed third placed Chelsea 5-2 at Stamford Bridge before beating Coventry City to regain top spot. Another five-goal thrashing, this time of West Bromwich Albion, in February underlined the more expansive approach Revie now advocated. The flipside was that United were also more liable to concede, a point illustrated by a clean sheet count that stood at 24 in 1968-69 being destined to fall by two-thirds come the end of the campaign. Nevertheless, Leeds continued to bear the look of a team destined to win trophies as winter turned to spring. Further progress had been made in the European Cup, Standard Liege having succumbed 1-0 in both legs to earn United a place in the semi-finals. Celtic, Legia Warsaw and Feyenoord completed the line-up for the last four, leaving both Revie and Jock Stein to hope the two British clubs could be kept apart and instead meet in the final. The two friends, who had attended the British Open at Lytham together the previous summer, were not to get their way as the names of the Polish and Dutch champions came out first in the draw in Rome to leave the mouth-watering prospect of a 'Battle of Britain' in April. The first leg would be played in Yorkshire and the return in Glasgow, where a phenomenal demand for tickets led to the tie being switched from Parkhead to Hampden Park. Six months earlier, a friendly between the two clubs had finished 1-1 but few believed it to be much use in terms of predicting how the semi-finals would pan out.

As enticing as the double-header against Celtic was, Leeds could not afford to allow it to serve as a distraction from their push for domestic honours. In the league, a win over Wolves just three days after booking their place in the semi-finals meant Revie's men were just three points behind leaders Everton with six games remaining. In the FA Cup, meanwhile, United had also battled through to the semi-finals thanks to victories over Swansea Town, non-League Sutton United, Mansfield Town and Swindon Town. As in Europe, any hopes of being drawn against the weaker of the other three remaining sides, Watford, were dashed as Leeds were handed a tough meeting with Manchester United in the last four. The semi-final was scheduled for March 14 to accommodate the need for Sir Alf Ramsey's England to acclimatise in Mexico ahead of the World Cup. As the fixtures backed up, Leeds badly needed the maxim of being '90 minutes from Wembley' to come true. Instead, what they got was two hard-fought goalless draws against the Reds at Hillsborough and Villa Park before the tie was settled in Leeds' favour by another timely goal for Bremner. His eighth minute strike at Burnden Park, an instinctive left-foot finish, capped a wonderful couple of days for the Scot, who the previous night had been named Footballer of the Year. Twelve months earlier, Bremner had finished third behind joint winners, Dave Mackay and Tony Book. Elevation to the top prize was recognition of the way the Leeds captain had harnessed his aggression and passion over the past 12 months. Chosen by the Football Writers' Association, the award was the ultimate accolade for a player - the Professional Footballers' Association's Player of the Year would not be launched until 1974 when Norman Hunter was the inaugural winner. Bremner's success in being named Footballer of the Year followed that of Bobby Collins in 1965 and Jack Charlton two years later, providing further recognition of the standing Leeds now enjoyed in the game. As proud as Bremner was, however, what mattered most was the team getting what he considered their just reward. Unfortunately for the Scot, his Cup semi-final winner against Manchester United would turn out to be the high point of United's season.

The push to retain the league title was the first to fall by the wayside. Just 48 hours after the semi-final win at Bolton, Leeds suffered a 3-1 home defeat to Southampton. Everton's defeat of Chelsea the same night meant any hopes of wrestling top spot off the Merseysiders were all but gone. Two days later, it was clear Revie had given up on the league as a host of first-team regulars were rested for the trip to Derby County. With the first leg of the 'Battle of Britain' against Celtic just two days away, the United manager was adamant his players needed to rest. The argument was one that would surely elicit plenty of sympathy today and lead to the authorities doing all they could to try and ease the burden. But, in 1970 and with Revie having fallen out with Football League secretary Alan Hardaker on numerous occasions in the past, the pleas fell on deaf ears and United were fined £5,000 for the weakened team that lost 4-1 at the Baseball Ground. Leeds would eventually finish second, nine points behind champions Everton, after winning just one of their final six league games.

Bremner had been one of many to sit the Derby game out but he was back two days later when the club he had supported as a boy came to Elland Road for a game that had generated huge excitement both north and south of the Border. Such had been the interest in Glasgow that many Celtic fans had queued overnight in the hope of securing one of the precious 6,000 tickets that had been allocated to the Scottish club by Leeds. For Bremner, the tie was one he had waited all his career to play in. Fatigue may have set in during recent weeks but he was sure United, still yet to concede a goal in Europe that season, would rise to the occasion. For Celtic, the train journey south was made in the knowledge another Scottish league title – their fifth in a row – had been sealed courtesy of a goalless draw against Hearts at Tynecastle the previous Saturday. Stein's men were also already through to the Scottish Cup final so were in relaxed mood ahead of kick-off. Within 85 seconds, the Scots' mood had been lifted even further when George Connelly capitalised on indecision in the home defence to open the scoring with a shot that deflected past Gary Sprake off Terry Cooper. Leeds, playing their 57th game of the season, offered little in response as Celtic dominated – the English side not being helped by Bremner having to sit out the final quarter with a bout of concussion after banging his head on the turf in a fall. Eddie Gray did strike the crossbar late on but, come the final whistle and with no further goals, the hosts were lucky to still be in the tie. Revie, crestfallen at his side's 1-0 defeat, tried to sound an upbeat tone afterwards by telling the *Yorkshire Evening Post*: 'It makes it very hard for us at Hampden but nothing is impossible in football.' Revie's refusal to accept the dream of a first appearance in the European Cup final was over was admirable. But, in truth, the homecoming afforded the Celtic players as 5,000 overjoyed fans flocked to Glasgow Central station spoke volumes for where the balance of power lay now lay in the tie.

As manager Jock Stein was afforded the biggest roar of all as he stepped on to the platform, the United team were heading south to London and a game against West Ham. Common sense would have dictated fielding a reserve team just 24 hours after such a draining encounter with Celtic. But Revie, still bridling at being fined for fielding a weakened side against Derby, named a handful of first-team players in the starting line-up. Among those was Paul Reaney, who suffered a broken leg in a 2-2 draw with the Hammers that would cruelly rule the full-back out of the return against Celtic, the FA Cup final and the World Cup. He would not return until December.

It was a shattering blow for Reaney and his team-mates. But, as had happened so many times in the past, they re-grouped ahead of the Cup final. Chelsea, who had thrashed Watford 5-1 in the semi-finals, had enjoyed an excellent season. A third place finish had been deserved reward for manager Dave Sexton. Under Tommy Docherty, he had helped lay the foundations of the attractive side that he had subsequently taken over in October, 1967. Now, Sexton was reaping the rewards of that work. At the Wembley final, however, even the most one-eyed of Blues supporters admitted Leeds were the better team. On a pitch covered in 100 tonnes of sand to try and improve a surface ripped apart by the Horse of the Year show, United rediscovered their early-season attacking verve with Eddie Gray leading the way. A week earlier, Gray had scored twice in a 2-1 win over Burnley. The second of those goals would, 25 years later, be voted by supporters the best in United's history as the Scot slalomed his way through the Clarets' defence before shooting past goalkeeper Peter Mellor. At Wembley, he proved equally difficult to handle with Chelsea's Dave Webb given the most torrid afternoon of his career. Perhaps inevitably, Gray was involved in the opening goal on 21 minutes when his corner was met by Jack Charlton just ahead of Peter Bonetti and the ball trickled over the line. It had been something of a freak goal due to the lack of power in the header but nothing compared to the near farcical circumstances surrounding Chelsea's subsequent equaliser as Gary Sprake allowed a speculative effort from Peter Houseman to squirm under his body just before the break. Leeds, with Gray again to the fore, regained control after the break and duly went ahead seven minutes from time when Mick Jones converted the rebound after an Allan Clarke header had struck the post. The Cup seemed destined for West Yorkshire only for Ian Hutchinson to equalise just four minutes later. Thirty minutes of extra-time were unable to separate the two sides, meaning the final would go to a replay for the first time in the Wembley era. It was the last thing United needed in this most unrelenting and punishing of seasons, especially as just four days after the drawn encounter with Chelsea they were due to return to action with the trip to Glasgow and a European Cup semi-final second leg tie. The one positive for Leeds was that Celtic had also been in Cup final action on the Saturday and had suffered a shock 3-1 defeat to Aberdeen at Hampden Park. Could United inflict something similar? Again Revie was sounding an optimistic note, telling the *Yorkshire Post*: 'We have been told that no team who are a goal down at home in a European Cup semi-final have ever reached the final of the tournament. But we won't let that worry us because we are history makers, we are record-breakers. If ever a record can go, then this one can.'

Celtic's decision to switch the game to Hampden Park was rewarded with 136,505 fans pouring through the turnstiles to set a new record crowd for the European Cup. To many in England, the move to another venue had passed almost unnoticed. But, to those such as Bremner, who had an intimate understanding of Scottish football supporters, the significance was clear. United goalkeeper David Harvey was born in Leeds but played international football for Scotland, qualifying through his father. "When the game was moved to allow a bigger crowd to watch, I remember thinking, 'This is going to be some atmosphere'," says a man who started the second leg on the bench that night but was destined to replace the injured Gary Sprake during the second half. "It would have been loud enough at Parkhead but Hampden Park was always something else. The atmosphere was unbelievable. We just could not hear ourselves think, never mind hear what each other was shouting. I think even the more experienced lads were surprised by the sheer volume of noise."

Amid the cacophony, Leeds started well with Bremner, who had faced bizarre calls from the more rabid members of the home support during the build-up that he be stripped of the Scotland captaincy for having the temerity to have been named 'Footballer of the Year' in England, to the fore. An initial flurry of Celtic attacks had come to nothing but a succession of corners when the United captain, who relished playing at Hampden for his country, brought the tie level on aggregate with a 25-yard shot that flew past Evan Williams in the home goal. The crowd momentarily fell silent as the Leeds players celebrated. Had Bremner, that scorer of so many game-changing goals in United colours, done the trick again? With the visitors still ahead on the night when the half-time whistle blew, those brave souls who had made the trip north from Yorkshire were increasingly beginning to believe he had. Should there be no further goals then a replay would take place at Sheffield Wednesday's Hillsborough, Revie having called correctly ahead of the game to decide whether the neutral venue should be in England or Scotland. Celtic were desperate to avoid being cast, effectively, as the away team for a second time against Leeds and stepped up their efforts after the break. Reward came within two minutes of the restart when John Hughes flung himself at a Bertie Auld cross to guide the ball beyond Sprake. Moments later, Sprake's involvement was over after a challenge by Hughes left the Leeds goalkeeper unable to continue. Harvey came off the bench but could do nothing to prevent Bobby Murdoch making it 2-1 on the night and 3-1 overall in the 51st minute. There was to be no second reprieve for Leeds as Celtic went through to the final, where they would suffer a shock defeat to Feyenoord. Harvey says: "When you are sat on the bench, you don't expect to get on – certainly not as a goalkeeper. But then the injury happened to Gary and I had to be ready. It is just a shame that I didn't have a bit longer to get used to the pace of the game and the noise out in the middle. It was hell after the game as all the Celtic fans were celebrating."

With the Glaswegian cheers ringing in their ears, the United squad returned south. Once again, Revie had an almighty job on his hands to lift spirits ahead of the FA Cup final replay against Chelsea at Old Trafford on April 29. The league game against Manchester City scheduled for the same night was pulled forward 11 days, while a rare helping hand from the authorities saw all nine players selected for international duty on the weekend before the replay released from their respective squads. Even so, it was still a tired group of players that limped into Manchester on the back of three straight defeats for their 62nd – and now most important - game of the season.

In the 18 days since their first meeting at Wembley, Leeds and Chelsea had both played three times. The difference was that while Chelsea beat Stoke and Liverpool in the league and lost to Burnley, the Yorkshire side's season had continued to implode with a European Cup exit that had been as draining physically as emotionally. During the gap, a feeling had grown in the Blues' dressing room that Leeds had missed their chance at Wembley. Alan Hudson, the precocious teenage playmaker who earlier in the season had come to the fore with Chelsea, missed both games through injury. But he says: "The lads' confidence had grown considerably since that first game. They really believed the Cup was Chelsea's." Such confidence would ultimately prove to be justified, even though it was Leeds who struck first in the replay when Mick Jones latched on to an incisive through ball from Allan Clarke to beat Peter Bonetti. Chelsea, just as at Wembley, then showed tremendous resilience to hit back 12 minutes from time through Peter Osgood. The equaliser sent the game into extra-time where, amid tackles that were becoming ever more ferocious, David Webb gained redemption for his tormenting by Eddie Gray at Wembley by heading the winner. The Cup was Chelsea's, leaving Leeds to work out just where it had all gone wrong. Some pointed to the opening stages of the Old Trafford replay when Ron 'Chopper' Harris, moved to full-back in place of Webb, deliberately scythed down Gray with a tackle that restricted the Scot's mobility for the rest of the night. Others, looking at the season as a whole, pointed at Revie's insistence that his side should chase an unprecedented treble and the consequence of how fatigue set in during those final few weeks. Another view, and one shared by Bremner, was that the early end to the season had worked against Leeds and that, the Scot told the *Yorkshire Evening Post*, 'Had we had an extra month, things would have been different'.

Either way, it was a disconsolate group of players who left the home of

Manchester United that night. David Harvey, who had replaced Sprake in the starting line-up, says: "It was an awful time. We had been so close to the treble, only to fall short in every competition. Losing to Celtic in the European Cup had made us even more determined to beat Chelsea but, again, it just wasn't meant to be. It was a horrible end to what had, until the final few weeks, been a good season."

Perhaps the final word on the treble-that-never-was should go to the journalist from *The Times* who, six months before that Cup final defeat, had left Bremner so in awe after downing two shots of the pungent local liqueur in Budapest Airport. Geoffrey Green wrote: 'Leeds, like Sisyphus, have pushed three boulders almost to the top of three mountains and are now left to see them all back in the dark of the valley.' Bremner, whose copy of *The Times* that day was destined to go unread as usual, would have been able to empathise with Green's words.

Chapter 10

Bridesmaid Revisited

In the early years that followed Leeds United's promotion to the top-flight in 1964, the failure to claim a trophy despite going close several times led to their critics latching on to an idiom whose origins could be traced back four or so decades. 'Always a bridesmaid, never a bride,' had first been used in a popular advertising campaign for a particular brand of mouthwash – the inference for the target audience of women being that bad breath would prevent them getting married. The intervening years had, mercifully, made such a slogan redundant. That was, however, until the phrase was brought back into the nation's lexicon by the Press as a way of describing the seeming inability of Don Revie's Leeds to make the final step towards winning a major honour. The subsequent winning of the League Cup, the Inter-Cities Fairs Cup and, above all, the League Championship had, temporarily, banished such talk. Now, however, in the wake of United's agonising near-misses in three competitions towards the end of the 1969-70 season had brought about a revival. The Yorkshire club, so the critics claimed, were, after all, destined to be remembered as the nearly men of English football.

To Billy Bremner and his Elland Road team-mates, such a label was annoying. Nevertheless, the disappointment of the previous April was weighing heavily on the players' minds as they returned for the by now traditional first few days of pre-season spent running around Roundhay Park in Leeds. Some, such as Bremner and Johnny Giles, had opted to spend a couple of relaxing summer weeks in Mexico watching the World Cup. Don Revie was another who had been in South America, working as an expert summariser for BBC Television. Allan Clarke, Terry Cooper, Jack Charlton and Norman Hunter had also been there as part of Sir Alf Ramsey's 23-man squad who, as if mirroring what had happened to Leeds a couple of months earlier, suffered a heart-breaking end as West Germany came from two goals down to knock the holders out in a thrilling quarter-final. The rest of the United squad, however, had opted to get as far away from football as possible – an understandable reaction with the memories of Celtic, Chelsea et al still so fresh. It made for a subdued few days as pre-season got under way. Revie, who for a second time had been named Manager of the Year despite his side having ended the campaign empty-handed, appreciated his players needed lifting. It would take all Revie's renowned powers of persuasion but, eventually, he managed to do just that – as illustrated by the scintillating start Leeds subsequently made to the new season by winning their first five games. Included among those victories was a 2-0 triumph at Tottenham Hotspur and a 3-2 defeat for champions Everton at Elland Road, meaning United had already beaten the two clubs Revie saw as their main rivals for the title. Such was the consistency shown by Leeds that they lost just once in the league, a 3-0 reverse at Stoke City, before the turn of the year. Defeats to Spurs and Liverpool in back-to-back home games handed Arsenal, the only side to stay with Leeds during their impressive start, the initiative only for Revie to again elicit a response as five of the next six games were won. By the first weekend in April, Leeds had opened up a six-point advantage at the top – helped by Bertie Mee's Gunners having played three games fewer. A fortnight later and three straight wins for Arsenal together with Leeds drawing against Newcastle and Huddersfield Town meant the advantage enjoyed by Revie's men had been cut to just two points. Arsenal also had two games in hand ahead of Newcastle United's visit to Highbury on a day their rivals were hosting West Bromwich Albion. The *Match of the Day* cameras duly selected the Elland Road game for broadcast later that night, hoping to capture more drama in what was turning out to be a thrilling title race.

West Brom were not expected to provide too much of a problem for Leeds with the Baggies having not won away from home in 16 attempts. A home win seemed a formality to all but those in the visitors' dressing room. John Kaye was the Albion captain for a game that was destined to go down as one of the most controversial screened by *Match of the Day*. "Funnily enough, we had quite a decent record against Leeds," recalls Kaye, who a few years later as Hull City manager would sign Bremner. "Earlier in the season, we had drawn 2-2 at The Hawthorns. A few years earlier, we had also knocked Leeds out of the League Cup. So, we were not overawed despite Leeds being such a good team. They had some tremendous players who weren't afraid to dish it out. Or, to their credit, take it, too. I remember one game when I was up against Billy. He had moved up front because Leeds needed a goal, so we were in direct opposition. Soon after moving up front, he whacked me a couple of times and I thought, 'I'm not having this'. So, I gave him an almighty whack back. As he got up off the floor, we just looked at each other and, although neither of us said a word, our faces said, 'Right, we can get on with playing now we've both had a crack'. And that was how we played the rest of the game, hard but fair."

Angered by what Kaye claims was over-confidence on Revie's part when talking about the game on television and saying, 'We could get five today', West Brom were fired up from the start and took a shock lead. They were still in front when referee Ray Tinkler blew for half-time. Leeds, though, remained confident – not least because Bremner, who had missed almost three months through injury, had returned to the side in midweek. All United had to do, Revie urged at half-time, was remain patient and the chances would come. What he and the 36,812 crowd could not have known during the interval, though, was how referee Tinkler was about to make one of the most controversial decisions of this or any season. A misplaced pass by Norman Hunter started the passage of play that would end with a pitch invasion and Leeds kicking off the following season with Elland Road closed by the Football Association. Tony Brown was the player who took advantage by blocking Hunter's attempted pass. The ball rebounded into the Leeds half in the direction of Colin Suggett, who was sauntering back towards halfway and standing a full 10 yards offside. Linesman Bill Troupe immediately flagged and the home defence stopped, as did Brown who had initially set off in pursuit of the ball. Under today's laws, the flag would not have been waved due to Suggett being deemed to be not interfering with play. But, in 1971, it was a clear case of offside. Despite that, referee Tinkler waved play on, the flag came down and Brown suddenly burst into a sprint before squaring for Jeff Astle to tap into an empty net. The Leeds players immediately surrounded the referee, while Revie was so moved by what he saw that he strode on to the field to plead his team's case. A number of home supporters also tried to get to Tinkler, though it is doubtful whether what they had in mind was a few quiet words with the official. Tinkler, though, was adamant. The goal stood. Viewers watching at home later that night were treated to an almost breathless commentary from Barry Davies on *Match of the Day*. 'Leeds will go mad,' said the BBC man. 'And they have every justification for going mad.'

As chaos ensued, all the Albion players could do was stand around and wait for the fuss to die down. Captain Kaye says: "We could see all the Leeds lads were fuming, they thought the referee had cost them the league. I must admit even when we were together at Hull City a few years later, I never asked Billy about that day. He would probably still have been angry. Leeds made all sorts of protests to the referee and the linesman but they wouldn't be swayed – thankfully for us." On the validity of the goal itself, Kaye adds: "I know Leeds still insist to this day that the goal was offside but I don't necessarily agree with that. Colin Suggett had closed Gary Sprake down when he rolled the ball out to Norman Hunter. When Norman's pass was then blocked by Tony Brown, Colin was still standing offside but, in my opinion, not interfering with play. Under today's rules, he definitely wouldn't be. Browny then ran through as the Leeds players stopped and squared it for Jeff Astle to score."

Once play had resumed, United did pull one goal back through Allan Clarke but it was not enough to prevent the initiative in the title race swinging the way of Arsenal, who, courtesy of beating Newcastle as the drama unfolded at Elland Road, had taken over at the top of the table. Leeds were furious, their anger only added to the following Monday when Tinkler was quoted in the *Yorkshire Evening Post* saying that he stood by the decision. He said: 'No offence was committed and I could let play go on. He was in an offside position and the linesman flagged him but he was not interfering with play.' Revie's response was to once again call for the introduction of professional referees, pointing out how decisions that could cost clubs tens of thousands of pounds were being made by part-time officials earning a flat match fee of just £10.50. Bremner was as appalled as anyone over what he perceived to be a gross injustice, though he did issue a rallying call to the *Yorkshire Evening Post*: 'Suggett was plain offside and the goal hung on that. We all stopped running. But we fight on. Make no mistake about that, it is not over yet.' The United captain's words were borne of defiance; though the sentiment would ultimately prove to be futile as Arsenal went on to clinch the title by beating Tottenham at White Hart Lane in their final game. By then, United's own league season had ended and the news that the Gunners had beaten Spurs was relayed to Bremner and his team-mates as they came off the Boothferry Park pitch following a testimonial for Hull's Chris Chilton. Five days later, Arsenal would seal a famous league and cup double with a 2-1 win over Liverpool at Wembley.

Leeds United's own Cup challenge had ended in rather more ignominious fashion courtesy of a 3-2 defeat at Fourth Division Colchester United. Without Bremner, who had missed the previous three weeks through injury, Leeds had fallen 3-0 behind shortly after half-time before launching a valiant late fightback. That shock defeat, together with Sheffield United ending Leeds' interest in the League Cup, meant the prospect of another season without a trophy was looming large. Europe, though, had once again proved to be to United's liking. Back in the Inter-Cities Fairs Cup following the failure to win either the league or European Cup in 1970, Revie's side had made light work of Norwegian amateurs Sarpsborg in the first round. Dynamo Dresden proved to be trickier opponents in the next stage but Leeds still progressed on the away-goals rule after Mick Jones had netted in East Germany as the hosts won the second leg 2-1. The only downside of the trip behind the Iron Curtain for the first leg was Bremner leaving behind a £150 watch presented to him the previous summer by United's official supporters club. Much to his relief, though, a Dynamo official took it upon himself to retrieve the watch from what had been the club's base and drive three hours to Prague to return it to Bremner ahead of the third round tie second leg against Sparta a few weeks later. The official then stayed on to watch Leeds win 3-2 to seal a 9-2 aggregate triumph.

The New Year brought a narrow 2-1 win in the quarter-final first leg at Elland Road against Vitoria Setubal. The return, as with the home tie, was played without an injured Bremner but a Peter Lorimer goal was enough to seal a 1-1 draw and a place in the last four. United's players were on the return flight from Portugal when news came through they had been paired with Liverpool in an all-English semi-final. The winners would face whoever prevailed from the other tie, FC Cologne v Juventus. With the first leg scheduled for Anfield in three weeks' time, Revie realised on that return flight just how vital it was that his captain be fit.

Bremner's ankle problem had been a huge source of frustration to the United captain, not least as it had led to his first long-term absence from the side since becoming a regular more than a decade earlier. He had already made one unsuccessful attempt at a return in the wake of United's FA Cup humiliation at Colchester. Now, he was facing a race against time to be fit for the trip to Anfield. Typically, during the run-up to the April 14 game, Bremner declared himself fit and available to play. Revie, however, was concerned that his captain's heart was ruling his head and that the injury had not healed sufficiently. A behind-closed-doors friendly against Bradford was arranged for the morning of the Liverpool game, which Bremner duly came through with no problems to claim a place in the starting line-up. It was a huge relief to someone who had always relished going head-to-head with Shankly's Reds. Mike Morgan, then of the *Daily Express*, recalls: "Billy loved the big games and few were bigger than against Liverpool at Anfield. I remember one year when we could see from the press box that Tommy Smith was particularly upset about something. After the game, Billy wouldn't say what had happened – though he did have a glint in his eye. It was a few years later before he finally told me how Tommy had come to be so upset. Leeds had won a corner and Billy ended up being stood next to Tommy, whose complexion is probably best described as 'pock-marked'. Billy saw it as a chance to wind Tommy up so turned and said, 'I won't stand too close, if that's all right Tommy – if I do then I won't know whether to sandpaper your face or Polyfilla it'. Only someone like Billy could come out with a comment like that to one of football's hardest players."

Revie's gamble, if that's how selecting one of football's most renowned competitors can be described, paid off handsomely at Anfield. First, Bremner won the toss – ensuring Liverpool would attack the Kop in the first half and not, as they preferred, after the break. Getting the inevitable onslaught that accompanied the Reds playing towards their most vociferous and passionate supporters out of the way was much preferable to waiting until the closing stages when the Kopites would work themselves into a frenzy. More important, though, it was Bremner's return to the side that proved to be the difference between the two teams as it was a guided header from United's talisman midway through the second half that ensured the visitors won 1-0. One man not surprised by Bremner's scoring return was John Helm, who had moved from the *Yorkshire Evening Post* a year earlier to become *BBC Radio Leeds* sports editor. "Billy was a magnificent footballer who had this amazing ability to pop up unmarked in the box to score a vital goal. And he seemed to do it in every big game. He had more energy than he knew what to do with, so would keep running just in case an opportunity arose when a lot of other players would have given it up as a bad job."

By the time of the return leg against Liverpool a fortnight later, Bremner had three more 90 minutes under his belt and felt much better as a result. It showed, too, as the Scot was everywhere as Leeds claimed the goalless draw that was enough to book a third appearance in the Fairs Cup final. Juventus, thanks in the main to a 2-0 home win that included a goal by future England manager Fabio Capello, were also through to the final at the expense of Cologne. The Fairs Cup, which would become known as the UEFA Cup the following season, may not have been the equal of the European Cup. But, after a couple of years that had brought no reward in terms of trophies, Leeds were desperate to prevail. A six-hour thunderstorm ahead of the first leg in Turin meant parts of the Stadio Comunale pitch were under water at kick-off. Peter Lorimer recalls: "The pitch looked more like a lake than anything else and the moment we got there I thought the game would be postponed."

Referee Laurens Van Raven, nevertheless, ruled the conditions were playable and United settled well. At half-time, the score remained goalless as heavy rain continued to pour. Once again, however, the official felt the second half should start only to call a halt after just six minutes. The game was abandoned and provisionally rearranged for 48 hours later. Under competition rules, if the pitch was still deemed unplayable then both legs would take place at Elland Road – which had already been named as the venue if a replay was needed. Revie, as he had been when Ferencvaros had been threatened with having to give up home advantage in the Fairs Cup final due to the Warsaw Pact's invasion of Czechoslovakia, was against the idea – wanting to win the competition 'the right way'. Much to his and Juventus' relief, the rain eventually eased and the first leg went ahead as planned. The Italians were the first to settle on a heavy pitch as Roberto Bettega opened the scoring in the 27th minute. Paul Madeley equalised shortly afterwards only for Capello to restore Juventus' lead with a fierce shot past Gary Sprake. Once again, however, Leeds hit back when substitute Mick Bates netted a precious equaliser 13 minutes from time. The draw had been preceded by a rare disagreement between Revie and his players over the manager's insistence that the team's planned reunion with their wives, who were staying in a different hotel, be delayed until after the rearranged game had taken place. Several players took exception but, eventually, the matter was smoothed over and Revie got his way. Once back in England, preparations continued for the return leg on June 2. Such a late staging of the tie was not ideal, not least as it meant Elland Road was bathed in sunshine when the two sides ran out. But it was infinitely preferable to United's two previous appearances in the Fairs Cup final, when the games had been held over until the start of the following season.

Allan Clarke's 23rd goal of the season settled home nerves on 12 minutes only for Juventus to again bring the aggregate scores level through Pietro Anastasi. Crucially, however, Leeds would lift the trophy on the away-goals rule if there was no further score. Play raged from end to end before the pleadings of the home fans in a crowd of 42,483 were answered when East German referee Rudi Glockner blew the full-time whistle. Leeds' two-year wait to get their hands on a trophy was over and the season had not, as their critics had suggested several months earlier, been a case of the Bridesmaid Revisited.

Chapter 11

It's Almost Cruel

It began, innocently, with a lazy pass from Allan Clarke to Billy Bremner. The game against Southampton had been over long ago as a contest. Ted Bates' team had beaten Leeds United at The Dell three months earlier but were still expected to struggle in the return at Elland Road. By half-time, such thinking had been borne out by Leeds netting twice without reply to move towards what looked like being their ninth win in 10 home league games. Now, as the game reached the closing stages, that lead had been extended to seven goals courtesy of a second strike of the afternoon for Clarke, Peter Lorimer completing his hat-trick and both Jack Charlton and Mick Jones getting their names on the scoresheet. All that was left, it seemed to the 34,275 crowd, was for Southampton's misery to be brought to an end by the final whistle. The *Match of the Day* cameras had been present to capture a near-perfect performance, meaning millions at home would also be afforded the chance to watch United's demolition of the Saints. The viewers did, indeed, get to see Leeds in all their glory later that night. But what they were also treated to was a passage of play so outrageous that it prompted BBC commentator Barry Davies to proclaim: 'To say that Leeds are playing with Southampton is the understatement of the season. Poor old Southampton just don't know what day it is. Every man jack of this Leeds side is now turning it on." Then, as Johnny Giles flicked the ball on to Clarke's chest with a pass that if made today would be called 'showboating' by the presenters of Sky's Saturday morning show *Soccer AM*, Davies added: 'Oh, look at that! It's almost cruel.'

The United players, courtesy of this unscripted passage of keep-ball, had taken on the role of matadors, teasing and tormenting the Saints players whose only response was to charge after the ball in the manner of an incensed bull. They rarely got close, as a succession of flicks, tricks and outlandish twists saw Leeds keep possession for what seemed like an age but was, in reality, a little over a minute-and-a-half. During those 90 or so seconds, however, Leeds displayed to the millions watching later that night on *Match of the Day* just what a fantastic side they had become. Gone was the stifling 'protect what we have' mentality that had brought 24 clean sheets and the League Championship in 1968-69. The approach of trying to sneak a goal and then, as happened when lifting their first trophy by beating Arsenal in the League Cup final, stifling the opposition by withdrawing both wingers to sit in front of the full-backs as an extra protective barrier was also at an end. Leeds now played the game on their terms. This transformation had begun with the signing of Allan Clarke a couple of months after the title win that had been built on defensive solidity. A year later, what Revie saw as an expert summariser at the World Cup finals when a flamboyant Brazil side romped to victory had further convinced the Leeds manager of the way the game was heading. He knew any team not willing to adapt risked being left behind, hence the gradual banishment of the conservatism that had characterised much of United's play since promotion. By early 1972, the result of this shift in emphasis was clear for all to see as a Manchester United side featuring George Best and Bobby Charlton were thumped 5-1. Two weeks after that humbling of the Red Devils came United's magnificent seven showing against Southampton.

To Bremner and his team-mates, Revie's insistence they were now free to express themselves had come as music to their ears. Mike O'Grady, a mainstay of the title-winning side of three seasons earlier, had left Leeds for Wolves in September, 1969 but remained in touch with Bremner. He recalls: "Billy was gutted when I left and Gilesy also wanted me to stay but the manager had made his decision and that was that. But I kept in touch with Billy as we were good friends. When we met up for a pint, he would say things like, 'You would love it now as the Boss has let us off the leash'. I could see how much he was enjoying it. I would have to grit my teeth as I knew I'd made a mistake in leaving Leeds anyway. Knowing I would have enjoyed playing in such an attacking side made it that bit worse."

The defensive and often dour approach that had once turned off the Press and opposition fans alike had been banished, replaced by a dazzling and fluent brand of football that, if not quite turning the critics into friends, did at least draw admiration. Duncan Revie says his Dad was delighted by the Leeds players finally receiving some recognition from the wider footballing public, though later in life the most decorated manager in United's history would admit to having regrets over not making the switch earlier. "Dad told me many times that he wished he had allowed them to play freely a lot earlier," recalls Duncan. "He accepted he had been too cautious in the first few years after Leeds had been promoted. The feeling he should have let the lads play more freely earlier only grew after Dad had become England manager. He would tell me things like, 'If I had known then what I know now about these so-called world stars at other clubs, I would have told my lads to go out and play earlier because they would have murdered them'. He hadn't realised that the other teams just weren't as good as his lads."

In the keep-ball session that had kept *Match of the Day* commentator Davies so spellbound, Bremner had been involved throughout. It had, in fact, been his deft back-heel to Clarke on the left flank that kick-started the outrageous succession of tricks. He was clearly relishing the change of emphasis by Revie, a feeling that was shared by the Scot's team-mates. Lorimer says: "I don't honestly think Don believed until the last couple of years what a great team he had. Everything was geared towards making sure we didn't lose in the early years, such as when we won the league that first time. It was only when Don was thinking about moving on that he said, 'Get out there and show everyone what a great team you are'. Those words were music to our ears. It was then that we started hammering teams, such as that 7-0 win over Southampton."

The football played by Leeds during 1971-72 may have been among the best seen at Elland Road. But the season had started under a cloud for the club due to the continuing fall-out from the previous April, when the controversial defeat to West Brom had all but ended hopes of a second League Championship. Ray Tinkler's decision to wave play on despite Albion's Colin Suggett standing in an offside position had led to a pitch invasion by irate fans. Linesman Colin Cartlich had also been struck by a missile in the melee. Afterwards, cars and shops outside Elland Road had been damaged while police had been forced to disperse around 100 fans waiting for the referee in the car park. The Football Association, understandably, took a dim view, while comments by Revie and United chairman Percy Woodward that Tinkler's woeful performance had partly justified the crowd's reaction did little to help matters. The punishment, when it came during the summer, was swingeing. Leeds would have to play their first four 'home' games at neutral venues. The club was also fined £500 and ordered to compensate visiting clubs for any resulting loss of income, the practice in those days being for gate receipts to be split and not, as today, kept by the home team. Revie and Woodward were also censured over the comments about Tinkler and warned as to their future conduct.

Once the coming season's fixture list had been announced, Revie, who had been forced to abandon a holiday in Spain with wife Elsie to deal with the verdict, was faced with having to find alternative venues for the 'home' games against Wolverhampton Wanderers, Tottenham Hotspur, Newcastle United and Crystal Palace. The priority was keeping Leeds in Yorkshire, which he duly achieved by striking a deal with Huddersfield Town to stage the Wolves and Palace fixtures. Likewise, Hull City agreed to host the Spurs game and Sheffield Wednesday the Newcastle encounter. It was hardly ideal, though the best that could be expected under the circumstances.

With United also handed legitimate away games at Manchester City, Sheffield United, Ipswich Town and Arsenal before their exile from Elland Road was due to end, it left Revie's men facing a tough start – especially for a team still smarting from what they perceived to be the injustice of the previous season. Revie, though, was adamant no-one be allowed to feel sorry for themselves – even if such a trait was hardly one associated with Bremner, Giles et al anyway. In the end, Leeds made a decent start by claiming six points from their 'home' games courtesy of two wins and two draws. They also collected maximum points at Maine Road and Portman Road. Less happily, however, the trips to Highbury and Bramall Lane ended in defeat. Further reverses on the road would follow at Huddersfield Town, Coventry City and Southampton before the turn of the year. United's form on the road all season would prove unusually erratic, so much so that in 21 league outings they suffered nine defeats. One school of thought was that the more expansive style of play now advocated by Revie was leaving his side vulnerable at the back. At Elland Road, however, it was a very different story.

The return from exile saw Lorimer net the winner against Liverpool in front of 41,381 fans. The players were not the only ones glad to be back, either, with the board rueing the loss of income caused by their four 'home' games in Hull, Huddersfield and Sheffield having attracted an average crowd of just 20,781. The win over Liverpool then kick-started an incredible run that saw just two more points dropped at Elland Road all season, Ipswich and West Ham the two teams to escape with a draw. Such an imperious record did not, though, transfer to the Cups with United being knocked out twice on home soil. The first loss came just 11 days after the league exile had ended. SK Lierse were the opponents for an Inter-Cities Fairs Cup first round second leg tie that, thanks to United having won the first tie 2-0 in Belgium a fortnight earlier, seemed a formality. Revie clearly agreed, as out went several first-choice players to be replaced by youngsters such as John Shaw and forward Jimmy Mann. Three goals in six first-half minutes snapped the United manager out of such a rare show of complacency as he brought Gary Sprake on for Shaw and Mann was replaced by Norman

Hunter. The damage, though, had already been done and Lierse, who boasted only seven full-time professionals, added a fourth goal towards the end to dump the holders out. West Ham United then followed the example of the Belgians by winning unexpectedly at Elland Road to end Leeds' interest in the League Cup. Going out of two competitions in quick succession inside just three weeks would, in the past, have troubled Revie. But, having learned the lessons of the treble-that-never-was season, the United manager had come to realise that narrowing his side's focus in terms of what trophies to chase was the way forward. Three months later, such thinking seemed to have its rewards with the demolition of Southampton in front of the *Match of the Day* cameras.

Ten more goals were scored in the three home games that followed the thrashing of the Saints, the 3-0 triumph over Arsenal, sandwiched between victories over Coventry City and Nottingham Forest, being particularly sweet due to the Gunners having pipped Leeds to the title the previous season. Swift progress had also been made in the FA Cup, a third round victory over Bristol Rovers followed by the edging out of Liverpool after a replay. Cardiff City had then been beaten in the fifth round to set up a quarter-final tie against Tottenham Hotspur. Goals from Allan Clarke and Jack Charlton ensured smooth passage to the last four but much of the Press coverage the following day centred on the US-style razzmatazz that Leeds had injected into their pre-match routine. Not only had the players embarked on an elaborate training routine half an hour or so before kick-off. But, on taking to the field, Bremner had led his team-mates in a pre-match salute of all four stands. The United fans lapped it up and the practice, which had been instigated by illustrator and budding sports marketing man Paul Trevillion, quickly became an established part of a matchday. Revie had been persuaded by Trevillion to adopt the gimmicks in the hope it would improve his players' public image. Most importantly, though, it was United's more flowing brand of football that was winning over the critics.

Birmingham City were paired with Leeds in the Cup semi-final but could do little to prevent Revie's men booking a fourth visit to Wembley via two goals from Mick Jones and another for Lorimer. Not for the first time, the prospect of a League and Cup double was on. Once again, however, the chase for success would bring its own logistical problems as the fixtures started to back up. Four days after making such light work of Birmingham at Hillsborough, Leeds travelled to Newcastle United. The game had been rearranged due to the Cup run and Revie was unhappy at having to play so soon. Football League secretary, Alan Hardaker, showed little sympathy, though, insisting that the build-up of fixtures was entirely down to Revie. Newcastle had, he claimed, offered to play the previous month following the lifting of a ban on midweek floodlit games that had been brought in by the Government to conserve power in the wake of the miners' strike. Hardaker passed on Newcastle's offer but Revie turned it down, saying Leeds did not play on Thursday nights. The upshot was the trip to St James' Park taking place just two-and-a-half weeks before the end of the season.

Compared to the often chaotic scheduling that had undone Leeds two years earlier when three trophies slipped through their grasp in a little over a month, the run-in was not overly arduous. After the Newcastle game, Leeds would have to travel to West Brom the following Saturday and then face a nine day wait before hosting Chelsea. Five days after that, Arsenal and the FA Cup final awaited United before the climax to the First Division campaign came at Wolves a little over 48 hours later. Apart from the close scheduling of the Cup final and the Molineux fixture, the run-in did not seem too burdensome. Injuries, though, were beginning to mount with Terry Cooper ruled out for the season to join Gary Sprake on the injured list. Fatigue had also set in, not least among those such as Bremner, Jack Charlton, Norman Hunter, Paul Madeley and Peter Lorimer who had missed just two league games between them all season. An attempt to strengthen the squad had been made the previous November when a fee of £177,000 was agreed with West Brom for Asa Hartford only for the deal to collapse after the player's medical had revealed a heart defect. The club's caution would turn out to be misplaced with Hartford going on to enjoy a long career and appear 50 times for Scotland. Had the deal not been abandoned in such haste, Hartford could have helped ease the burden in the closing weeks of the season by covering for Bremner and Giles. As it was, fourth placed Leeds travelled north to Newcastle with depleted resources and slipped to a 1-0 defeat. The damage was not, however, as serious as first feared thanks to leaders Derby County losing to Manchester City on the same night. The gap between Leeds and the Rams stood at four points with the Yorkshire club having two games in hand. By the following Saturday, the picture at the top of the First Division had cleared courtesy of United's 1-0 win at West Brom and a victory for Manchester City over Derby. The upshot was that Leeds were still fourth in the table, two points behind the new leaders from Maine Road who had, by now, completed their league programme. United still had two games to play. Derby and Liverpool, meanwhile, were both a point ahead of Leeds, with one and two games outstanding respectively.

Revie, with one eye on the looming FA Cup final, again approached the Football League for assistance in rescheduling one of their fixtures – namely the trip to Wolves. He reasoned a delay of 24 or, ideally, 48 hours would make all the difference. Again, however, the League refused to budge – arguing that a delay would impact on not only England's preparations for the following weekend's European Championships' game against West Germany but also Wolves' impending two-legged UEFA Cup final against Spurs. Leeds had to soldier on.

The eight days that would decide the destiny of the League and FA Cup began on May 1 with Leeds beating Chelsea 2-0 thanks to goals from Bremner and Mick Jones. Elland Road's biggest crowd of the season, 46,565, were then further cheered by the news that 100 or so miles away Derby had just beaten Liverpool. The Rams had moved to the top but, due to their own season now being over, Brian Clough and his players could only wait to see if they had done enough. Liverpool, meanwhile, were now a point behind Leeds but with a weaker goal average they knew victory in their own final game at Highbury could not guarantee a third league title under Bill Shankly. Only Leeds held the destiny of the title in their hands. A point at Molineux would be enough to be crowned champions for a second time, regardless of what happened at Highbury on the same night. Before then, however, there was the less than trifling matter of an FA Cup final to focus on.

Victory over Arsenal would leave Leeds just 90 minutes away from a possible League and Cup double, a reward that would more than make up for the disappointments of the past. The memory of those near-misses meant the United party arriving at Wembley after the short coach trip from their Hendon Hall base did so in determined mood. Revie, whose superstitious streak had by then become legendary in the game, had been left reassured by seeing a bride on her way to church during the journey. John Wray, Leeds correspondent for the *Telegraph & Argus*, explains: "Leeds United had so often been the bridesmaid as opposed to the bride in major finals that Don took it as an omen that his team would lift the Cup." The FA Cup was celebrating its Centenary year in 1972 so due pageantry was laid on to mark such a notable occasion. Ahead of kick-off, a procession in which all the previous winners from The Wanderers onwards were represented served as a curtain raiser. Bremner found it tiresome, being eager to get into the action after having led his players out of the tunnel. He soon had his wish as, after being presented to the Queen and the Duke of Edinburgh, the two teams were ready to do battle.

Both sets of players were expecting a hard-fought contest, while the neutrals in the 100,000 crowd merely hoped it would be a vast improvement on the dreary 1968 League Cup final between the sides. The omens were good with Revie's mindset having changed since United had lifted their first trophy a little over four years earlier. Arsenal, the double-winners, were also committed to taking the game to the opposition, albeit at Wembley this would take the form of a counter-attacking approach. The game, while by no means a classic, turned out to be an entertaining and dramatic affair worthy of the occasion. Arsenal settled first but it was Leeds who posed more attacking threat in a goalless first half as Bremner and Giles worked tirelessly in midfield. Allan Clarke hit the crossbar and Gunners goalkeeper Geoff Barnett bundled a low drilled shot from Peter Lorimer round the post, while at the other end Alan Ball's smart volley from 20 yards was kicked off the line by Paul Reaney. United then got the ball in the net when Peter Simpson turned Eddie Gray's centre into his own net only for the linesman to signal the ball had run out of play before the Scot had crossed. A goal seemed imminent.

The decisive moment came eight minutes into the second half after Jack Charlton had cut out an attempted pass by Alan Ball and found Paul Madeley. He, in turn, passed to Lorimer, who rolled the ball out to Mick Jones on the right. Clarke, showing the awareness that had justified countless times Revie's willingness to break the British transfer record three years earlier, raced into the penalty area in the hope his strike partner could get to the by-line. Jones duly obliged so, when an inch-perfect cross arrived in the Arsenal penalty area, Clarke was able to throw himself at the ball and power a diving header beyond the despairing dive of Barnett. The Gunners attempted to hit back and Charlie George rattled the crossbar but it was to be Leeds' day. The FA Cup was heading to Elland Road for the first time. As the players celebrated, however, a drama was unfolding in the Arsenal penalty area that would have serious consequences for United's hopes of clinching the League and Cup double. Mick Jones had, in the final minute of the game, collided with Barnett when trying to put the result beyond doubt and was still down. Les Cocker and the club doctor had run over to him the moment the final whistle had blown. A stretcher was ordered with the suspicion that Jones had dislocated his elbow. For Revie, the ramifications with the Wolves game a little over 48 hours away were immediately clear. He would have to travel to Molineux without a forward who had netted 13 goals in 30 games that season. Bremner, meanwhile, was determined to delay going up to collect the Cup as long as possible in the hope his prone team-mate could join in. Eventually, however, the Queen could be kept waiting no longer and Bremner started to climb the steps towards the Royal Box. Then, after reaching the top and wiping his hands on his shirt, he walked forward and collected the Cup. The Queen may have said, 'Very well done, you have earned it'. But Bremner, speaking afterwards, wasn't sure, understandably having been overtaken by the moment and the knowledge tens of thousands of Leeds supporters were waiting for him to hold aloft the most iconic trophy in English football. No other Leeds captain had lifted the FA Cup so Bremner was making history. Raising the trophy above his head to be met by a huge roar ranked as one of his proudest moments. Once back on the greyhound track that then surrounded the Wembley pitch, Bremner was unsure whether to embark on the lap of honour or take the trophy to Jones. The stewards tried to guide Bremner and his team-mates towards starting the traditional parading of the Cup but, instead, they delayed. Jones, by now his shoulder heavily-strapped, was back on his feet and determined to meet the Queen. Norman Hunter ran over to help his team-mate, first up the steps towards the Royal Box and then towards the monarch. Clearly in agony, Jones' determination led to the Wembley crowd rising as one. It was a special moment and an image that has endured for the best part of four decades. Jones was then whisked away to hospital as the Leeds players, with Bremner hoisted on the shoulders of Lorimer and goalscorer Clarke, proudly showed off the Cup.

Once back in the dressing room, the players were rationed to one plastic cup of champagne and a sip from the Cup as attention turned to the final game of the league season. Revie had decided the squad should head straight to Wolverhampton from Wembley, meaning the players missed out on the traditional banquet in London. They also left the Cup behind, club secretary Keith Archer being handed the task of ensuring it returned to Elland Road safely. Lorimer recalls: "We stopped at a service station just outside London on the way to Wolverhampton and 'celebrated' with a cup of tea and a sandwich. One of the lads joked, 'Great winning the Cup, isn't it?' It just about summed up the situation."

The following morning, Revie and his coaching staff assessed the Leeds squad. Many were carrying injuries, the price of having played so many important games in such a short space of time. Pain-killing injections were administered to Clarke and Johnny Giles, while Eddie Gray was struggling

Stan The Man: Billy Bremner, 18, shakes hands with 45-year-old Stanley Matthews before Leeds take on Blackpool.

A Perfect Match: Marrying childhood sweetheart Vicky.

Looking Forward: Captured at United's traditional pre-season photo-call.

The First Trophy: Billy holds aloft the League Cup in front of the Gelderd End a few days after Leeds had beaten Arsenal 1-0 at Wembley.

Triumphant Homecoming: The League Cup is shown off to supporters at a civic reception in Leeds.

Beautiful Budapest: Held aloft by team-mates Jack Charlton and Gary Sprake after a goalless draw in the second leg against Ferencvaros is enough to clinch the Inter-Cities Fairs Cup in 1968.

Success in Europe: Left, Paul Reaney and Terry Cooper watch their captain show off United's first European trophy to their adoring fans back in Yorkshire, before a lucky few are given a close-up (right)

Victory Salute: Billy waves to the crowd on the steps of Leeds Civic Hall as the city celebrates United's Fairs Cup success.

Leader of the pack: Billy leads United out at his beloved Elland Road.

Well Done, Boys: Along with Jack Charlton, Billy accepts
the congratulations of Bill Shankly after Leeds seal their
first League title with a goalless draw at Liverpool.

This Is For You: The First Division championship
is paraded on the steps of Leeds Town Hall.

Charity Begins At Home: Leeds beat Manchester City in the 1969 Charity Shield at Elland Road, allowing Billy and club president, the Earl of Harewood, to show off the trophy.

Rivals: Driving Leeds forward against Manchester United at Hillsborough in the 1970 FA Cup semi-final that ended goalless.

Fight for the ball: Opponents always knew they had been in a game when up against Billy.

Accusing finger: Billy lets the referee know what he thinks of his performance.

The Italian Job: Leeds beat Juventus on away goals in the 1971 Inter-Cities Fairs Cup final to land another trophy.

Wembley beckons: Billy shakes hands with Birmingham City captain Stan Harland ahead of the 1972 FA Cup semi-final against Birmingham City.

Up for the Cup: Birmingham's players are left in no doubt as to how badly Leeds want to reach the Centenary Cup final.

Marching On Together: Leading the team out at Wembley ahead of the 1972 FA Cup final against Arsenal.

Let Battle Commence: Greeting Arsenal captain Frank McLintock ahead of kick-off at Wembley.

Cup winners: Billy holds aloft the FA Cup as Peter Lorimer checks his winners' medal.

Teeing off: Relaxing at Leeds United's annual golf tournament.

Sporting Greats: Former heavyweight boxing champion Henry Cooper meets Billy and Don Revie at Pudsey Civic Centre in January, 1974.

Scotland The Brave: Showing off some of his 54 international caps.

World Stage: Leading out Scotland alongside Brazil captain Piazza before the two countries meet at the 1974 World Cup finals. (© EMPICS)

So Close: Denied by a brave save from Leao as Scotland are held to a goalless draw by Brazil in Frankfurt. (© EMPICS)

with a thigh injury. All would start on Monday night but Revie admitted later that, under normal circumstances, none of the trio would have played. Jones' dislocated elbow forced a reshuffle as Bremner moved to centre forward alongside Clarke and Mick Bates came into midfield. Despite the walking wounded, Revie was confident of claiming the necessary point to be crowned champions. All Liverpool, ahead of their own game at Arsenal that night, and the Derby County players who had been taken to Majorca by assistant manager Peter Taylor could do was hope for an almighty favour from Wolves. They got it, as Wanderers swept aside suspicions that being halfway through their own two-legged UEFA Cup final against Spurs could prove a distraction by taking the game to the visitors. Frank Munro opened the scoring shortly before half-time so when Derek Dougan added a second on 65 minutes, United's title hopes lay in tatters. A hobbling Clarke eventually admitted defeat and was replaced by Terry Yorath before Bremner gave Leeds a lifeline by converting a cross from Paul Madeley. It was the United captain's fifth goal of the season. A sixth would not come, however, and when Wolves full-back Gerry Taylor prevented a looping header from Yorath reaching the net with a goal-line clearance it was clear the game was up. Three earlier penalty appeals turned down by referee Bill Gow only added to the frustration of the night as Wolves clung on in front of 53,379 fans.

Leeds were not the only team left raging at the officials that night as Liverpool had what would, thanks to the result at Molineux, have been a League Championship-winning goal disallowed two minutes from time at Highbury. John Toshack was adjudged to be offside when bundling the ball into the net, leaving a furious Bill Shankly to tell the Press: "He (referee Roger Kirkpatrick) cost us the title." Liverpool's failure to collect the required two points together with United's defeat at Molineux meant the title went to Derby County on 58 points – one more than Leeds, Liverpool and Manchester City. It had been the closest title race in years but that was of little consolation to Bremner and his team-mates. Jack Charlton says: "We finished second in the league on five occasions and the biggest disappointment was when we had already won the FA Cup but were then beaten by Wolverhampton, which cost us the league. I thought the FA were completely out of order when we had to play on the Monday night after the Cup final two days earlier. That was wrong and it was done to suit the other side, not us."

For Bremner, the fall-out from that night would continue for many years thanks to allegations that three Wolves players had been offered bribes to 'take it easy'. The claim had first surfaced a few months after the defeat, appearing in *The People* but, on this occasion, no Leeds players were named. The Football Association and the police both investigated the claims but no charges followed. Several years later, however, the allegations were revisited during an investigation into Revie by the *Daily Mirror* following his decision to quit as England manager. *The People* followed up the claims in their sister newspaper on September 11, 1977, when Bremner was accused of trying to find takers for an alleged bribe during the game. The Leeds captain had, the paper claimed, offered Wolves player Danny Hegan £1,000 to trip him up inside the penalty area. Outraged, Bremner vowed to sue for libel.

The case was heard at London's High Court over six days in early 1982, Bremner having decided to sue both the publishers of *The People*, Odhams Newspapers Ltd, and Hegan, who had been quoted in the original article. Proceedings began with Patrick Milmo, Bremner's counsel, telling the Court how his client had been forced to endure insults in the wake of the article appearing and shouts of 'fixer' when playing for Hull City. After explaining how Bremner had retired as a player during the summer that followed the allegations being printed, Milmo then added: '*The Sunday People* can take credit, if that is the right expression, for ending the career of Billy Bremner.' It was also claimed that Bremner's three children had been taunted at school by comments such as, 'Your father is a fixer'. Over the next few days, several people appeared as character witnesses on behalf of Bremner, including Jack Charlton, Johnny Giles, Allan Clarke and Hegan's Wolves' team-mate Derek Dougan. All dismissed the story. Clarke, by then Leeds manager, told the High Court the claims were, 'Utter rubbish'. The referee of the Wolves game, John Gow, also spoke at his 'surprise' at the accusations. Gow, a Swansea schoolmaster, then went on to add: 'I noticed nothing unusual during the game and heard nothing that could be interpreted as attempts by Leeds players or anyone else to fix the result.'

On behalf of the defence, evidence was heard from Hegan, his Wolves' team-mate Frank Munro, two reporters and Bremner's former team-mate Gary Sprake. Ex Leeds player Bill McAdams also appeared to support the defence's allegation that Bremner had been involved in an attempt by Don Revie to 'fix' a game against Southampton in 1962. After hearing evidence from both sides, the jury of seven men and five women retired to consider their verdict on Wednesday February 3. They took just two hours to find in Bremner's favour, that day's *Yorkshire Evening Post* revealing to the people of Leeds the result with a front page headline of 'Billy Bremner Gets

£100,000'. Odhams Newspapers Ltd and Hegan were also ordered to pay costs of around £60,000. It was vindication for Bremner and an end to the shadow that had been cast over him by the original article in *The People* four and a half years earlier. Asked for his own verdict outside the High Court, Bremner, by now Doncaster Rovers manager, told the *YEP* of his 'delight' before adding: 'It has been the longest six days in my life. Now, I just want to get home to my wife and family.'

The settlement, at the time one of the highest awards for libel made in the High Court, brought the tawdry saga to an end. What it couldn't do, however, even almost a decade on was eradicate the memory of what had been a truly devastating night in the West Midlands for Leeds and their captain as another major honour passed the club by.

Chapter 12

Stokoe And Salonika

Leaving home at an early age to follow the dream of becoming a footballer is never easy. When that move as a teenager is to another country it can make life very difficult. That had certainly been the experience of Billy Bremner when he had headed to Leeds in 1959. He had never forgotten the feelings of loneliness and isolation that dominated those first few years away from Stirling in a foreign land called Yorkshire. It meant that when any fellow Scots made the move south in subsequent years, the United captain would try and ease any feelings of homesickness. Several who made the switch speak today of the kindness shown by Bremner, who would take a keen interest and often ask about their family and friends. Ditto many of the Scots who played for Bremner when he later moved into management. He didn't want anyone, as he'd almost done in those early years under Don Revie, to throw away their big chance due to a yearning for home. One of many to benefit was Gordon McQueen, who after impressing for St Mirren joined Leeds in September, 1972. Seen by Revie as Jack Charlton's successor, he would develop into an outstanding central defender who, within a year of arriving, had become an integral part of the side. In his first few weeks and months, however, 20-year-old McQueen found aspects of life at Elland Road difficult. He recalls: "It is a big thing at that age to move to another country, even if that country is only England. Life is very, very different and you do miss your pals from back home. What helped me after signing for Leeds was that there were quite a few Scots already at the club, and in particular Billy Bremner. He had been homesick himself after first joining Leeds so knew what us younger lads might be going through. So, he did everything he could to help. There were a few of us that Billy helped out. Me, Gary Liddell and David McNiven all appreciated it enormously. It was all the little things that made Billy special. Such as if a few of my pals from Scotland came down for the weekend to watch the first team, Billy would be straight over to talk to them. Later, when I started to play for the first team he was equally good in helping me settle. As I was still a young lad, Billy would make sure I was doing the right things and picking the right options on the park. There was no way he would allow me to slack, he was such an inspirational figure that I wouldn't have done anyway. But, as I got older, I appreciated how much of a help Billy had been to me. Not only when I first signed, but just as importantly when I started playing for the first team."

Another who moved south to Leeds from Scotland a couple of years before McQueen was Joe Jordan. Bremner had, again, been on hand to offer advice or just lend an ear for a forward who had been signed from Greenock Morton on the recommendation of former Leeds captain Bobby Collins. Including new signings in the banter that forms such a crucial, and cruel, part of dressing room life was seen as an integral part of the settling in process – hence Jordan being told by his new captain that a prized Arran knitted jumper made him, 'Look like Val Doonican'. Being no fan of the Irish folk singer, Jordan immediately dumped the offending item. The jibe may have been a tad cruel, not least as the jumper had been knitted by Jordan's mother, but it helped the new signing feel part of the dressing room.

As captain, Bremner didn't just take an interest in the young Scots at the club. He also made a point of trying to make all new arrivals welcome, even if their move had only been 15 miles or so down the A62. Trevor Cherry had been with hometown club Huddersfield Town for seven years when Don Revie paid £100,000 to bring the defender to Leeds. He had captained the Terriers to the Second Division title in 1970 and been a consistently impressive performer during the club's two-year stay in the top flight. Despite that, Cherry admits to having an inferiority complex on walking into a dressing room full of experienced internationals. He recalls: "I had played a lot of games for Huddersfield but still felt wet behind the ears compared to all these big names. At first, I wondered what I was doing there among all these great players. But Billy, as my skipper, was great in helping me settle. It probably helped that I was Billy's sort of player in that I hated to lose. I never saw the point in playing for the fun of it, even in training. Billy was the same." As with Jordan a year or so earlier, the moment Cherry knew he had been accepted in the dressing room came courtesy of Bremner's trademark humour. "It was my second or third game for Leeds," recalls the defender who, during his time at Elland Road, became an England international. "I came off thinking I had played really well so was delighted when the gaffer praised my contribution. But then suddenly, Billy started on me. He was shouting how I should be marking a lot tighter and that I needed to pull my socks up. It was in front of all the lads and all I could think was, 'Shit, I didn't think I played too badly'. Then, almost as suddenly as Billy had started shouting at me, he burst out laughing. He was winding me up and had got me hook, line and sinker. It was in that moment that I felt accepted as one of the lads."

With Cherry the only significant signing of the summer – Roy Ellam also joined for £35,000 from Huddersfield in August but was destined to make only 19 starts before returning to Leeds Road in 1974 – Leeds set off to Chelsea on the opening day in confident mood. Since winning promotion in 1964, United had proved to be strong starters with their seasonal bow having yielded six wins, one draw and just one defeat. At Stamford Bridge, however, the debut of Cherry and Ellam would end in a resounding 4-0 defeat. It was United's worst opening day loss in 24 years, though there were mitigating circumstances with goalkeeper David Harvey suffering concussion and having to be replaced by Peter Lorimer. Mick Jones was also forced out of the action with a twisted ankle as Revie's side finished the game with ten men. With Harvey back in goal and Jack Charlton replacing Ellam at the heart of the defence, normal service was resumed three days later as Sheffield United were beaten 2-0 at Bramall Lane. West Brom then suffered by the same scoreline in Elland Road's first game of the season as Leeds embarked on an eight-match unbeaten run. Back-to-back defeats followed against Newcastle United and Liverpool before a 5-0 thrashing of champions Derby County brought immense satisfaction at Elland Road. It also heralded the start of a run in the league that would bring just one defeat – at Arsenal in December – from the next 16 outings. United were, once again, firmly involved in the title race. It was a similar story in the European Cup Winners' Cup, the club's first appearance in the competition bringing a 2-1 aggregate victory over Turkish side Ankaragucu in the first round and a 2-0 triumph over two legs against Carl Zeiss Jena. The second leg victory over the East Germans at Elland Road had brought Cherry's second goal for Leeds, the first having come in a 4-0 win over Burnley in the League Cup second round. It further cemented the respect he had already won among his new team-mates by impressively stepping in at left-back to replace broken leg victim Terry Cooper. Cherry puts that early good form down to the welcome he received at Elland Road, plus a desire to follow the lead of his skipper. He says: "That Leeds team didn't have shouters and bawlers as such, instead it was more a case of everyone knowing what their job was. But if we ever needed a bit of inspiration, all we had to do was look across at Billy. He was someone who never accepted we were going to lose, even if we were 2-0 down and there wasn't long left on the clock. It might just be something he did in a game, but it gave us all a lift."

With the Cup Winners' Cup heading into the mid-season break afforded all UEFA's competitions, United's focus at the turn of the year was split between the league and FA Cup. As holders, United were determined to hold on to their trophy. Drawn against a Norwich City side destined to be relegated from the First Division come May, Revie's men made unexpectedly hard work of progressing to the fourth round, needing two replays to settle the tie. Routine wins over Plymouth Argyle and West Brom then put United in the quarter-finals for the sixth time in nine years. The draw paired Leeds with Derby, whose manager Brian Clough had become even more vociferous in his criticism of Revie's side since winning the title the previous May. Revenge, of sorts, had been exacted with a 5-0 hammering of the Rams in the league but here was a chance for Bremner and his team-mates to really make a point. It was an opportunity that was gleefully accepted as a goal from Peter Lorimer at the Baseball Ground put Leeds through to the semi-finals. Arsenal, Sunderland and Wolves made up the rest of the last four but there was little doubt who Revie's side wanted to play. Wolves had not only denied United the title the previous May but insult had been added to injury by the subsequent claims of how the Yorkshire club had tried to bribe their way to victory that night. A few of the Leeds players punching the air on hearing news that the draw had, indeed, brought a semi-final meeting with Wolves therefore spoke volumes. This was one game United were not going to lose, as Don Revie revealed when asked his thoughts on the FA decreeing that if the Wolves game finished as a draw then the replay would take place just two days later. This would leave his players facing the possibility of three semi-finals - the other being in the Cup Winners' Cup - in five days. Revie said simply: 'We don't mind as long as we reach Wembley.'

Revie's wish was granted as a tight game at Maine Road was decided midway through the second half by a strike from Bremner, the third time the Scot had netted the only goal to secure a Cup final visit to Wembley. Cherry, the only Leeds player at that time not to have played at the national stadium, remembers: "Billy had this amazing knack of scoring in the big games. Even in the relatively short time I played with Billy compared to most of the other lads, I saw that happen several times. It might be a Cup semi-final or a vital league match, but I always thought Billy would pull something out of the fire for us."

Bremner's strike in front of 52,505 fans at Maine Road meant the tantalising prospect of a league and Cup double was still very much alive. Five days before the win over Wolves, a 1-0 win at Coventry had left United five points behind leaders Liverpool with a game in hand. The elation of reaching Wembley was then added to when news reached the victorious dressing room at Maine Road that Liverpool had lost at Birmingham City in the league. Arsenal completed the trio of sides chasing the title and they sat a point behind Liverpool, but again they had played two more games than Revie's men. A week later, Bill Shankly's Reds extended their lead at the top by a point with a 1-0 win over West Brom as Leeds and Arsenal were both held. The initiative had swung the way of Anfield, paving the way for the killer blow to United's title hopes being struck by Manchester United with a 1-0 victory at Elland Road a few days later. In a strangely lethargic display, Leeds never got going and Liverpool's own win at Coventry the same night provided the impetus that would eventually see the League Championship go to Merseyside. Revie's men would eventually finish third behind Arsenal, despite ending their domestic campaign with a 6-1 hammering of the Gunners.

With any hopes of a second league title gone, United could, at least, console themselves with having reached two Cup finals. Rapid Bucharest had been swept aside in the Cup Winners' Cup quarter-finals to set up a two-legged meeting with Hajduk Split. For the first game at Elland Road, coach Zebec Branco sent out his Yugoslav side with the instruction to keep it tight. Allan Clarke did manage to snatch one goal, drilling a low shot across Radomir Vukceric in the Hajduk goal after 21 minutes. But, even though behind, the visitors refused to change their game-plan. As a result, no further goals were scored and, come the final whistle, the Yugoslavs were celebrating at the prospect of taking Revie's side back to Split with just a one-goal deficit to make up. Not only that, but the late dismissal of Clarke for dishing out his own form of retribution after being fouled by Mario Boljat meant Leeds would have to protect such a slender lead without their top scorer.

In the return, Revie's solution was to bring Joe Jordan in to play alongside Mick Jones. Played just two days after the 2-0 defeat at Anfield that had finally ended any hopes of a second First Division title as Liverpool were crowned champions, the tie was one the Yugoslavs expected to win. Bremner and his team-mates had been left in no doubt about this on the coach ride to the Plinaric Stadium as the locals held up their fingers to illustrate how many times Hajduk would score. Some went for two with a symbolic salute very similar to the one made famous by show-jumper Harvey Smith a couple of years earlier, while others had the temerity to wave all five fingers at the passing bus. As veterans of almost a decade of European combat, the United players responded with a mere shrug of the shoulders as if to say, 'We'll see'. Once out on the field, the visitors from England were met by a passionate 30,000 crowd intent on roaring their team forward. Leeds, however, were used to dealing with such a hostile reception and produced a display so polished that Revie would later describe it as on a par with the goalless draw against Ferencvaros in Hungary that won the Fairs Cup in 1968. Hajduk did fashion a couple of chances only for David Harvey to save from Micun Jovanic and Ivan Surjek to head wide when it seemed easier to score. Those apart, though, Leeds were rarely troubled and even managed to get the ball in the net at the death through Johnny Giles – only for referee Robert Helies to indicate he had already blown for time. Once again, United had prevailed in a hostile foreign land. Bremner, as captain, had played his customary important role in European combat – something football commentator John Helm always found admirable considering the Scot's fear of flying. "He didn't look forward to the times the team had to fly," recalls the man who accompanied United on many of their foreign trips after becoming sports editor of *BBC Radio Leeds*. "I am not sure exactly when it started but there was one European away game when one of the tyres burst on taking off that made it a hairy experience for everyone when we landed back in England. We flew over Heathrow for what seemed like an age before finally making it on our third attempted landing. By then, we all knew what had happened to the tyre on take-off and Billy's response had been to get drunk. It was the only way he could handle the fear. It didn't help matters that not long after that flight back to London, there was another trip where we had to circle Leeds-Bradford Airport three or four times. Eventually, the pilot decided it was just too difficult and we landed at Manchester instead. It did nothing for Billy's fear of flying."

United were, thanks to the goalless draw in Yugoslavia, through to their fourth European final, where they would meet AC Milan after the Italians had won 1-0 in Prague to seal a 2-0 aggregate triumph over Sparta. The final, unlike their previous appearances in three Fairs Cup deciders, would be a one-off affair and held in Salonika. Before the trip to Greece, however, United's focus was on preparing for their third FA Cup final in four years. Sunderland, the Second Division club who had started as 250-1 outsiders to lift the trophy in January, had battled their way through to Wembley for the first time since 1937. Even now, with the field of potential winners narrowed to just two, they were priced at 5-2 to lift the Cup as opposed to the odds of 3-1 on offered for a Leeds win. The Wearsiders had just finished sixth in

Division Two, recovering from the 21st place that the club had occupied when Bob Stokoe had been appointed manager the previous November. Even allowing for such a significant improvement in their league form, Sunderland's run to the final had still come as a major surprise. Only a stunning save by Jim Montgomery had prevented the club from falling 2-0 behind at Notts County with just 15 minutes remaining of their third round tie, a deficit that Stokoe later admitted would have been difficult to overcome. As it was, Montgomery's save together with an equaliser from Dave Watson earned a replay that Sunderland subsequently won 2-0. A second game was also needed to dispose of Reading in the fourth round before a battling draw at Manchester City paved the way for a memorable 3-1 replay victory over Malcolm Allison's side at Roker Park. Luton Town and then, incredibly, title-chasing Arsenal had been dumped out to earn Sunderland a crack at the team their manager wanted to beat more than any other.

Stokoe and Revie had been on opposing sides in the 1955 FA Cup final, the former claiming a winners' medal courtesy of Newcastle United beating Manchester City. But it was a game seven years later that had led to Stokoe despising Revie. Just four games of the 1961-62 season had remained when Leeds, in danger of dropping into the Third Division for the first time, travelled to Bury for the first of a double-header that would go a long way towards deciding the fate of Revie's men. Stokoe, then manager at Gigg Lane, went to his grave in 2004 insisting that Revie had offered £500 for Bury to forfeit one of the games. The allegation did not come to light until the 1977 *Daily Mirror* investigation that also included the attempted bribery claims surrounding United's defeat to Wolves in May, 1972. So, when Leeds met Sunderland in the FA Cup final, few realised the depth of Stokoe's resentment towards Revie. What was evident, though, during the build-up was how determined the Sunderland manager was to employ a touch of psychology in an attempt to give his side the edge. First, he complained that Leeds fans would occupy the Tunnel End of Wembley and then that the Yorkshire club had been handed the 'best' dressing room. These were, however, merely the prelude to what Stokoe considered the most important point to get across to Cup final referee Ken Burns. Namely, that he considered Bremner to have had an undue influence on the officials during United's semi-final win over Wolves. Stokoe said: 'I am not trying to knock Leeds in any way but we are playing a real professional side and, let's face it, the word professionalism can embrace a multitude of sins as well as virtues. The case about Bremner is the only comment I want to make about Leeds. My message is simple. I want Mr Burns, the Cup final referee, to make the decisions and not Mr Bremner.' The response from the Leeds captain was to tell the *Yorkshire Evening Post*, 'It is like Wilfred Pickles have-a-go week', Halifax-born Pickles having been the host of a BBC Radio show *Have A Go*. Bremner's flippancy was perhaps understandable, for the semi-final referee in question, Pat Partridge, had hardly seemed unduly concerned about the Leeds captain's conduct when quoted in the *YEP* the day after the Wolves game. He said: 'Billy never shuts up. He talks all the time. Sometimes that may look as if he is arguing. But it doesn't worry me. It is natural. I got in the way of one of his passes and he, er, rather suggested that I ought to watch where I was going. I just told him that it was a bad pass to start with. He laughed at that.'

Whether what Stokoe was implying was correct or not, Bremner's response was the last off-the-cuff remark made by a Leeds player before the final as Revie ordered there to be no display of public confidence during the last few days before the May 5 showpiece. This continued right until kick-off as the players provided taut, monosyllabic replies to even the most innocuous of questions when interviewed on television. In contrast, the Sunderland camp could not have appeared more relaxed with Stokoe inviting the cameras on to the team coach for the journey to Wembley – something unheard of at the time. Then, as Dave Watson was being interviewed by the BBC's Barry Davies, the viewers were left puzzled by an explosion of maniacal cackling after team-mate Billy Hughes had activated his new toy, a laughter box.

Once at Wembley, the contrasting mood of the two camps was again clear for all to see as Sunderland continued to milk the occasion by larking around and waving to family and friends. This relaxed approach was evident once the action got underway on the slippery, rain-soaked surface as the Second Division side went close when Mick Horswill hit a 20-yard shot that flew just past David Harvey's post. By now, it had become apparent that Sunderland's support at the game had been swelled beyond the 20,000 or so who had bought tickets from Roker Park. Instead, it was more like half the Wembley crowd who seemed to be cheering the underdogs on as the neutrals adopted the team in red and white for the day. The goal they had craved since welcoming the two teams on to the field with a huge roar arrived on 31 minutes, when Ian Porterfield capitalised on poor defending to cushion the ball on his thigh and thunder a right-foot volley past David Harvey. With so much of the game still to play, Leeds were not unduly worried despite having not been at their best in that opening half-hour or so. They did get the ball in the net shortly after half-time through Trevor Cherry only for referee Burns to, rightly, rule goalkeeper Jim Montgomery had been fouled. United continued to pour forward and it seemed only a matter of time before the equaliser was found. The moment that prompted commentator Brian Moore to shout, 'It's a goal', duly arrived midway through the second half as Peter Lorimer's shot arrowed towards the net. Trevor Cherry had created the opening with a diving header from a Paul Reaney cross that Montgomery had only been able to palm into the path of the on-rushing Lorimer. To ITV's Moore, the 100,000 inside Wembley and millions watching at home, the equaliser had arrived. Only it hadn't as Montgomery, in one motion, leapt to his feet before flinging himself in the path of the ball to pull off arguably the best save in Cup final history. Cherry, still on the floor after his initial effort had been blocked, stuck out a leg as the ball bounced back off the crossbar but Sunderland cleared and the Cup was on its way to Wearside. The final whistle saw Stokoe rush to thank his goalkeeper. As he danced the famous jig of delight on the Wembley turf that would later be replicated by Sunderland with a statue of their former manager outside the Stadium of Light, Revie had the difficult task of trying to lift his players.

This wasn't the first time the United manager had needed to find the right words. But, as quickly became apparent in the wake of the Cup final defeat, it was likely to be his last. Everton wanted Revie and, most worryingly of all for everyone at Elland Road, it seemed he wanted to go. The players feared the worst on hearing that one of Revie's trusted contacts in the press had broken the initial story. Trevor Cherry recalls: "Bill Mallinson of the *Daily Mail* was big pals with Don so because he had run the story about Everton wanting to make him manager then we knew it must be right." The news did little to lift the players' mood ahead of the Cup Winners' Cup, especially when Revie subsequently confirmed the story to be true shortly before the squad flew out to Greece. Terry Yorath recalls: "The gaffer was very frank and up front with us. He said everything was not signed and sealed but he looked set to leave for Everton when the season was over. He told us at the start of the trip, so it wasn't a happy one – even though we were setting off for a European final."

As the squad jetted out for Greece, they did so in the knowledge that several key players would be missing against AC Milan through either injury or suspension. One of the absentees was Bremner, who had accumulated sufficient bookings to be handed a one-game ban. His loss would be keenly felt after a season in which he had, for the third year in a row, been named by his peers in the PFA Team of the Year. The Scot's form had been such that Terry Brindle, of the *Yorkshire Post*, had been moved to write in the wake of Leeds reaching the FA Cup final: 'Bremner typifies the drive and spirit, and the deep-rooted will to win that has taken Leeds to success and near success for several seasons. He is abrasive, aggressive and, above all, competitive. Not everyone's idea of a gentleman, to be sure, but a man whose qualities and character and leadership have developed with United and helped spur them towards another sensational treble.'

Since those gushing words had been penned, United had missed out on both the FA Cup and the League Championship. That left just one remaining opportunity to ensure a season did not end with the club again left empty-handed. AC Milan, though, would be tough opponents, having just finished as runners-up in Serie A. One month after facing Leeds in Salonika, they would also retain the Coppa Italia by beating Juventus. Nevertheless, Leeds had become renowned for overcoming the odds and the players still fancied their chances despite the quality of the opposition and the key absentees.

Unfortunately, within four minutes of the start, Milan had been awarded a soft free-kick when Paul Madeley was adjudged to have fouled Alberto Bignon just outside the area. The Leeds players were fuming with the decision, which was then made worse when Luciano Chiarugi's free-kick clipped the heels of Madeley and spun beyond David Harvey into the net. The subsequent rejection by Greek referee Christos Michas of two strong penalty appeals – one for handball and the other when Mick Jones appeared to be fouled – only added to the disquiet of not only the Leeds players but also the Greek fans in the 40,154 crowd who started to jeer the referee. When a third appeal for a spotkick was turned down, United's patience finally snapped and Norman Hunter was sent off for retaliation after a foul by Gianni Rivera. Moments later, the final whistle was blown to confirm that, despite another almighty effort, Leeds had again finished the season empty-handed. Revie was distraught, as were his players, and the flight home was, understandably, a sombre affair. Missing out on another trophy was bad enough. But it was nothing compared to the sense of loss felt over the departure of the manager who had built Leeds United almost from scratch into one of Europe's most feared sides. To the already dejected players, it marked the end of an era.

Chapter 13

Back To The Summit

As Don Revie jetted off on holiday with wife Elsie a couple of days after returning from Salonika, his future was still undecided. Everton had raised the ante substantially, upping the original offer of a five-year contract worth £100,000 with an additional tax-free signing-on fee of £50,000. But still Revie was yet to make his mind up. His Leeds United players, to a man, wanted him to stay. They believed that, while none of them was getting any younger, there was still sufficient hunger and desire within the team to bring more success to Elland Road. Crucial to those hopes of winning trophies in the future, however, was the retention of Revie. So, as the squad went their separate ways for the summer, the hope was that the Leeds board could somehow persuade their manager to stay.

A few days later, the players got their wish – though it was less the intervention of the directors that proved the true catalyst for keeping Revie in Yorkshire than a bizarre twist in the form of a question being asked in the House of Commons. The previous year, the Government's desperation to curb inflation of around 10 per cent had led to the introduction of strict new legislation designed to keep a check on wages. Under the anti-inflation White Paper that was subsequently passed by 79 votes in the Commons, it was forbidden for any new recruit to an existing job to be paid more than his or her predecessor in the role. Millions would, ultimately, be affected by the new law. By far the most high profile was Revie, whose proposed move to Everton started to unravel the moment it became the subject of a question in the House from Dennis Skinner, the MP for Bolsover. Just eight days had elapsed since United's European Cup Winners' Cup final defeat to AC Milan when Skinner, dubbed the 'Beast of Bolsover' by his Parliamentary colleagues, asked if the Pay Board were investigating Revie's proposed switch from Leeds to Goodison Park. In support of the question, he drew the House's attention to the stories in the press that suggested Revie would be paid far more than the outgoing manager, Harry Catterick. Following Skinner's intervention, matters escalated very quickly. Within hours, it had been announced via an official statement from Whitehall that the matter was being investigated and that, 'Both clubs have been reminded of the Pay and

Prices Code'. The tide was turning and, by 9am the following day, Revie had telephoned Elland Road from his holiday near Athens to inform United secretary Keith Archer that he would be staying after all. Publicly, it was claimed a desire to finish the job at Leeds had brought about the U-turn and kept Revie at the club. Others, though, suspected the intervention of the Government had heavily influenced the decision. Either way, the United players were mightily relieved. Trevor Cherry recalls: "Everyone was delighted. We had not won anything in what had been my first season at Leeds but I still fancied our chances of winning at least a couple of trophies if the gaffer stayed. Finding out he was not going to Everton was a real lift, especially after how the season had just ended with the Cup final defeats to Sunderland and AC Milan."

There was still one more scare for United later that summer when Revie casually revealed that he had received a couple of lucrative offers to manage in Greece. Happily, though, neither came to fruition so when the players gathered for pre-season there had been only one notable departure from Elland Road. Jack Charlton, despite being offered a two-year deal that would have kept him at the club until the age of 40, had decided to become Middlesbrough manager, a move that brought about an end to a career that included 773 appearances in a Leeds shirt. Revie had wanted to keep Charlton, hence the contract offer that included a coaching role. But the United manager also recognised that 22-year-old Gordon McQueen had matured to such an extent that he had already replaced Charlton in his first-choice starting line-up. McQueen was, by no means, the only player to bring a more youthful feel to the squad with Joe Jordan, Trevor Cherry and Terry Yorath having also been gradually introduced to the first-team over the past couple of years. Teenager Frank Gray, brother of Eddie, had also made the step-up, leaving Revie pleased with the make-up of a squad that included only two 30-somethings - Billy Bremner (30) and Johnny Giles (33). The United manager felt the balance was just right, despite his players having been the subject of countless footballing obituaries in the wake of the FA Cup final defeat to Sunderland. Such was Revie's confidence, in fact, that he felt the time was right to set his players the ultimate target – to go through the whole campaign unbeaten. The challenge was laid down when the players re-assembled for pre-season training. 'We've been the best team for the last decade,' started Revie to his assembled squad. 'I know we haven't won as much as we should have, but that's in the past. Now I've had a thought this close season – can we go through the whole campaign unbeaten?'

It was a daunting challenge and one that no team in the modern era had come close to achieving. Preston North End had managed the feat once, though that had been in the Football League's very first season. Not only had the Lancashire club faced just 22 games and tackled opposition from only the Midlands and their own native county. But such had been the often chaotic nature of that 1888-89 season that a points system whereby teams were awarded two for a win and one for a draw was only settled on two months after the League had kicked off. It was going to take an almighty effort for Leeds to match Preston's Invincibles. Revie, though, was nothing if not persuasive – as Trevor Cherry recalls: "At first, I wasn't sure if I had just heard Don right. Go unbeaten for the whole season? But, soon, Don had us all believing it could be done."

After loosening the defensive shackles over the previous four seasons, Revie was adamant that attack was the key to achieving what would be tantamount to footballing immortality. With that in mind, training sessions began featuring much more shooting practice. The Leeds players were, once the season had begun, expected to let fly once in sight of goal. Billy Bremner, the scorer of so many important goals in the past, was also told to get into the opposition penalty area as often as possible to support the strikers. The instruction was just what Bremner wanted to hear, the United captain's goal tally having fallen in recent seasons due to the tweaking of tactics that had been made necessary by the signing of Allan Clarke and the blossoming of Peter Lorimer's talent. Bremner had netted four league goals in 1972-73, one less than the previous season. The two before that had brought just three apiece. Now, the Leeds captain hoped Revie's instruction to get forward in support of the attack would mean a return to the days when his name would feature more regularly on the scoresheet. An opening day 3-1 win over Everton certainly seemed to support such thinking, Bremner having opened the scoring to set United on their way to the two points. A 2-1 win at Arsenal followed three days later before Bremner was again among the goals in a 3-0 victory over Tottenham Hotspur at White Hart Lane, netting twice as Allan Clarke scored the other. Wolves were United's next opponents and, once again, Bremner scored in a 4-1 triumph to lead the club's goalscoring charts with four from as many games. Peter Lorimer duly eclipsed his captain with a hat-trick against Birmingham City three days later to take his own tally to six but, by the season's end, the licence to roam forward that Bremner had been so pleased to be granted had led to him reaching double figures in the league for the first time in 11 seasons. Such a healthy return was indicative of not only the expansive style of football now advocated by Revie but also the relaxed air that Bremner was exuding. John Helm, who by 1973-74 was in his fourth season covering United for *BBC Radio Leeds*, says: "Billy may have been this all-action player on the field but off it he loved to relax. I was the ghost-writer for a weekly column that appeared under his name in Shoot magazine. We agreed that I would chat to Billy on the 'phone for 10 minutes or so and then put his thoughts down on paper. Billy would then read it to check the piece reflected his own views. Well, that was how it went for the first two or three weeks at least. Then, he turned round and said, 'Just write what you want'. Most weeks I never even spoke to Billy, I would just write what I imagined he would be thinking. I took it as a sign of how relaxed Billy felt, and also that he trusted me. We had a great relationship and, later, he really helped me out on a couple of occasions, even coming to a couple of dinners I was organising and offering to speak for free. I tried to pay Billy a fee but he refused."

The goal output of Bremner and Lorimer may have slowed after the initial flurry that had seen the pair find the net ten times in the opening five games. But there was little chance of the brakes being applied to United, who made it seven straight wins with a 2-1 victory at Southampton. There was still a long way to go but Leeds were already wearing the look of champions. Trevor Cherry recalls: "We had all seen for ourselves in pre-season how set Don was in his mind that we could win the League Championship that year. He was such a persuasive man that we all believed it could happen, though I must admit there was a time during pre-season when I wondered if we still had the legs to do it. We had a couple of poor performances in friendlies that saw us draw and lose against Bradford and Huddersfield. I said to my wife Sue, 'What is going on? Maybe they just aren't the team I thought any more?' I needn't have worried as once the real action was under way, the team was quickly on top of its game."

United's 100 per cent winning start came to an end with a goalless draw at home to Manchester United. Two more draws against Stoke City and Leicester City followed after Norwich City had been beaten 1-0. Revie's insistence that winning the First Division title was the overriding priority meant a League Cup tie at Ipswich Town saw several first-team regulars rested in a 2-0 defeat. A similar approach was adopted in the UEFA Cup as, after beating Norwegian amateurs Stromgodset Drammen 7-2 on aggregate, Revie let it be known that it would not be a disaster if United's involvement was to be ended by Hibernian in the second round. Peter Lorimer recalls: "A couple of the younger lads were selected for the first leg at Elland Road and we drew 0-0. For the return, Don rested a lot of the lads and played the rest out of position. Billy played sweeper, for instance. Don dressed it up to the Press as wanting to give the Scottish lads a chance to play in their own country but he told the senior lads he wanted out of the competition. He told me before kick-off, 'Keep out of any tackles, I don't want you getting injured'. I am pretty sure he said the same to Billy and a couple of the others. John Shaw, who was still only a teenager, played in goal but, unfortunately for Don, had a blinder. Hibs just couldn't get past him, no matter what they tried. John saw it as his chance to really impress and was taking it. Thanks to him, there was still no score at half-time. We returned to the dressing room and it was almost comical to watch Don shake John's hand and say, 'I've never seen a performance like that, John. Brilliant. But I'm taking you off, son, so get in the bath'. Glan Letheran, our youth team 'keeper, was on the bench so Don brought him on. But the ploy didn't work as Hibernian still couldn't score and the game finished goalless, meaning the tie would have to be decided by penalties. Don, who looked absolutely gutted, came up to a few of the senior lads and said, 'You might as well win it now, we'll just have to go out in the next round'." Leeds duly won the shoot-out 5-4 to progress to the last 16 where they were paired with Vitoria Setubal. Two games against the Portuguese side were an irritation to Revie, though John Helm believes the unwanted penalty shoot-out victory against Hibernian merely underlined what a great competitor Bremner was. "Billy was a magnificent footballer and couldn't bear to be beaten," he says. "In the European game at Hibernian that finished goalless, he was outstanding. Hibs were a good team at the time but Billy produced one of the finest displays I've seen."

Revie got his wish in the next round of the UEFA Cup when, after winning 1-0 at Elland Road in front of just 14,196 fans, United lost the return 3-1 on a night when Bremner was rested along with Norman Hunter and Allan Clarke. As the United manager hoped, the December exit from the UEFA Cup allowed his side to focus on maintaining their unbeaten start. The weekend preceding the trip to Portugal had seen Leeds beat Ipswich Town to equal Liverpool's record of the longest unbeaten run from the start of a season. A 2-1 win at Chelsea a week later, therefore, meant that a new record had been set due to United losing none of their opening 20 fixtures. A 1-0 win over Norwich at Elland Road then ensured the halfway point of the season had been reached with the unbeaten record still intact. Just after Christmas, however, Revie's dream was almost ended when Birmingham City led United at St Andrews as the game entered the final stages only for Joe Jordan to pop up with a dramatic 87th minute equaliser. The United manager breathed a huge sigh of relief at his side having made it to the end of the year with a record reading 16 wins and seven draws from 23 league outings. It seemed, even at such an early stage of the season, a question of when and not if the title would be making its way to Elland Road. Bremner was just as delighted as his manager with United's form, viewing that season's title race as an opportunity to make up for previous disappointments. Trevor Cherry recalls: "Billy was exactly the same as Don that season – he just had to win the league. Billy, along with all the lads who had been together since the beginning, had been through so many disappointments that he was desperate to bring more success to Leeds. I also think he realised that he wasn't getting any younger and that there wouldn't be too many more seasons when that team would be at its peak. In a way, Billy was the man who ran the club for the manager on the field. Don treated all the players like sons but he seemed especially fond of Billy. He was the go-between and at the heart of everything. Even in the dressing room, little happened without Billy being in the middle of things - whether it was the banter or the jokes. To me, Billy really was our 'Captain Fantastic'."

The New Year began with a glut of draws as Tottenham Hotspur and Chelsea both returned to the capital from Elland Road with a point. Everton, who had worked so hard to try and entice Revie the previous summer, also held United at Goodison Park with United's solitary win of the first five weeks of 1974 being a 2-1 triumph at home to Southampton. Murmurings of Leeds possibly having run out of steam were then dispelled by back-to-back wins over Arsenal and Manchester United in February, the latter coming at Old Trafford via goals from Mick Jones and Joe Jordan to extend the unbeaten run to 29 games. More importantly, a nine-point lead had been opened up over Liverpool. Bill Shankly's side had been in scintillating form since the turn of the year, taking 10 points from a possible 12 courtesy of four wins and two draws. But, still, it seemed nothing could stop Leeds. That feeling was only strengthened in the opening 20 minutes of United's 30th league outing of the season at Stoke City as goals from Bremner, with a quickly-taken free-kick as goalkeeper John Farmer attempted to position his wall, and Allan Clarke put the visitors in control. In the Stoke side that day was Alan Hudson, the one-time Chelsea playmaker who a couple of months earlier had been sold to ease the crippling financial problems at Stamford Bridge that had followed the building of the East Stand. He recalls: "At Chelsea, I had always enjoyed playing Leeds because we hated them. I soon realised after joining Stoke that they felt the same. I hadn't been at Stoke long when they played Leeds so I was really looking forward to it. Everyone was determined to do well but, before we knew it, Leeds were 2-0 up and Bremner had scored with a goal that we couldn't believe was given. I am certain he only put it in the net as a joke as we lined up the wall but the referee gave it. At that stage, it looked like Leeds were going to make it 30 games unbeaten."

Two goals ahead and seemingly cruising towards another vital two points, Leeds were, after the early stumbles of the year that had brought three draws in four games, back on track. And with their next three games all at home, United were facing the tantalising prospect of being able to travel to Liverpool on March 16 with an unattainable lead at the top of the table. Such fanciful thinking was, however, soon dispelled as a rejuvenated Stoke made it 2-2 before the break at the Victoria Ground. Worse still for Leeds, Johnny Giles had limped off with a hamstring strain. Now the pressure really was on as the home side launched a second half onslaught that brought its reward in the 69th minute when Denis Smith capitalised on a bout of head tennis in the visitors' penalty area to power the ball past David Harvey. United had almost a quarter of the game to reply but, unlike at St Andrews in December, there was to be no late reprieve. Hudson again: "Once we got to half-time at 2-2, we just knew it was going to be our day. Leeds had gone and it was inevitable we would get the winner. It was a huge result, not least because Leeds had been unbeaten before kick-off. The confidence it gave us was huge and we ended up qualifying for Europe that season."

In public, Revie was magnanimous in defeat as he told the waiting Press: 'I always believed it would take a miracle for us to remain unbeaten. Some day, we were going to come up against a side who would hit top form and Stoke gave a tremendous display.' Privately, however, the United manager was fuming, making a point of allowing his team to overhear a conversation with Les Cocker in the dressing room afterwards where he said it was, 'Time to get the chequebook out and sign some new players'. The tactic was not a new one, he had said the same words directly to the team before a 1-0 win at Manchester City in late October. But Revie clearly felt he needed to try and provoke a reaction. It didn't work as draws against Leicester City and Newcastle United were followed by a scrappy win over Manchester City when Peter Lorimer scored the only goal from the penalty spot. Suddenly, the trip to Liverpool had taken on huge significance. Leeds still led the table by eight points but, thanks to having two games in hand, the Reds knew a win over their great rivals could throw the title race wide open.

Such was the interest in the game that the gates to Anfield were locked more than an hour before kick-off with 56,003 fans inside. Any hopes Leeds could repeat their heroics of five years earlier when a goalless draw had been enough to clinch the title were ended eight minutes from time when Steve Heighway netted the winner. The only consolation for Bremner and his team-mates as they headed back across the Pennines to Yorkshire was that United's destiny was still in their own hands. A week later, however, and this was no longer the case after Burnley had inflicted a stunning 4-1 defeat on Leeds at Elland Road. After the game, Bremner set a revised target of 12 points from the final seven games to win the title but it proved optimistic as another defeat – 3-1 at West Ham United – followed. Now, the initiative really did appear to have swung the way of Liverpool, who as Leeds were losing at Upton Park had been drawing 0-0 with Leicester City in the FA Cup semi-final. Not only was the gap between the two clubs still four points but now the Reds had an extra game in hand. Four days later, Shankly's men maintained their momentum by triumphing in the replay to book their place at Wembley. Liverpool, who had not lost since Boxing Day, were now chasing the double as Leeds' nightmare continued to unfold before their very eyes. Revie's response was to withdraw Norman Hunter and Paul Madeley from the England squad to face Portugal, a move that infuriated Sir Alf Ramsey ahead of what would turn out to be his final game in charge. Bremner, the one United player to regularly refuse his manager's request to pull out of international duty at the business end of a season, was saved a potential clash with Revie due to Scotland not having a game.

With Hunter and Madeley both fit enough to start, Leeds duly received a much-needed lift with a 2-0 win over Derby County at Elland Road. With Shankly's side also winning against QPR, the top of the table was unaffected as United led by four points with their rivals having three games in hand. The traditional Easter fixture pile-up brought three games in four days for Leeds as trips to Coventry City and Sheffield United sandwiched a home encounter with the Blades. Liverpool, meanwhile, had a slightly more demanding schedule with a visit to Bramall Lane plus two games against Manchester City either side of a long trip to Ipswich Town. With the title race now entering the final straight, nerves had become as apparent at

Anfield as they had at Elland Road and a 1-0 defeat for the Reds in Sheffield was followed by draws against City and Ipswich. Leeds also stumbled with 1-1 stalemates against Coventry and the Blades before both clubs returned to winning ways on Easter Tuesday – Leeds triumphing 2-0 against Sheffield United and Liverpool thrashing Manchester City 4-0. Revie's side were still top, four points clear but had just two games remaining as opposed to their rivals' four. It still seemed too close to call, though that did not prevent William Hill bookmakers all but declaring the race to be over by pricing Leeds at 9-2 on for the title with Liverpool on offer at 7-2.

Four days later, the bookmaker's faith was vindicated as the impetus swung decisively back United's way when Liverpool were held to a 0-0 draw in the Merseyside derby and United beat Ipswich 3-2 at Elland Road. The significance of the win was not lost on anyone as Bremner, Trevor Cherry and Allan Clarke were all booked for time-wasting in the closing stages. Liverpool, meanwhile, could only draw the Merseyside derby so, thanks to a vastly superior goal average, Leeds knew only defeat at QPR in their final game, together with Shankly's men winning all three of their own remaining matches, could prevent the League Championship coming back to West Yorkshire. The late rally in form had, it seemed, come just in time with Bremner believing his own change of fortune when calling heads or tails before kick-off had played a part. He told the *Yorkshire Evening Post*: "My luck with the coin this year had not been good up until we played Derby on April 6. In fact, I doubt whether I had won the toss more than a couple of times since the turn of the year. Few of our supporters will need reminding that since the New Year our form has not been as good as it was in the first half of the season. Now, I have won the last four and our results have been good." Bremner's belief that Lady Luck was finally smiling down on his side suggested that the players believed the title was almost within their grasp. Nevertheless, it was still to the immense relief of everyone at Leeds that they were spared any chance of suffering another last-day calamity when Shankly's men lost the first of their remaining trio of games to Arsenal. The race was over and the United players marked the occasion by meeting for an impromptu celebration drink at the Queens Hotel in the city centre.

A 1-0 victory at Loftus Road then ensured Leeds finished five points clear of Liverpool, who, by way of consolation, lifted the FA Cup a week later with a comfortable 3-0 victory over Newcastle United at Wembley. For Bremner, the season had been a personal triumph as well as a success for the team. Along with Norman Hunter, he had been one of only two ever-presents for the club in the league. The United captain also featured in all five FA Cup ties as Leeds beat Wolves and Peterborough United before bowing out to Bristol City after a replay in the fifth round. United's one game in the League Cup, the 2-0 defeat to Ipswich Town, had also seen Bremner lead the team out, while in the UEFA Cup he had been rested just twice – the away leg in Norway against Stromgodset Drammen and the third round tie against Vitoria Setubal in Portugal when Revie had been so desperate to get knocked out. Bremner also enjoyed his most prolific season in the First Division with 10 goals from 42 appearances. Only Mick Jones (14), Allan Clarke (13) and Peter Lorimer (12) scored more, while Bremner also netted once in the FA Cup when United drew 1-1 at Ashton Gate. It was an impressive record, and one only bettered by Bremner in 1961-62 when he found the net 12 times as Leeds battled successfully against relegation from Division Two in Revie's first full season as manager. The Professional Footballers' Association end-of-season awards also underlined Bremner's consistent form as he was one of five Leeds players named in the Division One Team of the Year. In the more well-established Football Writers' Player of the Year – the award Bremner had won in 1970 – he finished a very close second behind Liverpool's Ian Callaghan. To Bremner, however, such personal accolades were dwarfed by what he considered the true story of the 1973-74 season – just what a great team Leeds had become. Gordon McQueen, who missed only six games en route to United lifting the title, says: "It was great to be part of that Leeds team that won the league and went on such a long unbeaten run. But what really made it special was what Billy used to say, namely how it was the best Leeds team he had been involved in. Billy was a big one on everyone in the team pulling together so for him to say something like that was wonderful. Even the media realised in that title-winning season just what a good side Leeds had become. The club may have had a lot of bad press in the past but that started to change during the season. It was a great team to be part of."

For Bremner and his team-mates, the season did not end with the win at Loftus Road as there was still the United captain's testimonial to play. Usually, these games are less than robust affairs where both teams contrive to allow the beneficiary to score a late winner – often from the penalty spot. This being Bremner, however, such niceties were not on the agenda. Instead, he wanted revenge for one of the most disappointing episodes of his career – the 1973 FA Cup final defeat to Sunderland. He had initially wanted to face Scotland only for the SFA to veto the idea on the grounds that the national team were not allowed to face a club side. So, Sunderland would have to do. Speaking to the *Yorkshire Evening Post* on the eve of the May 6 game – a year and one day on from the final – Bremner said: "Quite honestly, I can't remember being quite as unhappy as I was after failing and I have not forgotten the sick feeling in the pit of my stomach as we sat numbed in the dressing room." Adding to the sense of occasion, the Football League had decreed that the League Championship trophy should be presented ahead of the testimonial. As League president Len Shipman did the honours ahead of kick-off, the crowd of 37,708 acclaimed not only the team that had brought the title to Elland Road but also the talismanic captain who had been such a driving force in the success. Once the game kicked off, it was a predictably hard-fought affair with Sunderland, who had again missed out on promotion from the Second Division, determined to prove their Cup triumph had been no fluke. Leeds, for their part, were so intent on avenging the previous year's Cup final that the original plan was for the same XI that had lost at Wembley to start. In the end, an injury to Mick Jones kept the striker out while Johnny Giles was away with the Republic of Ireland but, even so, there was a genuine competitive edge to a game that finished goalless. The result was less than satisfactory to Bremner, though he was able to seek comfort in the receipts of £32,500 – a sum that comfortably exceeded the previous highest for a Leeds testimonial of £27,000, set by Jack Charlton the previous year when Celtic had been the visitors.

Bremner could also look back with satisfaction on a job well done. Leeds may not have delivered on Revie's pre-season challenge of remaining unbeaten but no-one at Elland Road cared as, for a second time, they had been crowned champions. The promise of a second tilt at the European Cup also lay ahead. Before that, however, Bremner had the fulfilment of a boyhood dream to realise. Leading his country at a World Cup.

Chapter 14

The World Stage

When Del Amitri implored Scotland's footballers *Don't Come Home Too Soon* ahead of the 1998 World Cup finals, it was the first recorded instance of an official song urging a national team not to embarrass themselves in a major tournament. The downbeat message brought much criticism of lead singer Justin Currie, who was accused of waving a musical white flag of surrender before a ball had been kicked in France. However, to those all too familiar with Scotland's 'previous' in major finals, the impassioned plea was an understandable one. In their seven appearances at the World Cup prior to France '98, the Scots had failed to go beyond the first round so why would it be any different this time? Sadly, Del Amitri's urgings proved in vain as Craig Brown's side managed to muster just one point and finished bottom of a group featuring Brazil, Norway and Morocco. Even allowing for the pessimism of the official World Cup song, it was a desperately disappointing performance by the Scots with the nadir a 3-0 defeat to the Moroccans in the final group game. What few among the Tartan Army making their way disconsolately back across the English Channel could have predicted, however, was that it would be their team's last appearance at a major finals for some time. So far, in fact, has Scottish football fallen in the intervening years that if Del Amitri were today asked to write a song to sum up the feelings of their nation towards the football team then it would surely be difficult to do so without a liberal amount of swearwords being included. To the older legions of the Tartan Army, the decline from serial qualifiers – Scotland competed in six of the seven World Cup finals held between 1974 and 1998 – to also-rans has been a painful one. The current side's on-going struggles have only added to that sense of anguish with an upturn in fortune seeming further away than ever. To those, however, who believe football moves in cycles and that Scotland can once again return to the top table of world football, solace can be sought in history. Namely, how the Scots bounced back from going 16 years without appearing in a World Cup finals to become a mainstay of the tournament over the following quarter-of-a-century or so.

The Scots' exile from top-level international football ended in 1974. Until then, their World Cup record had been distinctly unremarkable. Having withdrawn from FIFA in 1929 over a dispute about payments to amateur players, Scotland were not involved in the qualifying campaign for any of the three finals held before the outbreak of the Second World War. Then, after ending a 17-year self-imposed exile from FIFA, they turned down the chance to play in the 1950 finals despite having qualified by finishing second behind England in the previous year's British Home Championship – which FIFA had decreed would double up as the qualifying group for the Home Nations. George Graham, the Scottish Football Association chairman, had been the reason for the withdrawal after stating before the qualifying group began that the Scots would only travel to Brazil if they finished top. Despite the pleadings of captain George Young, Graham refused to change the SFA's stance and Portugal went in Scotland's place. Four years later, Scotland did deign to take part only, by the end, to wish they probably hadn't bothered. Andy Beattie had been appointed as Scotland's first manager ahead of the tournament in Switzerland only to then be undermined by the SFA, who ignored his selection of a 22-man squad by deeming he could take only 13 players. The first game against Austria in Zurich ended with a 1-0 defeat before further interference prompted Beattie, who was only part-time, to inform the SFA he would be leaving after the meeting with Uruguay that would act as the climax of the group. The resulting 7-0 defeat remains Scotland's heaviest. In 1958, Scotland would not suffer such an embarrassing reverse but defeats to France and Paraguay would still ensure a bottom place finish in the group stages that not even a first ever point – from a 1-1 draw against Yugoslavia – could make any less disappointing.

For the next 16 years, that would be it regarding Scottish involvement in a World Cup finals. It was an absence made all the more galling by Northern Ireland qualifying during that period and, worst of all, England's success at Wembley in 1966. Just how a nation that had spawned the Lisbon Lions side that won the European Cup plus the likes of Jim Baxter, Dave Mackay and Denis Law could miss out on not only qualifying for the World Cup but also the European Championships was a mystery that the SFA moved to solve by appointing Tommy Docherty in September, 1971. By then, any hopes of claiming a place at the following year's European Championships had been all but ended thanks to defeats in Belgium, Portugal and Denmark. The Home Championships had also brought a 3-1 defeat to England at Wembley that had seen the team booed from the field by the thousands of fans who had travelled south. Docherty knew changes were needed so, for his first game in charge against Portugal, only Hibernian's Pat Stanton survived from the starting line-up that had lost 1-0 to Russia in a friendly three months earlier. Among those changes was the return of an available-again Billy Bremner, who collected his 26th cap as the Portuguese were beaten 2-1. It was a promising start for Docherty and one he built on admirably with subsequent victories over Belgium, Peru, Northern Ireland and Wales. The latter two of that quartet of wins had come the May following his appointment in the Home Championships, meaning the Scots' final game against England at Hampden Park would be the decider. A draw for Scotland would be enough to clinch a first outright Championship success since 1967. Instead, however, it was the English who prevailed through an Alan Ball goal to ensure the 1972 title was shared between international football's two oldest competitors. For Bremner, defeat was a bitter disappointment – especially coming so quickly after the loss to Wolves in Leeds United's colours that had ended any hopes of claiming a historic League and Cup double south of the border. He could, though, also see that progress was being made under Docherty ahead of the all-important World Cup qualifiers getting under way in October. The Scots had been drawn in a three-team group that also featured Czechoslovakia and Denmark. Unlike four years earlier when beaten finalists West Germany had stood in their path, this was a much kinder draw and one that to Bremner, who was fast approaching his 30th birthday, offered one last chance to play in a World Cup. It was an opportunity he was determined to accept, so much so that ahead of the traditional return to pre-season with Leeds the Scotland captain made himself available for a mini-tour of Brazil in late June and early July.

The original thinking behind the Brazil Independence Cup had been for all previous World Cup winners to compete against each other. When this proved to be unfeasible, entry was made by invitation only. Scotland were not initially on the guest list but, as soon as it emerged England had declined the invitation, Docherty moved quickly. Initially, the SFA were sceptical but the national team manager soon talked them round by pointing out what invaluable preparation taking on Brazil, Argentina and Uruguay would be for the forthcoming qualifying campaign. Once permission had been granted, Docherty quickly turned his attention to the club managers who would also need to give the go-ahead to their players taking part. Some were reluctant but one player who was not going to miss the trip was Bremner. The captain's dedication was rewarded by an unforgettable experience as the Scots drew with Yugoslavia and Czechoslovakia to earn a semi-final meeting with Brazil in the Maracana Stadium. The visitors from Britain would, ultimately, lose 1-0 to a Jairzinho goal 10 minutes from time but not before producing an impressive display in front of a 133,000 crowd. It was the biggest attendance Bremner had played in front of since the 1970 European Cup semi-final second leg against Celtic at Hampden Park.

The defeat in Rio was Scotland's last outing before the opening qualifier against Denmark in Copenhagen on October 18. Bremner again captained the side as the Scots triumphed 4-1 on a night when a young Kenny Dalglish was a late substitute from the bench. A month later, Dalglish had been promoted to the starting line-up for the return against the Danes and he rewarded Docherty's faith by opening the scoring inside two minutes. Peter Lorimer then added a second just after half-time to ensure Scotland went top of the group. Their next qualifier was 10 months away so, in the meantime, all the Scots could do was hope Denmark would do them a huge favour in their double-header against the Czechs in May and June. It duly came in the first of those two meetings when a crowd of 21,000 in Copenhagen saw the two countries share a 1-1 draw. The Czechs exacted revenge a month later with a 6-0 win in Prague but the damage had been done. Scotland needed to win just one of their own home and away meetings with Czechoslovakia to book a place at the 1974 finals in West Germany. By now, Willie Ormond had taken over as manager following Docherty's decision to accept an offer to become Manchester United manager. The loss of someone who had reinvigorated the national side had been a big one, as illustrated by the shock 5-0 defeat to England that marked the start of Ormond's reign. But, still, the feeling in Glasgow ahead of the first meeting with the Czechs was that little could stop the Scots in front of a passionate Hampden Park crowd. That belief did take a hit on 33 minutes as the partisan locals were momentarily silenced when Zdeněk Nehodac put the visitors ahead with a shot that left goalkeeper Ally Hunter embarrassed. Within eight minutes, however, parity had been restored when Jim Holton headed a Denis Law corner into the net. As the tackles continued to fly, Bremner was in his element as the Scots poured forward for the goal that would end their long absence from a major tournament. The moment an entire nation craved arrived 15 minutes from time when Bremner crashed a shot against the post. The ball ran to Willie Morgan, who looked up and sent over an inviting centre that Joe Jordan threw himself at to power a header into the corner of the net. As Hampden Park erupted, the Czechs were stunned. As befitting a side who a couple of years later would win the European Championship, they soon came back strongly as the home team were forced back. This, though, was destined to be Scotland's night and the celebrations that met the final whistle continued well into the small hours. As much as Bremner enjoyed the party atmosphere that came with World Cup qualification, he made a point of insisting that he and Jordan get back to Leeds as quickly as possible the following morning. England had not played the previous night and were still overwhelming favourites to qualify from a group also containing Wales and Poland. But Bremner, the proud Scot, had waited a long time to be able to walk into the Elland Road dressing room holding the upper hand over his English team-mates. Sure enough, as the Leeds squad came off the training pitch, Bremner was there to proclaim his pride at Scotland's success. A month later that sense of satisfaction would grow immeasurably as on the night Scotland lost what was effectively a dead rubber against the Czechs, England were knocked out by the Poles at Wembley. The injured Bremner had not been in Prague with the rest of the Scottish lads watching Jan Tomaszewski have the game of his life in the Polish goal. But he, nevertheless, enjoyed being able to bask in the knowledge that only Scotland of the four Home Nations would be competing in West Germany.

Adding to his happy mood come the end of April was Leeds having sealed a second League Championship. Success in both domestic and international football meant he approached the Home Internationals in confident mood. A 1-0 defeat to Northern Ireland, therefore, came as something of a shock but wins against Wales and England at Hampden Park meant for the second time in three years that Scotland finished as joint-winners. It was not, however, deeds on the field that were destined to attract the headlines ahead of the World Cup but events off it. First, on a night out midway through the Home Internationals, Jimmy Johnstone had been walking back to the team hotel in Largs along the pebbled beach with a few team-mates when, suddenly, he had clambered into a rowing boat. Unfortunately, as he then started to sing 'Bonnie Scotland', the boat started drifting out into the Irish Sea. With no oars to be found on board, his by now panicking team-mates on the beach had no option but to telephone the Coastguard. Inevitably, the newspapers soon found out and the story was splashed across every back and front page. Manager Ormond was incensed, forcibly telling his players that any repeat would leave Scotland's first World Cup in 16 years in danger of becoming a media circus. Unfortunately, more negative publicity involving Johnstone lay just around the corner. This time, Bremner was also a central character in the drama that unfolded on Scotland's visit to Norway for their final warm-up friendly. The pair had decided to go for a walk late at night and bumped into a group of travelling journalists drinking in a student bar. A couple of drinks later, a communal sing-song was under way when Willie Ormond walked in. Again, the Scottish manager was unhappy with what he deemed to be unprofessional behaviour and this time it seemed disciplinary action would follow. At one stage, there was even a suggestion – later confirmed by the SFA in an official statement – both Bremner and Johnstone would be sent home for what was termed, 'A serious breach of discipline'. Eventually, however, it was announced after an emergency meeting of the SFA committee that, 'After receiving very profuse apologies, (we have) decided with some hesitation to accept the apology of the players concerned and take no further action'. The following day, Ormond, who had appealed to the SFA not to send the pair home, confirmed Bremner would remain as captain.

Once the Norway friendly was out of the way - Scotland winning 2-1 thanks to goals from Jordan and Dalglish - the travelling party moved on to West Germany to begin their final preparations. The Scots had been drawn in a tough group that included holders Brazil, a skilful Yugoslavia side managed by Miljan Miljanic and rank outsiders Zaire, who today exist as the Democratic Republic of Congo. With the top two teams progressing to the second group stage, Scotland had all on to reach what equated to the last eight. A fixture schedule that brought a meeting with Zaire on June 14 followed by games against Brazil four days later and Yugoslavia on June 22 meant a strong start against the Africans was needed. Little was known about Zaire, other than they had successfully negotiated a path to the finals that was distinctly longer than any other of the 16 competing nations. With just one team to qualify from the continent, Zaire had faced two preliminary rounds before winning their place in West Germany by triumphing in a three-team final that also featured Zambia and Morocco. The often chaotic nature of African football in the 1970s had seen Zaire do the double over Zambia before beating Morocco in a game that the Moroccans found so controversial they refused to take part in the return. That apart, though, little was known of Scotland's first opponents other than the fact Zaire was, later in the year, set to host the fight between George Foreman and Muhammad Ali that would become known as the 'Rumble in the Jungle'. The hope within central Africa, which before Zaire had never provided a qualifier for a World Cup, was that a decent showing in West Germany could really boost the profile of the sport in the region. Instead, Zaire would leave the reputation of African football in tatters courtesy of erratic performances, calamitous defending and a seeming lack of knowledge when it came to the rules of the game. The nadir of what was a disastrous few weeks in West Germany came in their final group game against Brazil when Illunga Mwepu came racing out of the defensive wall to hoof the ball away despite the World Cup holders having not yet taken the free-kick. Mwepu was then booked, only to respond by bowing to the applauding crowd. His actions quickly became a symbol of the naivety Africans allegedly showed towards football, though in later years Mwepu would claim it was instead a protest on behalf of the team who had discovered they would not be paid by the Zaire FA. Whatever the truth, Mwepu's actions and Zaire's performance undoubtedly put back the cause of African football by years. All this, however, was in the future when Bremner led his Scotland team-mates out to face Zaire in Dortmund's Westfalenstadion. It was a proud moment, as Gordon McQueen readily recalls. "Billy loved his country and loved captaining his country," says the defender whose Scotland debut had come just two weeks earlier in a friendly against Belgium in Bruges. "I was part of the World Cup squad and remember looking at Billy before that first game and thinking, 'I doubt anyone could be prouder right now than Billy'." David Harvey, who made his eighth appearance for Scotland against Zaire, concurs: "Billy was a patriotic man who adored playing for his country. He was intense as our captain at Leeds but, if anything, he was even more intense when it came to leading Scotland. It had been a big relief to everyone when we qualified for the 1974 World Cup. But when England then didn't make it, we all saw it as a chance to make our mark. I wouldn't say I was pleased England hadn't made it but I did want to do well in their absence. Billy was the same." Gordon McQueen, part of the squad in West Germany but destined not to make an appearance, more readily recalls the fun the Leeds captain had at the expense of his club-mates. "Billy was really proud that we had made it but England hadn't," he says. "There was a lot of banter at Leeds about it during the few weeks before we went to Germany. The rivalry was fierce between the two countries then so we didn't want to miss a chance to rub it in to the English lads."

The tournament had begun the previous day with its customary anti-climax as Brazil and Yugoslavia played out a dull goalless draw in Frankfurt. It meant a win for Scotland would be enough to claim pole position in the fledgling table. First-half goals from Peter Lorimer and Joe Jordan duly did just that as the Scots claimed a first victory at a World Cup finals with a 2-0 triumph. It was a solid start, though one criticism made in the immediate aftermath was how Ormond's men had eased off in the second half rather than pushed on for more goals. The players, for their part, were just happy the action had begun. David Harvey recalls: "The thing with a World Cup is you are cut off from everyone and everything, including friends and families. I don't think that is necessarily a good thing as it means all you end up doing is living, breathing and sleeping the World Cup 24 hours a day. It means you don't get a break and that can make things seem bigger than they actually are. In my opinion, there should have been more of a balance. In the end, I was just relieved when the tournament got under way as it gave us all something to focus on."

Next up for Scotland were Brazil, who since the triumph of 1970 had forsaken their adventurous style for a much more defensive-minded attitude. The two countries had met the previous summer at Hampden Park when Brazil triumphed 1-0 courtesy of a Derek Johnstone own goal. Bremner had won his 41st cap that afternoon and felt the Scots had caused the South Americans sufficient problems to suggest his 50th international appearance could end in a famous victory. It didn't, though not for the want of trying on the part of the Scotland captain as he urged his side forward. After an opening 20 minutes where Brazil had played what would be their best football of the 1974 World Cup, the Scots were the better side. On the balance of play across the full game, Ormond's side deserved to win. But they could not apply the final touch as the game ended goalless, Bremner coming the closest to breaking the deadlock when the ball rebounded off his shin and trickled wide of the post after the Brazilian goalkeeper had failed to collect a Jordan header cleanly. David Harvey recalls: "We were unfortunate not to win the game. Brazil might have been the world champions at the time but beforehand we had not been overawed. The thing we knew was that we had a good team. Billy was captain but it wasn't just Billy that made that team such a good one. There were so many good players and I would describe it as one of the best Scotland ever had. With that quality, there would have been no need to be intimidated by Brazil. Throughout the game, I never really felt our goal was under threat and when the final whistle blew I got the impression Brazil were glad to see the back of us." This view that Scotland – and their captain – had made a big impression was, more than 30 years later, confirmed by Carlos Alberto Parreira, a member of Brazil's backroom staff in 1974 and later destined to lead his country to

World Cup success. Speaking ahead of his then South Africa side taking on the Scots in 2007, he said of the World Cup meeting in Frankfurt: 'I remember a troublemaker in midfield called Billy Bremner. When I say 'a troublemaker', I mean that he was a fighter and very determined. I remember the game very well. It was 0-0 and a very difficult game for us.' Bremner had also come in for praise in the immediate aftermath of the Brazil game, Pele telling *The Times*: 'I really was most impressed with Bremner, he is a great improviser and a very good leader of his team'.

Far more important, however, than personal plaudits for the Scotland captain was his team's prospects. A battling point against the world champions had been an admirable effort, but any feelings of satisfaction at the final whistle were soon tempered when news came through of how the other game in Group Two had finished. David Harvey recalls: "It was a real sickener to see Yugoslavia win 9-0. Zaire were nothing like the team that we had played. Why that was, I don't know. But maybe they had exerted so much energy against us in the first game that they were dead on their feet by the time they faced Yugoslavia. Zaire had been okay against us and even had two or three chances. But they just collapsed in that second game and it made things very difficult for us. Basically, we were going to have to beat Yugoslavia as there seemed little chance of Brazil not beating Zaire in their final game."

The upshot of such a dramatic run of events was that Yugoslavia were top on goal difference from Scotland, both countries having three points. Brazil were third, one point adrift. For the Scots and their travelling army of by now 15,000 fans, the action moved on to Frankfurt. Not all of the visitors were welcome, *The Times* reporting on the eve of the game how, 'Boisterous Scots football fans upset staid Frankfurt'. The English newspaper went on to reveal: 'The jubilant Scots, many dressed in tartan from head to toe, last night took over Frankfurt's sin-strip. Kilted fans sent local drinkers scurrying for safety as they jumped on tables, smacked the bottoms of infuriated waitresses and forced other customers to drink out of their beer mugs. The band leader in one beer hall shouted in exasperation, ''You are not in Scotland now, this is orderly Germany. Behave, gentlemen'. His appeal was greeted with predictable gestures.' Any hangovers among the Tartan Army the following morning were, though, soon forgotten as the countdown continued towards kick-off. Spirits were high, as was the fans' confidence in their players delivering the required result. Unfortunately, it was the Yugoslavs who took the lead in the second half when Dragan Dzajic, on the right, cleverly spun past a Scots defender to centre for Stanislav Karasi to head past Harvey. Ormond responded by bringing Tommy Hutchison off the bench to replace Dalglish and he crossed for Jordan to net the equaliser. But, try as they might, a winner could not be found as Yugoslavia held on to finish in front of the Scots on goal difference. With Brazil also winning – 3-0 against Zaire – it meant Scotland were out by the cruellest of margins, one goal. That Brazil's third and decisive strike by Valdomiro had come courtesy of a miscued cross from the right wing that had rolled under the hapless African goalkeeper's body only added to the sense of frustration. David Harvey recalls: "In that final game, we were so close to going through. Maybe it just wasn't meant to be. It was certainly not through a lack of effort but so disappointing all the same. We were going out yet had not lost a game." Back in the dressing room, the players cut disconsolate and forlorn figures. Harvey again: "I think Billy knew it was his last chance to do well in a major tournament so he did feel it badly. We had gone so close, only missing out by the skin of our teeth, and that really upset him. He knew there would not be another World Cup for him." Gordon McQueen, who would miss out on playing for Scotland in the 1978 World Cup due to a freak injury, adds: "Billy knew it was his last chance and had been so determined to do well. The disappointment was etched all over his face afterwards. It was the same with a lot of the lads who knew that was it for them. The worst thing is we had gone so close. We had done well in a very tough group and not lost a game but were out of the competition. It didn't seem fair. If a side remained unbeaten in the group stage of a World Cup now, they would sail through."

As the Scotland players made their way home, the World Cup moved to the second group stage. Yugoslavia, who had topped Scotland's group, would finish bottom but Brazil finished second behind Holland to earn a third place play-off tie against Poland. The Poles won a dull encounter 1-0, while in the final hosts West Germany came back from conceding a penalty inside two minutes to triumph 2-1. That the victorious side had lost in the first group stage to East Germany meant only the Scots of the 16 teams who had competed in the 1974 finals had returned home unbeaten – a fact that only added to the frustration. Peter Lorimer, who played in all three games and scored one of Scotland's three goals, says: "We had a terrific team and really felt we could win the World Cup as we set off. The other teams definitely saw us as a threat but, unfortunately, we got knocked out despite not losing a game. What made it worse was watching the final a couple of weeks later and thinking, 'We are every bit as good as the Dutch and the Germans'. That really brought it home to me just how close we had been to being successful. I think we were unlucky in that we played the games the wrong way round. Facing Zaire first did us no favours at all. Had we played them last – and by then we would have known just how poor they were – I am sure we would have treated the game very differently and scored a lot more goals. Instead, we treated it merely as a game we needed to win with a minimum of fuss and no injuries. We were due to play Brazil just a few days later so cruised a little bit in the second half against Zaire. In the end, it cost us as just one more goal would have put us through. Billy, as captain, took a lot of stick after the tournament. Many fans said it was him who slowed things down against Zaire. That wasn't the case, it was just how the game turned out because we went to keep the ball and pass it around."

The draw against Yugoslavia in Frankfurt was Bremner's 51st appearance for his country. It was also his 36th as captain. He would, however, win just three more caps as an international career that had included so many notable victories and inspiring performances came to a less than glittering end.

Copenhagen was the setting for a drama that would have far-reaching consequences for not just Bremner but four other Scottish players. By the time of the ill-fated trip to Denmark, a little over 14 months had elapsed since the World Cup. Bremner had ended the tournament held in such high esteem that calls had been made for him to be appointed as Willie Ormond's assistant, a position that would have included taking charge of the Under-23 side. The much-touted appointment never came to fruition but Bremner remained a key figure, even though in those intervening months leading up to the trip to Copenhagen he had missed six internationals due to Leeds United's run to the 1975 European Cup final. The last of those absences had come in a 1-1 draw against Romania in a European Championship qualifier played just four days after United's 2-0 defeat to Bayern Munich in Paris. With the Scots having already dropped three points against Spain courtesy of a 2-1 defeat at Hampden and a 1-1 draw in Valencia, any hopes of qualifying were all but over following the draw in Bucharest. Despite that and Bremner being less than three months short of his 33rd birthday, he was desperate to continue representing his country. So, as Ormond's side took to the field in the Danish capital on September 3, Bremner once again led the way. The ensuing 1-0 victory achieved with a goal by Joe Harper may have made little difference to Scotland's hopes of finishing top of Group Four. But it did, at least, regain a sense of pride by ensuring the Scots could not finish bottom of the four-team group. A celebration was in order, starting in the bar of the team hotel. Also staying with the senior squad were the Under-23 players, who had beaten the Danes the previous night in Frederikshaven. It meant the bar quickly became busy, as Peter Lorimer recalls: "Everyone was pleased with the win and most of us headed to the bar. We just wanted a nice, quiet drink. Unfortunately for Billy, his night ended up being anything but quiet after he teamed up with some of the younger lads from the Under-23s squad. Before the game, I remember saying to him, 'Billy, the young lads from Aberdeen have a bit of a reputation so it might be best to steer clear of them'. So, what does he do once we are back in the bar? He only heads straight over and joins them. Within 20 minutes, they were going to fight everyone. But that was Billy, he had to be in the middle of things. He couldn't just sit with the older lads, talking football and eyeing the birds up. He wanted to be where things were going on. I was sitting with Tommy Hutchison, Peter Cormack and Kenny Dalglish in the lounge bar and couldn't believe it when I looked across and there was the Scotland captain sitting with the rowdy youngsters."

After a row with the bar staff over the price of drinks, Bremner and his cohorts left for the bright lights of Copenhagen. Later, the police would be called to a nightclub following complaints of rowdy behaviour and bad language. No arrests were made but matters took a further turn for the worse on the players' return to the Marina Hotel when the room belonging to Jock McDonald, a member of the SFA council, was trashed. There was also talk of Bremner being allegedly punched by McDonald. By the time the rest of the Scotland party woke in the morning, it was clear there would be serious repercussions for the five players allegedly involved – namely Bremner, Aberdeen duo Arthur Graham and Willie Young, Celtic's Pat McCluskey and Joe Harper of Hibernian. Lorimer says: "I was rooming with Billy in Copenhagen and knew something serious must have happened. He had been delivered to the room in the early hours by two people whose identity remained a mystery due to me pretending to be asleep at the time. Billy was swearing and there was a lot of banging about but I just lay still. I wanted no part of whatever had happened. After a couple of hours, I woke up again and rolled Billy over to reveal his badly swollen face – it was clear he'd been in a bit of bother. I went down to breakfast and the atmosphere was terrible. The lads were saying, 'Have you heard about last night? Billy is in a lot of trouble'. The thing was I had just left Billy in our room and he had no recollection of what had happened the night before so I couldn't add anything to what was being said. Details started to emerge, including the police having been called during the night and then the incident with one of the selectors. It was clear it was all about to kick-off."

Lorimer's foreboding proved correct as the Scottish Football Association launched an immediate inquiry, any hopes the 'Copenhagen Five' had of the punishment being a lenient one soon dispelled by SFA secretary Willie Allen referring to the players as, 'The hooligan element'. The verdict when it came just a few days later was a damning one: All five were banned for life from representing Scotland. Bremner, who at the time stood just one cap away from equalling Denis Law's record for international appearances, was devastated. On September 9, he told the *Yorkshire Evening Post*: "I honestly never expected to be banned like this for something I still consider to be a small happening. It is bad for all of us, but it is particularly so for the three younger lads – Arthur Graham, Willie Young and Pat McCluskey – who were only just starting out on their careers at international level. In my case, I could only have hoped for a couple more games. But it is still a sad way to end my career with Scotland, with whom I have had many enjoyable times. The whole thing has been exaggerated so much it isn't true. The players' side of the case has not yet been put and I do not want to say much at present other than to stress there was no fight in the nightclub." As if to back up the players' belief that the SFA were guilty of over-reacting, the secretary-general of the Danish Football Federation, Erik Hyldstrup – who compiled a report on the alleged incidents for his Scottish counterpart – told the Danish newspaper *Politiken* that the verdict was 'harsh' before adding: 'My report indicated there was very little basis for the charges against the five. There was no police complaint after the incident in the nightclub, when the Scottish players were ejected. And no names were given in the police patrol's report.' The manager of the hotel in which the nightclub was situated also confirmed the disturbance had been 'minor' but the SFA, clearly mindful of this not being the first disciplinary problem involving Scotland, were determined to come down hard on the errant players. A year later, Graham and Harper – who had always maintained their innocence – successfully overturned the SFA's decision and resumed their international careers. Graham went on to make ten appearances for the senior side, while Harper earned his fourth and final cap as Scotland were held to a 1-1 draw by Iran in the 1978 World Cup finals. For Bremner, however, there would be no reprieve as he suffered the ignominy of an international career stretching back 10 years being brought to an end in such an unseemly manner. Lorimer, who won 21 caps, insists the SFA need not have been quite so draconian when dealing with his team-mate. He says: "I drove Billy back to Leeds after we flew home from Denmark and he still didn't really know what had happened. In many ways, that was typical of his attitude – he could be the sort of character who thought he could get away with anything. But I still believe the matter could have been handled differently. It wasn't a great night for Scottish football, I admit that. But instead of banning Billy, they should have sat him down and said, 'We think this is the right time for you to retire'. That way, Billy could have finished with his head held high rather than because of a ban. Unfortunately, the SFA made their decision and that was that. The problem was that Billy was captain and they felt the need to take a stance. Either way, it was a desperately sad way for a great player to finish his international career."

Chapter 15

Doomed United

Breaking up a family is, invariably, a traumatic affair. So, when Don Revie – a father figure to the boys he had turned into men while transforming Leeds United into a force in European football – accepted the offer to become the manager of the England national team in July, 1974, there was an indelible feeling at Elland Road that life would never be the same again. Revie had been such an all-powerful figure that few, if any, decisions were taken without his say-so. Contract negotiations, travel plans, even ground improvements – nothing happened without the say-so of the manager. This control extended into the life of his players, Revie even going so far in the days when his squad were in their late teens and early 20s as having prospective girlfriends checked out. "If Don didn't like what he heard, he would say, 'She's not the right kind of girl for you – get rid," remembers Peter Lorimer. The devotion Revie felt towards his 'lads' was mutual, so the news he was leaving came as a blow to the players – even if, as Johnny Giles explains, they understood. "We were gutted to see Don leave," says the former Republic of Ireland midfielder and manager. "But he had to take the England job. He had earned that chance through the amazing work he did at Elland Road."

Few felt this sense of loss over Revie's departure more than his captain, Billy Bremner. Trevor Cherry recalls: "Leaving was a big decision for the manager and very hard for everyone, but in particular Billy. He was so close to the Boss and they had such a bond between them that it was difficult for him."

The seeds of the bond Cherry mentions had been sown when Revie, then the senior pro, and Bremner had roomed together on the eve of the Scot's debut for Leeds at Chelsea more than 14 years earlier. Over the years, it had grown and strengthened so Bremner was, understandably, hugely disappointed to hear the news. He was also, in common with many at Elland Road, surprised, considering the coming season would see United compete in the European Cup – the one glaring omission from the club's roll of honour under Revie. The appeal of managing his country was obvious. But Bremner felt the pull of winning the one trophy to elude Leeds would hold sway. It didn't, though many close to Revie wondered as to the real reason behind his decision to leave. "I never asked him outright about this," says Revie's son. "But I have always had the suspicion Dad took the England job because he could not bear to break up the Leeds team he had built. The lads were growing old and I just don't think he could face the prospect of moving them on after 10 years together. He would have to dismantle a team he loved so, to me, I think when the England job came along it was a case of 'problem solved'." Eddie Gray concurs, adding: "Don could see the day fast approaching when he would have to break up the team. It would have been very difficult for him and maybe taking the England job was his way of avoiding that."

Whatever the real motivation behind Revie's decision to leave, what his departure did was create a vacancy at Elland Road. The United board had wanted Revie to stay on until his successor was found but, instead, he was gone within 24 hours. His final act before leaving, however, was to recommend Johnny Giles for the job. Initially, it seemed the board were willing to act on the advice – only for Bremner to get wind of the move and apply himself. Eddie Gray recalls: "Peter Lorimer and I were standing on Fullerton Park before training when Johnny came up to us and said, 'I'm the new manager'. But it turned out Billy had also applied, which he had every right to do as captain, and the directors panicked. They thought there would be a split in the camp but they should have spoken to the boys as we would have told them that was nonsense." Football reporter Mike Morgan, who since 1969 has covered the Yorkshire patch for a variety of national newspapers, adds: "Billy was hurt to discover Don had recommended Johnny for the job and not him. He saw it as a natural progression, him as manager with Johnny as his assistant." Another motivation, it seems, behind the board's discarding of Revie's advice was to make one final point to their departing manager. For at least the last decade, few decisions had been made at Elland Road by anyone other than the manager. To some on the board, this had caused resentment – as Ray Oddy, who covered United for more than three decades on behalf of Gosnay's Sports Agency, readily recalls. "I will always remember a chat myself and Colin Durkin of the Press Association had with director Bob Roberts shortly after Don left," he says. "A new manager had not yet been appointed and the board were in a bit of a quandary. Don had recommended his successor but Bob said to us both, 'We can't stop Revie leaving but he is not going to choose his successor as well'. To this day, I still believe that was the major reason why they brought in Brian Clough, the one man that no-one could have predicted. Don had run the club almost single-handed for several years before leaving for the England job, so much so that the first the directors knew that Leeds had signed Allan Clarke was when Don told them Leicester had to be paid £165,000."

Suddenly, the board were faced with a huge dilemma. Common sense would have been to back the judgement of the man who had led their club to unprecedented success. Instead, they prevaricated publicly and dithered in private. Peter Lorimer believes United's history could have been very different had Bremner not staked his own claim. And that some of the blame lay with Revie. He says: "I am certain Don told Billy all the time they were together, 'I want you to manage the club after I leave'. It will have been Don's way of getting the best out of Billy, making him feel like he was the main man when really it was Johnny who he felt best suited to the job of Leeds manager. Don will have kidded Billy along, which is why Billy messed it up by going in to the see the directors when he found out Johnny was going to get the job. The directors lost their nerve. It was a real shame and the start of Leeds' downfall. Billy never even apologised, either, even though Johnny was upset about what had happened. A few days later, Billy was on his way out to train when he called Johnny over. Johnny thought he was going to say something about what had happened, something like 'Revie always promised me the job'. But all Billy did was point to his leg and say, 'I think I've injured my calf, what would you do to treat it?' It was as if nothing had happened. Johnny just looked at him as if to say, 'You've got some cheek'."

With the board fearful of a split in the camp should Giles get the job ahead of Bremner, a fresh search was begun that would culminate in the disastrous appointment of Clough. What is less well known even today, however, is that other candidates were spoken to by Leeds, including Ian St John. The former Liverpool forward had, by now, left Anfield to take charge of Scottish Premier League club Motherwell. Having served his coaching apprenticeship on the staff at Coventry City, St John had been in charge at Fir Park for 18 months when a recommendation from one of football's biggest names was made to the Leeds board. "Jock Stein put my name forward," recalls St John, who during the 1980s would become one of the most recognisable faces on television through the football show *Saint & Greavsie*. "Leeds were interested so I met the chairman at Scotch Corner. We discussed everything from wages to transfers and the current squad. We covered the lot and it looked like the job was mine. I was really excited. But then, just as the chairman got up to leave, he said they had one last candidate to meet. Unfortunately for me – and, as it turned out, Leeds – that other candidate was Brian Clough. Life could have worked out very differently for everyone." A few weeks later, St John got his move south when offered the chance to manage Portsmouth but it didn't work out. The same can be said about Clough at Leeds, his appointment confirmed just a couple of days after the meeting between St John and Leeds chairman Manny Cussins just off the A1.

The decision was a staggering one. Not only had Clough been such a vehement critic of Leeds that, just a year earlier, he had called for the club to be relegated. But his antipathy towards the players was such that he had once insulted Peter Lorimer – accusing Leeds' all-time top goalscorer of, among many things, 'making a meal of challenges' – when making a speech at a Yorkshire Sportsman of the Year dinner. "I'd actually won the award and Clough was only supposed to be there to present me with it," laughs Lorimer today. Clough's vitriolic attacks on Leeds United, Don Revie and their players made the appointment an unlikely one right from the start. Gordon McQueen recalls: "It was a ridiculous choice, absolutely ridiculous. Don leaving was always going to be difficult for all those lads like Billy, Norman, Peter and Eddie who had been with him since they were kids. What they, and the club, needed was continuity. Instead, Brian Clough walked in."

Clough's appointment, based solely on footballing merits, was a sound one. He had taken a provincial club in Derby County from the lower half of Division Two to the league title before a fall-out with the Rams' board had brought an abrupt end to his reign. He had moved on to Brighton when the opportunity to manage Leeds arose. Peter Taylor, who would be by Clough's side at both Derby and later Nottingham Forest, had also decamped to the south coast. Crucially, as Clough headed north to Elland Road, Taylor elected to stay with the Seagulls. It meant Clough was taking on the biggest challenge of his career without his trusted right hand man, someone whose value he had once underlined by describing their managerial partnership as, 'If I'm the shop window, Peter is the goods on the shelves'. The absence of the much less abrasive Taylor would, Clough admitted later in life, prove to be a telling factor in what subsequently went wrong at Leeds. Taylor would, for instance, have strongly advised against Clough, at his first meeting with the squad, uttering those now infamous words about how they should, 'Chuck your medals in the bin because you have won them all by cheating'.

Telling Eddie Gray how, 'If you had been a racehorse, you would have been shot by now' would also surely have never happened had the calming influence of Taylor been at Elland Road. Instead, a relationship that had always seemed unlikely to work was already moving towards breaking point.

Clough had decided that changes had to be made and was soon busy in the transfer market, signing Duncan McKenzie from Nottingham Forest for £250,000. The new arrival sensed straight away an atmosphere. He recalls: "Cloughie's appointment had clearly come as a shock to Billy and the rest of the lads so it was an uneasy place. Happily for me, the lads accepted me straight away – even though people outside the club might have seen me as a 'Clough man'. It may have helped that, when Brian saw me smoking in the dressing room he said, 'Hey Smokey Joe, get rid of those fags or you'll be on your way'. To which I replied, 'That's fine, but where's my five per cent signing-on fee?' The lads loved that. It meant that the only thing I was on trial about was being the new boy and whether I was any good. The lads weren't bothered about anything else." McKenzie's debut came at Wembley in the Charity Shield against Liverpool as a substitute. It was the first time the traditional curtain-raiser to a season had been shown live on television so, when Billy Bremner and Kevin Keegan were sent off for fighting and subsequently shown ripping their shirts off, there was a furore. The game ended 1-1 with Liverpool winning on penalties but the headlines the following day were all about the clash between the two players. Both were subsequently fined and banned until the end of September by the Football Association. It was bad news for Leeds and their new manager, but perhaps just as significantly the affair suggested all was not well behind-the-scenes at Elland Road. John Helm, then of *BBC Radio Leeds*, recalls: "I always felt Don Revie had pulled off a masterstroke when making Billy captain of Leeds. Up until then, Billy had been a bit of a problem for the management and Don saw making him captain a way of coping with his rebellious streak. What happened with Kevin Keegan at Wembley suggested to me that things were maybe not too good between Billy and the new manager, as that was something he would never have done under Don."

Bremner played in the first game of the league season against Stoke City due to, at that stage, not having appeared before the FA's disciplinary committee. But he could do little to prevent Leeds slipping to a shock 3-0 defeat. Four days later, QPR won 1-0 at Elland Road in the first of 14 games Bremner would miss through a combination of suspension and injury. By the time the United captain returned, Clough had been sacked and his 44-

day reign was destined to become part of football folklore. Results under Clough had been poor, Leeds won just once during his time in charge. But, far more telling, was the disintegration of the relationship between manager and players that had taken place. Matters came to a head during the build-up to a League Cup tie at Huddersfield Town in early September when the board called a meeting with both players and management. It was clear the appointment of Clough had backfired and that a parting of the ways was inevitable. Clough was destined to go on and become one of the managerial immortals by steering Nottingham Forest to two European Cups. But there were few tears shed at Elland Road over his demise – even among those who had got on well with Clough. Cherry says: "As one of the younger lads, Brian seemed to like me but, in terms of the club, his arrival spoiled things."

The book and subsequent film version of *The Damned United* – a fictional account of Clough's ill-fated reign – suggested Bremner had been one of the conspirators-in-chief behind the removal of Clough. Such an assertion is perhaps understandable as the pair didn't see eye-to-eye, as illustrated after Clough's departure when he said of Bremner in *Shoot* magazine: 'When Bremner called me 'Boss' it meant nothing. He had to call me 'Boss' and believe it. What Bremner has to establish is he is not the manager of Leeds United.' Bremner's response in the *Yorkshire Evening Post* was to firmly refute the allegation he had somehow undermined Clough. He said: 'It is ridiculous to suggest anything of the sort. He is trying to make me a scapegoat to cover his own shortcomings. I honestly expected something like this to crop up. What he doesn't realise is that as the captain of Leeds United it is I who has to speak on behalf of the team.' But what those behind the making of *The Damned United* got wrong, according to those in the Leeds dressing room at the time, was the accusation Bremner was in some way responsible for Clough's sacking. Duncan McKenzie recalls: "I'll admit the relationship between Brian and Billy was, shall we say, quite tepid. But it was thoroughly professional and certainly nothing like as glum as made out in *The Damned United*. He and Billy may not have been the best of friends but there was nothing objectionable between them. It was the same with Johnny, the other senior player at the club. He and Billy may not have been over-enamoured with Brian but they were definitely not objectionable, as was suggested in the film." Likewise, any accusation that the players were deliberately not trying for Clough is also firmly refuted by McKenzie. "No team goes out to lose games," he says. "That just doesn't happen and it certainly wasn't the case at Leeds. What was missing was the spirit that

Leeds had always been renowned for under Don Revie. It had disappeared, and that was what told me that things couldn't go on as they were. The board had made an extreme decision in going for Brian and it just hadn't worked out, simple as that." Another who shares the opinion that Leeds, and in particular their captain, could never have gone deliberately easy in games is football reporter Mike Morgan. He says: "Billy just wouldn't know how to go through the motions. His personal pride would not allow it, nor would his love for the club. It was the same for all that team."

With Clough gone, the Leeds board looked around for someone capable of steadying the club. A safe pair of hands was needed and their search would, ultimately, end a couple of weeks later in Bolton. By then, however, Lorimer insists irreparable damage had already been done to Leeds United. He says: "Billy applying for the job after finding out Johnny was in line to take over was the start of the club's downfall. In my opinion, if Johnny had taken over then Leeds would have stayed at the top. He would have sorted the club out and done what needed doing. But Billy messed it up."

Chapter 16

Enter Gentleman Jim

If ever a football team has been in need of a calming influence, it was Leeds United in the wake of Brian Clough's abrupt departure. His reign may have lasted just 44 days but such had been the upheaval and stress for those involved that it had felt to be a good deal longer. After such a traumatic time, what the players needed was someone capable of making Leeds united once again. The Elland Road board were well aware of this, so turned to a man known as 'Gentleman Jim' due to his immaculate temperament. Jimmy Armfield had, during his playing career, been the ultimate one-club man, spending 17 seasons with Blackpool and making more than 600 appearances. He had also won 43 England caps and been part of the squad that had won the World Cup in 1966. More importantly, however, Armfield had enjoyed success since moving into management with Bolton Wanderers – leading the Lancashire club to the Third Division title in 1973 – and was considered the type of character to bring harmony where there had been discord under Clough. For the man himself, the offer to manage Leeds was one he could not turn down – especially once Don Revie, by now in charge of the England national team, had stepped in to invite Armfield to London to discuss possibly taking over as manager of the Under-23s side. To this day, Armfield believes the offer of a position on the England staff was a pretence, and that Revie knew full well he had been offered the Leeds job. "I can't believe Don didn't know as he was better informed on what was happening at Elland Road than anyone," recalls Armfield, now a hugely popular expert summariser with *BBC Radio 5 Live*. "He then asked if I was interested in the Under-23s job but when I said Leeds had offered me the manager's job, he said, 'Forget all about this, take that instead'. Don then told me all about Leeds as a club and the players. I didn't really need convincing but Don's words did stick in my mind. I accepted the job."

The gap between Armfield's appointment and the departure of Clough was a little over three weeks. During that time, Maurice Lindley and Syd Owen had looked after first team affairs with Billy Bremner, still suspended following his red card in the Charity Shield, also having some input in selection. The first league game following Clough's exit had ended in defeat to Burnley at Turf Moor. A 5-1 home win over Sheffield United the following Saturday then briefly raised spirits only for Leeds to crash again a week later at Everton, meaning Armfield was taking over a side who had already suffered more defeats than in the whole of the previous season. He recalls: "As you can imagine, there was an air of uncertainty among the players. They had just been through a traumatic time, while there was also the added factor of a couple of the players having fancied being manager themselves when Brian got the job. I could see on the faces of all the players, many of whom I had played against, that they were wondering what came next. What I stressed was that I would be very different to the previous manager and that it was time to look forward." Duncan McKenzie was one of those players who had been wondering what to expect when Armfield took over. He says: "Jimmy was very different to Brian in his approach, we saw that straight away. He was such a nice man, it was impossible not to like him. I remember Norman Hunter heading into Jimmy's office one day, determined to have a row with him. But, as soon as he got in, Jimmy started asking how the family were etc. In the end, Norman came out without having made his point – just because Jimmy was too much of a nice man to row with."

Armfield's bow as Leeds manager came at home to Arsenal on the first Saturday of October and he drew an immediate response courtesy of a 2-0 win. A draw at Ipswich Town and a defeat to Birmingham City at St Andrews followed before Wolves were beaten at Elland Road. Any hopes that the 2-0 victory would bring about a change of fortune were, however, soon shot down by back-to-back defeats against Liverpool and Derby County. It meant that by the first week in November, Leeds were sitting 19th in the table. Some in the boardroom believed changes in personnel were required but Armfield was adamant there were still sufficient miles left in the legs of his admittedly ageing squad. He says: "I thought when I took the job that the players had one last season in them, providing they were handled carefully. I decided to adopt the approach of being respectful and reminding the players what they were good at. I even put my arm round one or two of them."

What Armfield was also banking on was the impact the return of the club captain, whose time on the sidelines through suspension had since been extended by injury, would have. He recalls: "Bob English, the Leeds physiotherapist at the time, said to me when the early results went against us, 'Don't worry, it will all change when Billy gets back'. I asked what he meant, and he just said, 'You'll see'. Bob was right, too, as Billy made a big difference once back in the team. His legs might not have been as strong as when I had played against Billy but he brought invaluable experience to the team." Bremner's importance to Leeds had been illustrated vividly a couple of years earlier when a rumour had swept the city that he had been involved in a road accident. Fans had been so concerned that they had inundated the *Yorkshire Evening Post* with anxious telephone calls, prompting the newspaper to run an article the following day dismissing the rumour under the headline, 'He's alive and well'. The fans' understanding of just how important Bremner was to Leeds was shared by his team-mates. Duncan McKenzie says: "Billy was one of the most infectious characters I ever met. The only one who compared in my football career was Dave MacKay when I played for him at Nottingham Forest. Both lived for their football and were men I viewed as inspirations. At Leeds, Billy was always the first to dish out a rollicking or give out praise. And if I scored, I knew the first one jumping on my back would be Billy."

Bremner returned to action the week after Derby had triumphed at Elland Road to help inspire Leeds to a 3-1 win at Coventry City, just for good measure adding the third goal of the afternoon. Four days later, though, United's season suffered another setback when Fourth Division Chester claimed an almighty League Cup giant-killing with a 3-0 win at Sealand Road. For the first time, Armfield dispensed with the niceties to tear into his players. "We were awful and got exactly what we deserved," he says. "But, in a funny way, it acted as a turning point. It was the first time I really got at them. Initially, my approach had been designed to get them going again but this was different. I felt the time had come to say a few harsh words." It did the trick as Leeds embarked on a run that brought just five further defeats during the rest of the league season to finish ninth. For a team who had been crowned champions the previous year, a place in mid-table would be cause for concern. But, by then, United had their eye on the biggest prize in club football – the European Cup. Armfield says: "I had thought on taking over that the Cups were going to be our best hope of success. Chester put paid to us in the League Cup, but we had a decent run in the FA Cup to the quarter-finals where we went out after a third replay against Ipswich. That left the European Cup, the one everyone at Leeds wanted due to it being the prize that had eluded the club under Don Revie."

Leeds had already progressed to the second round by the time of Armfield's appointment, the caretaker management team of Lindley and Owen guiding the club to a 5-3 aggregate triumph over FC Zurich. Bremner missed both games against the Swiss side through injury but returned as

United took on Ujpesti Dozsa in the second round, marking the unusual sight of him sporting the number '9' jersey by scoring as the home leg was won 3-0 en route to a 5-1 triumph. It meant Leeds would still be in Europe's premier competition come the New Year, by which time Armfield was determined to have further raised spirits. To do so, he hit upon a novel idea – staging a pantomime as part of Paul Reaney's testimonial year. Armfield explains: "Barney Colehan, who ran the Leeds City Varieties at the time, was a regular at our games and one day we were discussing ideas for a Christmas party for the players. I thought fancy dress might be fun, though strictly in-house as this was a time before football club's Christmas parties became such big affairs. Anyway, one thing led to another and, eventually, I suggested writing a panto for the players. Barney thought it to be a great idea and said, 'If you do that, we'll stage it at the City Varieties and make a few bob for the testimonial fund'. I started to work on a script, even though I thought there was little chance of it happening. To my surprise, though, the lads really got into it once over the initial shock of the idea. We decided on *Cinderella* and Duncan McKenzie was cast in the lead role. Billy was Buttons. I got my secretary, Maureen, to type up the scripts and the players went away to learn their lines." Rehearsals continued for a few weeks before the City Varieties decided to go public, revealing the pantomime would be staged on two successive nights in February. The box office was besieged and the shows quickly sold out. Armfield recalls: "Fair play to the lads, they really put some effort into it and the nights were a huge success. I was Master of Ceremonies, while those who took a starring role along with Duncan and Billy were Gordon McQueen as the Good Fairy and Paul Reaney as Prince Charming. Everyone was terrific, especially Billy who played the best Buttons I have seen – before or since. He came down the aisle wearing this bright blue outfit handing out sweets to the kids and was brilliant with them. As he jumped on stage, he turned to the audience and said, 'They're our sweets, if anyone comes near them – you tell me'. You can imagine how much the kids loved that. The shows went down brilliantly; Barney even wanted us to do more nights. Everyone enjoyed themselves, but the most important part for me was how it helped further re-build and strengthen team spirit. The players had been through a difficult time before I arrived and I wanted to put the smiles back on their faces, which is what the pantomime helped to do."

Less than a month after the successful staging of *Cinderella* at the City Varieties, Leeds were back in European Cup action with a two-legged quarter-final against Anderlecht. The first game at Elland Road was played in such a heavy fog that the players had to be taken off the field for 17 minutes. At the time Leeds were 2-0 ahead so there was understandable concern in the home dressing room that the tie may have to be abandoned. Fortunately, the fog then cleared and Peter Lorimer was able to add a third goal before the end. The away leg two weeks later in Brussels saw United complete the job with a 1-0 victory, Bremner scoring the only goal with a delightful chip from the edge of the penalty area 15 minutes from time. That set up a semi-final meeting with Barcelona, the undoubted aristocrats of European football and whose numbers included the incomparable Dutchmen, Johan Cruyff and Johan Neeskens. The Catalan giants, able to sign the best talent money could buy, were unsurprisingly considered to be favourites to lift the trophy. Even Barcelona's arrival in West Yorkshire ahead of the first leg caused a stir, while their decision to train at the unlikely setting of Bradford non-League club Thackley led to many locals taking the chance to watch at close quarters some of European football's biggest names. For Gordon McQueen and the rest of the Leeds players, it was clear they would have their work cut out if the club was not to be knocked out at the semi-final stage for a second time in five years. He says: "Up until the semi-finals, we had found it quite easy. The European Cup was nothing like the Champions League of today. We only had to play a few games to get to the last four, none of which had really given us any trouble. We knew that wouldn't be the case against Barcelona. Add to that the older lads like Billy knowing this was their last chance of winning the European Cup and that gave everything that little bit more significance. The lads wanted to do it for Don Revie."

Come the night of the first leg, the atmosphere inside Elland Road was electric as 50,393 fans – an attendance that has not been matched since at the ground – squeezed through the turnstiles. The vast majority were soon celebrating a goal as Bremner beat Salvador Sadurni with a ferocious shot into the corner of the net. It was the first time the Barcelona defence had been breached during their run to the semi-finals but they hit back midway through the second half through Juan Manuel Asensi. United refused to be denied, however, and Allan Clarke struck with 12 minutes remaining to ensure they would at least travel to what was certain to be an intimidating Nou Camp with a one-goal lead.

Ahead of that return, Armfield hit upon a tactical switch that, he felt, may just give Leeds the edge. He explains: "I wanted to try and fool Barcelona's two full-backs. They both man-marked so I asked Peter Lorimer, who usually played on the right of front three with Allan Clarke and Joe Jordan, to start on the left before switching to the right after a few minutes. I thought the Barcelona right-back would follow him, which is exactly what happened. It worked a treat with Peter getting away from his marker, who was out of position, to score from a knockdown."

Lorimer's seventh minute strike meant Leeds held a precious two-goal lead, though any hopes the rest of the game would be plain-sailing were soon dispelled as Barcelona proceeded to bombard Dave Stewart in the visitors' goal. With 20 minutes remaining, the breakthrough all of Catalonia craved came when Manolo Clares equalised on the night. One more goal and the tie would go into extra-time. Worse was to follow for Leeds, who were reduced to ten men when McQueen was sent off following a skirmish in the goalmouth. Barcelona immediately upped the tempo but United held on to secure a first European Cup final appearance. Trevor Cherry, handed the unenviable task of marking Cruyff in the Nou Camp, recalls: "It was one of those nights when everyone showed tremendous resilience, especially after Gordon had been sent off. There were 110,000 fans there and, at times, it seemed like every single one of them was against us. Billy was in his element that night, our leader really led from the front in Barcelona. It was such a memorable game and everyone was jubilant afterwards." Everyone that is, apart from McQueen. "The sending-off was stupidity on my part," says the Scot. "As you can imagine, the dressing room afterwards was euphoric but I just didn't feel part of it. I knew I would be suspended for the final and it really hurt." For Bremner and the rest of the more experienced players, the celebrations were also tempered by knowing the job was only half done. Leeds had, during their considerable time together, come close to success before having it snatched away so many times that no-one was going to get carried away. Nevertheless, the one prize that had eluded the club throughout Revie's reign was, finally, within touching distance. It was all such a contrast from when Armfield had first walked into Elland Road seven months earlier with a sense of belief not only restored but also the team spirit that had been so conspicuous by its absence under Clough. The man himself believes a number of factors helped to bring about the change, not least the number of games United played. He says: "Due to runs in the European and FA Cups, we played something like 31 games from Christmas onwards. They talk about fixture congestion today but we played four games in a week at one stage. Basically, we all lived out of a suitcase for six months and it was during that time on the road that I really got to know the team." Trevor Cherry also believes credit is due for the manner in which Armfield helped the players move on after Clough. He says: "If compared to some of the managers we'd had, Jimmy probably wasn't in the same league but he was a smashing bloke. The older players probably thought they could do things better but Jimmy was someone who was impossible to fall out with and it just seemed to work in that first season."

Armfield's softly-softly approach to coaxing one final season out of an ageing team had worked, the reward being an appearance in the biggest game in club football. May 28 was set as the date for the potentially crowning moment for a team built by Revie and Paris's Parc des Princes the venue. With United's final league game, a 4-2 defeat to Tottenham Hotspur at White Hart Lane, taking place exactly a month earlier, it meant a long gap before the final against Bayern Munich. To keep the players' fitness ticking over, Armfield organised a handful of friendlies. He also spent time pondering how best to cope with the suspension of McQueen, eventually settling on a line-up that saw Paul Madeley move into the centre of defence and the more combative Terry Yorath start on the left instead of Eddie Gray.

Bayern were the holders of the European Cup, having thrashed Atletico Madrid 4-0 12 months earlier in a replay after the first game at the Heysel Stadium in Brussels had finished level at 1-1. It meant confidence was high among Franz Beckenbauer and his team-mates from the moment St Etienne had been defeated 2-0 on aggregate to set up the showdown with Leeds. The Germans were, though, also wary of their opponents' reputation – a feeling that was only strengthened in the Parc des Princes tunnel. Bjorn Andersson, a Swedish international who had joined Bayern the previous summer, recalls: "I remember it was a really bad atmosphere. I can only speak for myself and say I have no hatred for English players but that was not the case for the Leeds team playing a German team that night. In the tunnel, they were shouting, 'You fucking Germans will lose'. I am not sure if this was what always happened when an English team played a German team but we tried to shut it out of our minds and make sure we got ourselves up for the game."

Bayern, as befitting the holders of the European Cup, boasted a formidable array of talent with Beckenbauer joined by the likes of Sepp Maier, Uli Hoeness, Gerd Muller and Franz Roth. In total, the line-up to face Leeds included seven German internationals – and West Germany had lifted the World Cup a little over a year earlier. Despite that, United were in confident mood – a feeling Bremner revealed on the eve of the final to the

Yorkshire Evening Post: 'If it is decided on skill, Leeds will win.' It was an admirable sentiment, though one that Bayern's Andersson may have had cause to query within five minutes of the final getting underway after being left in agony by a horror tackle from Yorath. There was, as the Welshman later admitted, nothing skilful about the challenge, which had come after French referee Michel Kitabdjian had already blown for a foul against Frank Gray. Andersson says: "I knew I was going to be up against Billy Bremner, who was what Englishmen call a 'hard player'. After two or three minutes, I felt a punch in my eye and thought, 'What is going on?' Two minutes later, I was off the field after a tackle by Terry Yorath and had to sit on the bench for the rest of the night. I remember I could not move my knee and I found out later it was kaput, destroyed. I did not play again for eight months."

With Bayern forced into a reshuffle by Andersson's substitution, Leeds seized control and had two strong appeals for a penalty turned down during a one-sided first half. The two decisions by referee Kitabdjian left United's players incensed but that was nothing compared to the anger that followed after the break. Sixty-six minutes had been played when Lorimer, standing 12 yards out, volleyed an unstoppable shot past Maier and into the net. It seemed deserved reward for United's dominance, only for the French official to cut the celebrations short by walking over to speak to the linesman, who by now had raised his flag. After what seemed like an age to everyone in the stadium plus the millions watching at home, Kitabdjian then disallowed the 'goal' due to his belief that Bremner had been standing in an offside position. Today, the sense of injustice over that disallowed 'goal' has not gone away in Leeds. Peter Lorimer says: "I am as certain now as I was that night, it was a goal. The referee agreed initially, too – the first thing I always did after scoring was to look at the referee to check it had been given. He signalled a goal, so I turned away to celebrate. Franz Beckenbauer then raced over to the linesman to put pressure on him and it worked as the flag belatedly went up. There was no doubt it was a goal, but the referee went over to talk to him with Beckenbauer still offering his opinion and, surprise surprise, the goal was ruled out. Billy had been coming out when I caught the ball cleanly. It went straight in the net so there was no way he could have been interfering with play. The goalkeeper certainly had no complaints at the time."

Shattered by the injustice, Leeds capitulated and within four minutes Bayern had taken the lead through Roth. Muller added a second goal nine minutes from time and United's dream was over. Lorimer says: "We all knew it represented our last chance because the team was starting to split up. A couple of the boys had already left, Johnny Giles was thinking over an offer to go to West Brom while several others were coming to the end of their careers. It had been a fantastic team and a fitting end would have been to win the European Cup. So, to be denied like that was heart-breaking – especially as we had all wanted to win the trophy for Don Revie."

Armfield was also left distraught by the turn of events, his mood of dejection not helped by angry Leeds fans rioting inside and outside the stadium after Lorimer's 'goal' had been chalked off. He adds: "Losing in Paris was a crushing blow, not just for the older players but everyone. What probably made it worse, though, for Billy and the others who had come through under Don was that it was their last chance. Changes were on the way and they knew that, so it was very sad." So dejected were the United players that they left their losers' medals in the Paris dressing room. Armfield felt like leaving his too, but instead scooped them all up into a plastic bag. He distributed the medals the following day, though the recipients still showed little enthusiasm.

Further misery would be heaped on Leeds as a club a few weeks later when they were handed a four-year ban from European competition as punishment for the riot involving their supporters in Paris. The sentence was later halved on appeal after Armfield took it upon himself to plead in person on the club's behalf, but by the time United did return to European action in 1979 they were a pale shadow of the side that had terrorised the continent for so long. The inevitable breaking up of the team built by Revie had begun within weeks of the defeat to Bayern Munich when Giles, by now 35, was appointed West Brom manager. Mick Jones, such a perfect foil for Allan Clarke down the years, was then forced to retire the following October through injury. With Terry Cooper having joined Middlesbrough two months before United's European Cup final appearance, there was an inescapable wind of change sweeping through Elland Road.

Bremner, at 32, still felt he had plenty to offer – a sentiment shared by Armfield, who retained the Scot as captain. In the 1975-76 season, he made 38 league and cup appearances. There had been just one lengthy absence from the side early in the New Year, by which time Leeds were in second place and firmly in the hunt for the title. During that spell on the sidelines, however, results dipped with the seven games without the captain, yielding just one win and three draws. Any realistic hope of success were at an end. Nevertheless, United finished the campaign in a creditable fifth place – nine points behind champions Liverpool. The rebuilding of the squad continued during that summer with Duncan McKenzie, the only one of Clough's signings at Leeds to be a success, moving to Anderlecht for £200,000 and Mick Bates joining Walsall for £35,000. Terry Yorath also departed to join Coventry City in a £140,000 deal but it was early in the 1976-77 season that finally signalled the end of the Revie era as two of the club's stalwarts moved on. Trevor Cherry recalls: "Billy and Norman left at a similar time and that really was the end of an era. I thought Jimmy did the breaking up of the side very well. On a personal level, I see Jimmy as something of a double-edged sword as he dropped me for the European Cup final despite having played in every round. Syd Owen persuaded him that the older lads who had come through under Don should play and I lost a bit of respect for Jimmy. But, in terms of breaking up that team, he did a difficult job very well. No-one was made to feel like they were being forced out. He handled the moving out of established players very tactfully. Cloughie had been brought in to do the same job but he tried to change things too quickly. No-one ever wants the good times to come to an end but the way Jimmy did it at least made things easier. In terms of Jimmy's relationship with Billy, they got on all right."

Bremner had made 773 appearances, including one as a substitute, when the curtain came down on his Elland Road career in September, 1976. The last of those came in a 2-2 draw at home to Newcastle United, by which time he was a little over two months short of his 34th birthday. Armfield recalls: "It was only when I became Leeds manager and started to work with Billy on a daily basis that I realised what a tremendous player he was. He was hugely talented and gave everything for the Leeds United cause. I find it entirely appropriate that the club erected a statue of Billy outside Elland Road shortly after his death. Billy was wonderful for me at Leeds but time catches up with everyone in the end. An offer came in from Hull City and Billy was tempted. I actually pleaded with him not to drop down to the Second Division, it is one of my pet hates – seeing a great in the game struggle towards the end of their career in the lower divisions. I much prefer the public to remember those great players at their best. I said that to Billy but, as with most players who want to eke out their time in the game as long as possible, he just wanted to keep playing and decided to join Hull. I was sad to see Billy go. At first, I think he had been a bit doubtful about me. There was an initial resentment that he hadn't got the manager's job. Bob English, our physiotherapist, said when I first arrived that Billy was never short of an opinion, which I later found out to mean I would need a thick skin. But he soon realised what my strategy was and that I was going to be very different to Brian Clough and, in the end, I like to think we got on well."

The first inkling the public had of the club's most successful captain possibly leaving was when the *Yorkshire Evening Post* splashed the news across their front page under the headline, 'Bremner sensation – United skipper on the move?' There was an inevitable sadness in Leeds when the story became fact a couple of days later, not least as it signalled the true ending of an era at Elland Road. No-one was more upset to leave than Bremner, though typically any sadness was tempered by his excitement at taking on a new challenge.

Chapter 17

The Hull Truth

As a symbol of Hull's new-found confidence and ambition, it was both powerful and persuasive. For centuries, Kingston-upon-Hull had been considered an outpost by the rest of England. On the way to nowhere other than the North Sea, anyone wishing to visit the city had to make a special effort to do so. A train journey from London could take the best part of a day, while the natural barrier of the Humber Estuary made travelling by road even more of an arduous experience. Such a splendid sense of isolation was why Philip Larkin, the poet who shunned the limelight and once rejected the Laureateship, made Hull his home for the final three decades of his life. Not everyone, however, shared Larkin's pleasure in being all but cut off from the rest of the country and plans were already afoot to rectify the situation by the time he moved to the East Riding in 1955. The first proposal was a motorway linking Yorkshire and Lancashire that would, ultimately, stretch from Hull to Liverpool. Work began on the first stretch around Manchester two years after Larkin's arrival in Yorkshire, but it would not be until 1976 that the final section to North Cave was completed. By then, a far more symbolic development of Hull's desire to open up new frontiers could be found on the banks of the Humber as the longest single-span suspension bridge in the world started to take shape. For the people of Hull, the days of a river that flows inland almost as far as Goole acting as a barrier to both trade and the development of their city were soon to be at an end.

Three or four miles away from where the newly-constructed North Tower of the Bridge could be found at Hessle, plans were being drawn up to bridge a similarly unassailable gap between ambitious dreams and reality. Hull City had, by the time the skeletal frame of the Bridge's two towers were completed in 1976, developed a reputation for being a club whose deeds never quite matched expectation. Hull was, and would remain until 2008, the largest conurbation in Europe never to have hosted top-flight football. There had been moments of promise, not least when the Tigers reached the FA Cup semi-final in 1930 and only bowed out against Arsenal after a replay. The mid-Sixties were also a time for optimism as promotion from the Third Division came amid significant improvements to Boothferry Park that suggested the club was, finally, ready to make the breakthrough. As ever, however, it proved to be a false dawn for City, who in the decade following promotion from the third tier in 1966 made a place in mid-table their own. A 14th place finish in 1975-76 merely seemed to confirm to the outside world that rugby league would always remain the city's true sporting success story. In Hull, however, there was a sense that the local football club was stirring. John Kaye, who during his playing career lifted the FA Cup and League Cup with West Bromwich Albion, had been appointed manager two years earlier. During that time, he had put the emphasis on youth and built a promising side. Future England Under-21 international Peter Daniel was making a big impression as a full-back, while much was expected of promising youngsters John Hawley, Jeff Hemmerman, Dave Gibson, Dave Stewart and Stuart Croft. Kaye, who had been signed as a player by then Hull manager Terry Neill for £20,000 in 1971, recalls: "We had been building gradually and felt to have the makings of a good team. A lot of the lads were young and everyone could see their potential." Jeff Wealands, City's first choice goalkeeper for five years from the start of the 1973-74 season, agrees: "We were a promising team and had a lot of good younger guys. We had finished eighth in 1974-75, when only a ridiculous amount of draws prevented us from having a real go at promotion. We were 14th the following season but, by the summer of 1976, confidence was high that we could do well."

That confidence was borne out in the first week of the season when, after being unfortunate to lose a bruising opening day encounter at newly-promoted Hereford United, Hull claimed resounding back-to-back wins. Luton Town were the first to be beaten as Kaye's decision to hand starts to Hawley, Gibson and Hemmerman was rewarded with a 3-1 victory. Better was to follow on the second Saturday of the campaign when FA Cup holders Southampton were the visitors to Boothferry Park. Less then three months earlier, Lawrie McMenemy's Saints had caused a huge upset at Wembley by beating Manchester United courtesy of an 83rd minute winner by Bobby Stokes. Unsurprisingly, the bookmakers had made Southampton favourites to win promotion. Hull, and particularly the defence who were due to face a strikeforce of Mick Channon and Peter Osgood, were expecting a tough afternoon. Instead, it turned into a procession towards the visitors' goal as the Tigers triumphed 4-0 in front of 7,774 fans. In the fledgling Second Division table, City were sitting second and Kaye was determined to build on such a promising start. "I was delighted with how the young lads had done," he recalls. "But I knew we needed some more experience. During the summer, I had tried to sign Alan Ball. I had roomed with Alan when I was in the England squad, but unfortunately the move didn't happen." While watching Ball in Arsenal's reserves, Kaye also spotted a young striker who he felt could make an impact in the Second Division. David Bond, who at the time was the football correspondent for the *Hull Daily Mail*, says: "John really liked the look of Frank Stapleton and wanted to buy him, but the board refused. Arsenal were asking for £45,000, which considering the career Frank went on to have would have been a steal."

With his hopes of bringing Ball to Hull thwarted, Kaye continued his hunt for an experienced campaigner capable of helping develop the club's promising youngsters. The search became more pressing after a League Cup exit at Orient had been followed by a draw with Carlisle United and a 5-1 thumping at Bolton Wanderers. It was then that a breakthrough was made. *Hull Daily Mail* reporter Bond recalls: "Every Tuesday afternoon, I would go down to the ground and interview John Kaye in his office before popping over the road to the Three Tuns pub for a drink with him and Mac Stone, the club secretary. This particular Tuesday, there was no sign of John and Mac was being all evasive so I knew something was going on. I headed back to the office to find a message to phone Barry Foster of the *Yorkshire Post*. He informed me there had maybe been some interest in Billy from Hull. In those days, evening newspapers still had a proper edition structure rather than printing one edition at breakfast as they do today. That meant I could get the story in our final edition. It really put the cat among the pigeons in Hull."

City had first enquired about Bremner during the summer, just after Leeds United had signed Tony Currie in a £240,000 deal from Sheffield United. Kaye hoped, with his chances of signing Ball by now all but dead, that Leeds would be tempted to sell. Bremner, by then 33, had been an important member of the Leeds side that had just finished fifth in Division One, the midfielder having missed just eight of 42 league games. But with Jimmy Armfield's desire to re-model his team having already seen several long-serving players depart Elland Road, Kaye felt his United counterpart could be persuaded. It didn't happen but Kaye refused to give up and, by mid-September, the deal was back on.

Hull's offer of £25,000 was accepted on Tuesday September 21, but it was not until two days later at a meeting in a Leeds hotel that Bremner finally gave Kaye the answer he craved. Andy Davidson, City's record appearance holder with 520 games between 1952 and 1967, was then the assistant manager at Boothferry Park. "Billy had played in my testimonial a few years earlier," he says. "I found him to be a really decent bloke so when the chance came up for Hull to sign him from Leeds I was all for it. Billy had been one of the best players I had ever seen. He was a bit older by now, but there was no doubt in my mind that Billy would fit in. The fans seemed equally keen, as the moment the news broke that the transfer had gone through there was a real buzz in Hull. It was all anyone was talking about for the next week."

Bremner's capture was seen as a real coup for the club. Just like the spectacular bridge that was steadily growing on either side of the Humber, it was a real statement of intent. Hull was a city on the up and so, it seemed, was the local football team. Due to Bremner's signing having come three hours after the deadline to be able to play the following day, his debut would have to wait another week. Not, it has to be said, that the Hull directors were too upset with the prospect of his bow in amber and black coming at Boothferry Park as opposed to Burnley's Turf Moor, where Kaye's side claimed a goalless draw in the absence of the club's new signing. The sense of anticipation built steadily all week, not just in Hull but also elsewhere in the country – something that had a lot to do with the opponents for Bremner's debut: Brian Clough's Nottingham Forest. The pair had enjoyed a tempestuous relationship during Clough's ill-fated 44-day stint as Leeds manager in 1974, a point underlined by Bremner's cutting response to the *Yorkshire Evening Post* a few days after Clough's sacking: 'People say you cannot get to know a man in such a short space of time, but seven weeks was long enough for me to get to know Brian Clough.'

Muhammad Ali's third and final bout with Ken Norton, who three years earlier had famously broken the champion's jaw, in New York's Yankee Stadium may have been the true heavyweight clash of 1976. But Bremner v Clough was not too far behind, at least in the minds of the two protagonists. It meant Bremner, who in John O'Hare and John McGovern was also facing two former Elland Road team-mates who had been brought to Leeds by Clough, had an extra motivation to impress. He didn't disappoint, either, much to the delight of a 16,096 crowd – double the previous season's average.

Bremner running out sporting the amber and black of Hull may have felt unusual, but the tenacity and drive that had characterised his 18 years in a Leeds shirt was evident from the first tackle. Every challenge was fought as if Bremner's life depended on it as he urged his new team-mates forward against a Forest side who had started the day above City in the table. He even, as had so often been the case during his time at Elland Road, grabbed the goal that would settle the game. *Hull Daily Mail* reporter David Bond recalls: "City had not been watched by 16,000 fans in quite some time and it created a real air of expectation. Billy was credited with the winner, though whether he got the final touch or not is open to debate. His free-kick could or could not have got a touch off someone else on the way in but, using journalistic licence, everyone in the old press box at Boothferry Park made sure Billy was given the goal. It was a much better story!" Another journalist at Hull that day was Mike Morgan, who had got to know Bremner well during his time chronicling the fortunes of Leeds United for the *Daily Express*. He recalls: "Billy was a one-off. After scoring on his debut, I remember we all waited to interview him in the tunnel and he wandered up with a fag in one hand and a cup of tea in the other. But when we got to talking about football, he became deadly serious. He talked about the challenge at Hull and was as passionate as he had ever been at Leeds." The 119th goal of Bremner's career ensured it was not only a perfect debut but also a modicum of revenge over Clough. The bloodbath forecast by the rest of the country had also not materialised, though warring supporters did do their bit on the terraces as 32 arrests were made for fighting.

Bremner's impact on the field together with his demeanour off the pitch had also led to his immediate acceptance by the dressing room, as Jeff Wealands recalls: "The great thing with Billy is he didn't arrive with this attitude of 'been there, done that', which is something you can get with big-name players. Instead, he was a real down-to-earth lad, who loved hanging around with his team-mates. We respected him because of what he had achieved with Leeds but he never played on that." Bremner's immediate acceptance by his new team-mates also pleased his manager, who had been conscious as the signing went through that the club's pay structure was being smashed. "The lads weren't stupid and knew Billy would be on more money than them," says John Kaye. "So, I sat them all down soon after the deal had been done and explained the situation. I said, 'He is going to be on bigger wages than you, but if we are successful then you will get the same money through bonuses and so on'. Fair play to the lads, they accepted that straight away."

Bremner's second game ended in defeat at Charlton Athletic but a 2-0 win over Wolves with John Hawley netting both goals was enough to push Hull up to fifth in front of the *Match of the Day* cameras. The portents seemed encouraging, but soon results started to dip and by Christmas it had become clear City were neither going up nor going down. Bremner, for his part, was giving his all but a lack of goals – as illustrated by full-back Peter Daniel finishing the season as joint top scorer with six penalties – meant the team plateaued in mid-table. It was frustrating for Kaye, not least because a lack of funds meant the signings he planned to make in the wake of Bremner never materialised. "I had sold Roy Greenwood to Sunderland for £110,000 the previous year and was hoping to use that money to bring a few players in but it didn't happen."

Defeat to Port Vale in the FA Cup third round at the start of the New Year meant interest in the city inevitably began to wane. There were still high points, notably a 4-1 thrashing of Burnley that saw Malcolm Lord net a hat-trick. Bremner also managed one more goal to go with his debut strike, though tellingly the crowd that witnessed the 1-1 draw with Orient in April was just 4,495. Two weeks later, the final home game against Cardiff City was watched by just 3,511 – then the lowest ever to watch the club in the Second Division. The optimism of Autumn had long since evaporated, though manager Kaye insists Bremner was still a great signing. "Billy was terrific," he says. "The younger lads learned so much from him in games and training. His enthusiasm rubbed off on everyone. The unfortunate thing was Billy picked up a back injury very early on that he never really recovered from. It definitely impeded him." Jeff Wealands agrees: "It must have been hard for Billy to leave Leeds after so many years, especially as it was to drop down a division. The gap was nothing like what exists now between the Premier League and the Championship but it was still a gap. After being at the top for so long, it must have been difficult to adapt. But, credit to Billy, he never once complained. He was great to have around the club."

Bremner's desire to repay Hull's faith was such that he played through the pain barrier on numerous occasions during that first season. In the end, he missed just five league games – and three of those came in the final ten days of the season. Even so, Bremner knew more than anyone that the clock was ticking on his career. One year remained on his contract at Boothferry Park, by which time he would be six months short of his 36th birthday. Retirement was becoming an increasingly attractive proposition. And what better way to sign off, he thought, than by helping Hull City into the top flight for the first time in history.

Chapter 18

Calling Time

When Billy Bremner first signed for Hull City, he did not have to delve too far into the past for a role model. A little over 14 years, in fact, to the day he, as a homesick teenager, had first played alongside Bobby Collins for Leeds United. Don Revie, knowing his fledgling group of youngsters needed an experienced older head, had signed Collins from Everton. Paying a fee of £25,000 for a 31-year-old seemed excessive, especially as the Goodison Park club had paid Celtic the same amount for the midfielder four years earlier. Revie, though, knew it would be money well spent. Not only would Collins bring desire and a will to win to Second Division Leeds, but the Scot could also be relied upon to instil the same qualities in the promising group of youngsters who were coming through the ranks at Elland Road. Bremner had never forgotten the lessons learned playing alongside Collins. Now, as the elder statesman at Hull, he had the chance to pass on similar tips to the next generation. What Bremner could not have known, however, when signing a two-year deal at Boothferry Park, was that within a few months he would be reunited with his former team-mate.

The departure of first team coach Phil Holme in the spring of 1977 had been the catalyst for Collins' arrival on Humberside the following July. Bremner, realising his playing days were numbered, had initially shown an interest in replacing Holme on John Kaye's coaching staff, as *Hull Daily Mail* reporter David Bond recalls: "John wanted to freshen up his staff and I remember discussing it with Billy on the team bus to Plymouth for a game in mid-April. I certainly got the impression Billy was interested, though I could tell he was also being careful not to give too much away. The season was petering out and Billy sounded like he was thinking of moving into coaching, though also remaining as a player. I stored it away in my mind, but then once the summer came it was announced Phil Holme's successor would be one Robert Collins. Straight away, I wondered if Billy had played a part in the appointment as he had been bosom buddies with Bobby at Leeds." Not so, insists manager John Kaye: "Billy had no input on the decision, it was totally my own. I had played against Bobby so knew what he was all about. Plus, Bobby was the one who came across best in interview."

With Collins joining Kaye and assistant Andy Davidson for pre-season, thoughts turned to potential signings. Goal-scoring had been a major problem for the Tigers during the previous campaign, so the priority was to find a quality striker. Kaye, who had initially considered Duncan McKenzie, eventually settled on Bruce Bannister, the former Bradford City forward who had also played for Bristol Rovers and Plymouth. A £15,000 fee was agreed with the Pilgrims and Bannister, who was also wanted by newly-relegated Tottenham Hotspur, admits a return to Yorkshire – and the opportunity to play with Bremner - was too good to turn down. He recalls: "Just as I was about to sign, John confessed that Spurs were also in for me but it made no difference to my decision. I had only been at Plymouth a few months but it was a chance to come home and to play with Billy Bremner. He had been such a special player at Leeds so it was great to think I would now have the chance of playing in the same team as him. Later, I got to know him quite well. My father died when I was playing for Hull and I came over to Bradford to live with my Mum for a bit. I would then drive to the A1, where I would meet Billy and Alan Warboys, and the three of us would travel on to Hull in one car. He was, basically, a quiet guy and a lovely man."

Bannister, aping Bremner's achievement of the previous season, enjoyed a dream debut by scoring as Hull beat Sunderland at home in front of a bumper crowd of more than 16,000. Bremner had missed the win, as he had done the whole of pre-season, with a recurrence of the knee injury he had sustained against Millwall the previous April. He was, however, fit enough to start at Sheffield United three days later as Hull lost an ill-tempered encounter 2-1. A 1-0 win over Crystal Palace, City's first win in the capital in 15 attempts, was then followed by September yielding just two points from four games, plus a narrow League Cup second round victory over a Southport side who would be voted out of the League the following summer and replaced by Wigan Athletic. The pressure was starting to mount on Kaye as City prepared to host bottom club Mansfield Town. A terrible 90 minutes followed as the Stags won 2-0. By 5.30pm, the axe had fallen on the manager. David Bond recalls: "The season had started poorly but it still surprised a lot of people when Christopher Needler, the chairman, sacked John within an hour of the final whistle against Mansfield. Then, as chairmen tend to do, he went straight on holiday!" John Kaye, who had confided in his backroom team ahead of kick-off that he feared defeat would spell the end of his three-year reign, had become the first Hull manager to be sacked

Just Champion: Celebrating
winning the First Division
title in 1973-74.

Taking On The Best: Going head-to-head with Johann Cruyff as Leeds claim a first leg lead in the European Cup semi-finals with a 2-1 win.

Bidding to be Kings of Europe: Billy, far right, lines up alongside his United teammates ahead of the 1975 European Cup final against Bayern Munich in Paris.

Travesty Of Justice: Leading the protests as referee Michel Kitabdjian disallows Peter Lorimer's 'goal' for offside when the score is 0-0.

Bitter taste of defeat: The injustice of losing to Bayern Munich in the European Cup final is written all across the United captain's face.

Best of friends: Allan Clarke and Billy take a breather to share a joke at Elland Road.

Dream Debut: After joining Hull City, Billy marks his first appearance in amber and black by netting the winner against Brian Clough's Nottingham Forest.

Going Down: Taking a tumble as Hull draw 2-2 with Blackpool at Boothferry Park.

Still Deadly: Netting his penultimate goal as a professional in March, 1978, as Notts County claim a 1-1 draw from their visit to Humberside.

In The Notebook: His career may be winding down but Billy still has the capacity to get into trouble with referees.

Rovers On The Up: Billy, in his first managerial job, reflects on Doncaster Rovers' progress along with the club's chief executive, Les Holloway.

Father Figure: As Doncaster manager, Billy was like a father figure to countless players. Here, one of his many 'sons', John Buckley, signs on at Belle Vue.

All Smiles: Watched by chairman Leslie Silver (far right) and vice chairman Manny Cussins (with glasses), Leeds United's new management team sign in. Right to left, Dave Blakey, Billy and Dave Bentley.

Back Home: Billy surveys his Kingdom after returning as manager.

Down To Work: Settling into his new office at Elland Road.

United again: Billy watches training at Elland Road along with his long-time mentor, Don Revie. Don Warters of the Yorkshire Evening Post is on hand to chronicle the meeting.

Cup Run: Goalscorers Micky Adams and John Stiles celebrate putting Billy's United into the FA Cup semi-finals with a 2-0 win at Wigan Athletic.

Wembley-bound? David Rennie puts Leeds 1-0 up against Coventry City in the FA Cup semi-final.

Get in! Keith Edwards celebrates United's equaliser at Hillsborough to send the semi-final to extra-time.

Peace-maker: Tempers boil over during the 1987 play-off final second leg against Charlton Athletic at Elland Road.

Concern: Watching United captain Brendan Ormsby being carried off with a serious Achilles injury during the 1987 play-off final replay against Charlton Athletic in Birmingham.

Going Up? Ian Baird, left, wheels away in celebration after John Sheridan's curled free-kick puts Leeds 1-0 ahead against Charlton in extra-time at St Andrews.

Sinking Feeling: Two goals from Peter Shirtliff mean Leeds are 2-1 down and their promotion hopes almost at an end, leaving Billy in dejected mood.

Dream Job: A pre-season photo-call as Leeds United manager.

That's How To Do It: Running through instructions with his Leeds players.

The Don's Final Return: Billy, as United manager, greets Don Revie on his final visit to Elland Road in May, 1988, for a testimonial to raise funds for research into Motor Neurone Disease. Revie died the following year.

Sacked: After being
axed by the Leeds
board in September,
1988, Billy leaves
Elland Road with
his head held high.

Leeds United: The author
meets Billy at a Sportsman's
Dinner in enemy territory -
Turf Moor, Burnley.

City In Mourning: The gates at Elland Road are quickly adorned with tributes following Billy's death at the age of 54.

Final Journey: The funeral cortege makes its way to St Mary's Roman Catholic Church, Edlington, Doncaster.

Cast In Bronze: Billy's death
led to Leeds commissioning
a statue of their greatest ever
captain outside Elland Road.

in 20 years. "I did think it was harsh," he says today. "I still do. But I had fallen out with a couple of the directors in the September and before long I was gone."

Jeff Wealands, who had played in nearly every game of Kaye's reign, felt the blame for City's failure to become genuine promotion challengers lay in the boardroom rather than dugout. He says: "The board didn't back John. He had wanted a seasoned goalscorer but was told, 'No'. We had a good nucleus of players but the club just didn't have the ambition. A manager needs the tools to do the job. I felt really sorry for John because, in my opinion, he had been doing a good job. Just how good a job was shown by what happened next."

City, 15th in the table after the Mansfield defeat, named Bobby Collins as caretaker manager, but indicated the job would be advertised. Bremner, who had spoken to chairman Needler in the immediate aftermath of Kaye's departure on the Saturday, was still giving little away publicly when talking to the *Yorkshire Post* two days later. He said: 'What was discussed is between me and the chairman. As far as applying, I have not applied. I am not rash enough to rush into anything as important as this without giving it a great deal of consideration.'

As the press and supporters speculated as to who was favourite to succeed Kaye, the squad regrouped at training on the Monday to prepare for the following night's home game against Tottenham Hotspur. One of only three clubs in the Football League still unbeaten, Spurs boasted an enviable array of talent with Glenn Hoddle, Steve Perryman and future Hull manager Peter Taylor all in the squad that travelled north for Collins' bow as caretaker manager. Two goals from Alan Warboys, however, ensured the Londoners suffered the first of what would be only six defeats en route to clinching a return to the First Division at the first attempt. After ending a scoring drought that had reached 353 minutes when Warboys netted against Spurs, Hull claimed a draw at Millwall and a 2-0 home win over Blackpool. Collins had done his hopes of landing the job on a permanent basis the power of good, though Bremner was still hoping to pip his old Leeds team-mate to the post. David Bond recalls: "Bobby was interviewed by Christopher Needler on the morning after the win over Blackpool. Then, he told me later, he was driving back along the A63 and who should he see coming the other way but Billy? It was only then that he knew Billy was in for the job as well. Both had been great players, but their approach to trying to win favour with the board was quite different. Bobby was much more relaxed about what his role might be, he had joined City as a coach and was quite happy with the role. It was my impression that Bobby would have been quite happy to remain as coach if Billy had got the job. I was told Bobby was very relaxed in his interview, whereas Billy was much more forceful. He told the chairman exactly what he expected and wanted in terms of resources. Human nature being what it is, the chairman thought Billy might be a bit hard to handle so he gave the job to Bobby instead."

The appointment of Collins as Hull's ninth post-war manager was confirmed on October 18, chairman Needler revealing the Scot had beaten 30 other applicants to the post. Andy Davidson would remain as assistant manager, while Ken Houghton returned to the club as youth team coach. There was no place in the new-look management team for Bremner, which came as a surprise to many at Boothferry Park. Jeff Wealands, who made 240 league appearances for the Tigers, says: "To be honest, we had all expected Billy to get the manager's job. I think Billy expected to as well and not getting it probably played a part in him leaving at the end of the season."

Bremner, who had been disappointed to be overlooked, kept his counsel in public. Tellingly, however, within a couple of days of Collins' appointment being confirmed, Bremner was telling the *Yorkshire Post* about his plans to retire at the end of the season. He said: "I always thought I would be someone who would wake up one morning and say, 'That's it, my playing days are over'. But that is not really fair on your club. It doesn't give them time for the change-over. I went to Hull on a two-year contract and I intend to honour it. At the end of that time, I think it will be about time for me to go. I have had 18 happy years at Leeds and two tremendous years with Hull so next May that will be it. Obviously, at 34 there are things you can't do that you were able to do at 27. I decided a bit back that this would be my final year but it would be nice if I could end with Hull going up. I might want another year in the First Division but, at this moment, this is my final year."

Bremner had not taken the rejection well, something that David Bond quickly picked up on. "A real wedge was driven between Billy and Bobby," recalls the then football correspondent of the *Hull Daily Mail*. "Billy didn't handle it too well and their relationship definitely suffered. They had been bosom buddies before but not any more. Maybe there were just too alike in terms of being fiery, diminutive Scots who had been such big parts of that great Leeds United team. But it made life at Hull very uneasy. Bobby would continually say to me, 'I understand why Billy is so disappointed so I don't want to come down on him hard'. But a few of the players thought it should have been nipped in the bud. They felt Bobby, as manager, should have taken his big pal in hand, but he didn't."

Relations between the two former Leeds team-mates may have been strained, but there were never any question marks over Bremner's commitment on the pitch. In the first game of Collins' reign as permanent boss, he netted City's goal in a 1-1 draw at Burnley and produced an all-round display that was described in the following Monday's *Yorkshire Post* as 'dominant'. Four days later, Bremner netted the second goal in a 2-0 win over Oldham Athletic that earned the Tigers the glamour draw of a League Cup fourth round tie at Arsenal. Assistant manager Andy Davidson says: "Billy was a class act. Even though he was in his 30s at Hull, he was still quick where it mattered the most – in his brain. He could see a pass before anyone else. Billy was also a great professional and a real positive influence on the younger lads. They could see that if someone who had been as successful as Billy was working hard, there was no excuse for them not doing the same. Even if he was unhappy with something, he never moaned or groaned in front of the young lads." One of the older members of the squad could also see what a positive influence the City captain was having both on and off the field. "I had played against Billy," recalls Bruce Bannister, who had just passed his 30th birthday when he signed for Hull. "But it was only when I was in the same team that I realised just what he was all about. Billy read the game superbly, there was no-one quicker over the first five yards and that is because he saw things before anyone else. He was coming towards the end of his career by the time he joined Hull but there was no doubting his quality. Off the field, Billy was a great influence as well. He knew the importance of taking the pressure off because players can get swept away with the hype before a game. Billy had played in so many big games that it was second nature to him. But I always found it fascinating to watch him in the dressing room before we went out, calming everyone down – and, in particular, the young lads. He was a great captain."

Bremner may have been upset to miss out on becoming manager, but he continued to enjoy being one of the lads – though, sometimes, it could hit him in the pocket. Jeff Wealands says: "Billy loved the banter, and particularly playing cards on the team bus. Unfortunately for him, he was probably the worst cards player in the world. What Billy didn't realise was that whenever he had a good hand in something like three-card brag, he would give himself away with a nervous tick he had. The better the hand, the more pronounced it became. We picked up on it, so whenever the tick returned we would all fold straight away. Billy never cottoned on and would always end up £20 or £30 down after an away trip, which was quite a bit of money in those days. I don't think we ever confessed the truth!"

A trip to London for the League Cup at Arsenal may well have cost Bremner a few quid, but it was nothing compared to the damage that had been done to City's league position in the preceding weeks. A run of just one win from the previous six games meant the club had slid into lower mid-table. It was still very early days in Collins' reign, but the optimism of his first few weeks had already evaporated. Nevertheless, the chance to play at one of English football's great football stadiums was something to savour for not only Hull's youngsters but also Bremner. It was almost two years to the day since he had last played at Highbury in a 2-1 win for Leeds and the League Cup tie meant a return to the limelight. Bremner had actually won in each of his last three visits to the home of the Gunners but this time there was to be no fairytale ending as Liam Brady and Graham Rix dominated the midfield in a 5-1 home win. For the Tigers captain, it was a humbling evening that ended in him being substituted by John Hawley. Bruce Bannister admits it was a disappointing night, though one incident has stuck in his mind. "It was totally bizarre," he says. "Arsenal were 5-0 ahead when we were awarded a late penalty. I was the designated penalty taker but, suddenly, John Hawley picked the ball up and marched towards the spot. I said, 'What the hell are you doing?' We ended up having an argument about who should take it and I just couldn't get the ball off him. In the end, I let him take it but I have always wondered, 'Would John have insisted on taking it at 1-1 when the pressure was really on?' It was strange because John's character wasn't like that. I did complain to the management afterwards but they just said, 'The game's over, let it go'. It was a very, very strange incident."

Back in the League, City's troubles continued as December brought just three points from six games. Matters hardly improved in the New Year, either, with a home defeat by Leicester City in the FA Cup being accompanied by a further slide down the Second Division table. Boothferry Park was not a happy place, as Jeff Wealands recalls: "I got injured just after Christmas but continued to watch all the games and it was clear we were on the crest of a slump. We couldn't buy a win, the confidence had gone and it seemed the only way we were heading was down. There were a lot of problems behind the scenes."

The season had begun in an acrimonious fashion due to eight members of the squad being in dispute with the club over pay. Dave Stewart, Vince Grimes, Dave Gibson, Eddie Blackburn, Peter Daniel, Stuart Croft, Ian Dobson and Wealands were the players in question. All took their case to an independent tribunal and although agreement was eventually reached – Grimes and Stewart being the last two to sign new deals in early October – the saga had an unsettling effect on the squad. The sacking of a popular manager in Kaye then further dented morale, something Collins' management style did little to improve. Jeff Wealands recalls: "Bobby was a fine coach, who I enjoyed working with. But, once manager, he became very different and the lads didn't like it."

The relationship between manager and his players is key at any football club. Get it right, as Sir Alex Ferguson has done for so much of his time at Manchester United, and success will invariably follow. Get it wrong, however, and the end-result is the mess that was England's 2010 World Cup campaign. At Hull under Collins, the cracks had started to appear within weeks of the Scot taking permanent charge. Bruce Bannister says: "As a trainer, Bobby had been excellent. Training had been varied and he had gained everyone's respect. Unfortunately, the management side was not his strength. He didn't suit the role at all, which was a real shame as I had the utmost respect for Bobby as a trainer. You need to be a bit more subtle as manager, use psychology to get the best out of the players. But that was not Bobby. What should have happened after John Kaye was sacked was to make Billy manager with Bobby as his trainer. Unfortunately, the board made the wrong decision in sacking John and then compounded it by not giving the job to Billy. The club ended up paying the price."

A 4-1 win over Cardiff City soon after the appointment of Collins on a permanent basis should have been a springboard for further success. Instead, the manager had chosen to publicly criticise his players. The intention was to ensure no-one rested on their laurels, but the comments backfired spectacularly as Hull drew three and lost six of the following nine games. Further discord was caused by Collins' choice of his number two, Syd Owen.

At Leeds, Owen had been a key member of Don Revie's back-room staff. A former Footballer of the Year, he had also played three times for England before moving to Elland Road in 1960 when Revie was still a player. Along with Les Cocker and Maurice Lindley, Owen had gone on to play a major part in Leeds' success – not least in the compiling of the dossiers that Revie became synonymous with during his time with Leeds and England. He was, however, someone who Revie knew how to handle, as former Scotland winger Eddie Gray recalls: "Syd was a great coach, but a bit of a perfectionist so Don would try and keep him away from the first team at times because nothing was good enough. Some of the Leeds boys would go home in tears after what Syd had said."

That Collins should turn to Owen two months into his reign at Hull was not a surprise, as the pair had formed a bond during their time together at Elland Road. But the move quickly antagonised the players. "Bringing Syd Owen in was Bobby's big mistake," says Jeff Wealands: "Syd, basically, became Bobby's henchman and no-one liked him. He had a superior attitude about him, making sure we all knew that he considered Hull to be a big step down from Leeds. Syd lost the players almost straight away. He seemed to expect Bobby Charlton or Peter Lorimer to be playing for Hull City, ignoring the fact we were in the Second Division. I will always remember a training session when Syd belittled one of the lads. We used to train at Hull University and a few students were watching us play a practice match one day. One of the lads mis-controlled the ball, and Syd's response was to turn to this group of students and say, 'What chance have I got when he can't even control a football?' It was completely unnecessary and really wound the lads up."

With discord growing behind the scenes, City's league position continued to nose-dive. A series of crisis meetings between the players, Collins and Owen allowed grievances to be aired, but did little to improve results on the pitch. The appointment of Mac Stone, City's club secretary, as general manager working alongside Collins, a move new chairman Bob Chapman insisted did not undermine the manager, further added to the chaos at Boothferry Park.

A 1-1 draw at home to Brighton & Hove Albion on February 4 did little to raise spirits and, by the following Friday, Collins had gone. City had won just two of 16 league games since the Scot's appointment had been made permanent. Jeff Wealands says: "I wasn't surprised when I found out Bobby had been sacked. Confidence was rock bottom, the players were unhappy and it simply wasn't working out. Even in the short space of time he had been in the job, we had three or four crisis meetings when the gloves were really off. Syd Owen really copped it."

The experiment of trying to follow the Elland Road blueprint was over. Collins had been manager for only four-and-a-half months, Owen his assistant for just two. Hull were searching for a new manager, though this time there was no suggestion Bremner was interested. David Bond of the *Hull Daily Mail* recalls: "Billy was never in the running this time. A new board had taken over and I am sure they knew Billy had been overlooked last time. His name was never mentioned and the job instead went to Ken Houghton, who stepped up from the youth team."

The freezing weather bought Houghton time, causing the trip to Stoke on February 11 to be postponed along with the following Saturday's home game against Southampton. It meant Houghton's managerial bow would instead be the crucial relegation battle with Mansfield Town. Victory would have been a major boost not only for Houghton but also City's survival hopes, but it was the Stags who triumphed. A 3-2 win over bottom club Millwall the following week lifted the Tigers back out of the relegation zone, but it proved only a temporary respite. Successive defeats against Stoke City, Blackpool and Burnley started a truly shocking run of just one win from the final 13 games. Relegation was confirmed with a 2-1 defeat at Orient, by which time Bremner had played his last game for the club. His farewell appearance in amber and black had come the previous week in a 1-0 home defeat to Fulham in front of just 3,901 fans. The end of a truly glorious playing career spanning almost two decades and more than 900 appearances was in sight. It was time to open a new chapter in the life of Billy Bremner.

Chapter 19

Donny

For nigh on a century, the story of Doncaster Rovers had been largely an undistinguished affair. Sure, there had been five promotion successes. But these instances of upward mobility had been more than cancelled out by six relegations. There had been good times, not least during the 1950s when Rovers spent eight years in the Second Division and crowds regularly topped 20,000. There had also been Alick Jeffrey, considered by many supporters to be the best player to grace Belle Vue, and the record-breaking season of 1946-47 when Rovers lifted the Division Three North title after netting 123 goals and collecting 72 points. If the current three-points-for-a-win system had been in place during that first post-war campaign, Doncaster would have become the first club to smash through the century mark. But, on the whole, a year short of their 100th anniversary, Rovers had rarely troubled the country's football radar with the club even suffering the ignominy of twice being voted out of the Football League before returning in 1923. Fifty years on from being accepted back into the League fold for a third time, the club were struggling. All but three of the previous 19 seasons had been spent in the Fourth Division and there appeared little hope of improving that record any time soon, a point vividly illustrated by the start of October, 1978, as Rovers slumped to third bottom.

Stan Anderson, who during his playing career had become the first to captain the North East trio of Newcastle United, Sunderland and Middlesbrough, had been in charge since 1975. But progress had been minimal and unrest was growing among supporters. Anderson's hopes of repeating the promotion success he had enjoyed as Middlesbrough manager had been undermined by a chronic lack of funding at Belle Vue. So, when a possible route out appeared in November courtesy of an offer to become Ian Greaves' assistant at First Division Bolton Wanderers, Anderson jumped at the chance. His final act was to oversee a 2-1 home defeat to York City that ended with fans, ignorant of Bolton's advances, chanting for the manager to go. Within 48 hours, the calls had been answered and Rovers were looking for their 15th post-war manager. It was going to be a hard sell, as former midfielder Dave Bentley remembers: "I had joined the previous year from

Chesterfield and Doncaster were not in great shape. It was rundown and, generally, lacking in a bit of pride. There was no money around and it showed. The club was badly in need of a lift."

That lift came a week after Anderson's departure when chairman, Tony Phillips, revealed Billy Bremner was to be the club's new manager. Glynn Snodin, who went on to make more than 300 appearances for Doncaster, remembers the buzz the appointment caused in the dressing room. "We just couldn't believe the news," says Snodin, whose first-team debut had come a year earlier at the age of 17. "Here was this icon of football coming to manage Doncaster Rovers. It was a real coup for the club and one that lifted everyone, whether they were players, staff or supporters."

Bremner had been looking for a new challenge since calling time on his playing career the previous May. His appetite for management had been whetted as a pundit in the 1978 World Cup, where he worked alongside Jock Stein, Lawrie McMenemy and John Bond. The big question, however, as the summer wore on was whether any club would be willing to take a chance with an untried manager. Doncaster provided the answer and, once in charge, Bremner set about the task with all his customary relish. Glynn Snodin says: "After getting over the initial excitement of the news and then meeting Billy for the first time, I suppose we were all a bit nervous. Would he be a disciplinarian? How would he get us to play? Which of us would he want to move on? There were a lot of questions, but it was still a thrill to know Billy Bremner was our new manager." Unfortunately, it seems the sporting public of Doncaster did not initially share the players' excitement with just 1,750 fans coming through the turnstiles for Bremner's managerial bow at home to Rochdale on December 2. The snow that had fallen in south Yorkshire during the previous few days may have been a factor along with the apparent poor quality of the opposition. Rochdale had finished the previous season rock bottom of the Football League and little had improved in the intervening six months. Not only had Dale not won away from home in 36 attempts, but the previous week had seen the club knocked out of the FA Cup by non-League Droylsden. In many ways, managerless Rochdale – Mick Ferguson having been dismissed in the wake of the Cup exit - were the perfect opposition for a manager's first game due to the chances of starting on a high. For Bremner, though, it was a different story, believing that Rovers would receive little credit for winning and, therefore, had everything to lose. It was not, however, an opinion he was going to share with the team as they sat expectantly in the dressing room ahead of kick-off. Glynn Snodin, who was in the squad to face Rochdale, recalls: "Billy was only 5ft 5in tall but, when he walked through that dressing room door, he filled the place. You could hear a pin drop as he got up to speak and outlined what we had to do. Man-management was a skill he excelled at and it meant the lads went out really fired up. Billy was great like that." Buoyed by Bremner's words of encouragement, Rovers dominated on a snow-covered pitch but had only a Bobby Owen goal to show for their efforts against a Rochdale side who were fortunate to escape with a 1-0 defeat. It was a solid start, though one that would soon be undermined by the inconsistency that had dogged Doncaster for more years than anyone at Belle Vue cared to remember. The following week brought a 2-1 defeat at Aldershot that was followed by an FA Cup second round exit to Shrewsbury Town, who coasted to a 3-0 triumph at Belle Vue. A cold snap then meant Rovers' first taste of action in the New Year was delayed, though the wait was worth it as a 3-1 triumph at Port Vale became the first of five wins from the next six games. As if to underline how inconsistent the team could be, however, that one blemish was a horrendous 7-1 thrashing at Bournemouth - Doncaster's worst reverse in 26 years. The result was made even worse by the Cherries having started the afternoon level on points with Rovers. Publicly, Bremner was philosophical – pointing out to reporters how Leeds, after conceding seven goals to West Ham in the League Cup one year, had bounced back by lifting the trophy at Wembley the following season. Privately, however, he was fuming with what he saw as a lack of pride in the closing stages. Glynn Snodin says: "As a rule, Billy was not a manager who shouted and bawled at the players. He had been a special player but, unlike some managers, was not the sort to criticise you for not being able to do what had come naturally to him in his career. But if he felt anyone was not working hard enough or putting the effort in, then he would let rip."

Results continued to fluctuate wildly with a four-game unbeaten run in March sandwiched by losing streaks of three and five games respectively. A 4-3 win at already promoted Grimsby Town on the final day was a rare highlight, even if a fifth away triumph of the season was not enough to prevent Rovers having to apply for re-election for only the third time since being re-admitted to the League. Happily for Bremner, the League's Annual Meeting on June 1 subsequently handed Doncaster a reprieve along with Darlington, Halifax Town and Crewe Alexandra as all four polled sufficient votes to stay up.

Finishing 90th out of 92 clubs may have been the joint lowest position in

Rovers' League history but, to those involved at Belle Vue, progress was being made behind the scenes. Dave Bentley says: "Billy had come in with his eyes open and could see a lot needed improving. The facilities, the training ground, the scouting and so on all needed overhauling. But Billy realised money was tight and that things would have to be done gradually. He was not one to moan about it, more the sort to roll his sleeves up and get on with sorting out any problem that arose. Billy, basically, loved a challenge. I soon realised that determination to overcome the odds was probably a big factor in why he had been such a good player." Glynn Snodin was another at Doncaster who could see how the club was changing. "It was a gradual process," he says. "He brought in things like massages for the players, which was something that he'd had at Leeds. He wanted to make sure the canteen was right, along with the kit. It was all about wanting to make the set-up more professional, the reasoning being that the players would feel more professional as a result. We might have been in the Fourth Division, but Billy did not want us to have a Fourth Division attitude."

One man who found Bremner's move into management fascinating was football commentator, John Helm. He had first interviewed the then Leeds captain as a budding journalist with the *Yorkshire Evening Post*. A mutual respect developed, so much so that Helm was later asked to be Bremner's ghostwriter for a column in *Shoot* magazine. Through his work with Yorkshire Television, Helm could see at close quarters just how Bremner was adapting to the demands of his new role. He recalls: "Stepping up to manager can be difficult. Billy had seen that for himself when Don Revie first took charge at Leeds in 1961. Don had made a point of making sure everyone called him 'Boss' after becoming manager, it was his way of putting a boundary down. In Billy's case, he had joined a club where he had no playing links and that does make it easier. Funnily enough, though, he did love being called 'Gaffer' and it led to one of our only altercations. At YTV, we used to do a feature about a player's interests away from football. One week, we did Glynn Snodin who loved playing the board game Trivial Pursuits. I asked him a couple of jokey questions, one of which was, 'Who is the gaffer?' Glynn said, 'Billy Bremner', to which I replied, 'Wrong, it is Frank Sinatra'. Glynn fell about laughing but, after it had gone out on YTV, Billy hit the roof. He thought it had belittled him, which was never the intention. Thankfully, Billy was not a man to bear grudges and everything was smoothed out very quickly."

Central to Bremner's vision for the future at Doncaster was a flourishing youth set-up. With the club coffers, as ever, bare, being able to promote from within was always going to be vital if progress was to be made on the field. Bremner had watched and learned during 13 years as a player under Revie at Leeds, and had quickly put those lessons into practice after taking over at Belle Vue. Ian Snodin, three years younger than brother Glynn, recalls: "I had just passed my 15th birthday and playing for Rovers' juniors when Billy was appointed manager. He took an interest straight away. Providing the first team were playing at home or not too far away, Billy would come down and watch us in the Northern Intermediate League on a Saturday morning. He wanted to see if there were any decent young lads coming through as a strong youth set-up was important to him. He was very encouraging and would find time to have a chat with us all."

Bremner's desire to shake up the youth set-up also saw him approach Dave Bentley about a change of direction in his own career. "It happened about a year after Billy had arrived," recalls the midfielder who played in all but seven of Bremner's first 47 league games in charge. "He called me into his office one morning and said, 'Do you want to join the coaching side?' I was only 29 and wanted to keep playing, but Billy made it clear the offer might not arise again. So, I accepted. I doubt I would have done that for many other people but Billy. I continued to play, but mainly in the reserves where I was able to help the younger lads with coaching and the like. Billy thought it vital that the young lads, who he really rated, had a bit of experience alongside them."

Another lesson learned at Leeds was the importance of a good backroom staff. In that respect, Bremner felt his best business of the 1979 summer had been in persuading Les Cocker to become assistant manager. Cocker had been an integral part of Revie's coaching staff, putting the United players through their paces in training. He had also been the team trainer for Sir Alf Ramsey's victorious 1966 World Cup winners. Cocker had stayed on in the international set-up when Revie took charge of England in 1974, later following his former club manager to the United Arab Emirates. Bringing Cocker to Belle Vue was seen as a real coup by Bremner, whose other summer arrivals included former Hull City team-mate Alan Warboys. Only Bobby Owen had reached double figures in the previous season so it was clear more firepower was needed, hence the arrival of Warboys and Sheffield Wednesday forward Ian Nimmo. Another summer signing from Hillsborough was defender Hugh Dowd, while Celtic duo John Dowie and Billy Russell completed the additions to the squad. The existing players could see the squad was starting to evolve, as Glynn Snodin admits: "Billy wasn't one to come in and have a huge clearout straight away. He spent the first six months or so assessing things, and only then did he start to change the squad. It was fair, as it meant everyone was given a chance."

All five of the summer signings featured in the opening game of the season, an encouraging 1-1 draw at Sheffield United that ensured the League Cup first round tie was finely balanced ahead of the second leg at Belle Vue. The Third Division Blades duly attracted a bumper crowd of 8,444, who were treated to a magnificent display as the home side triumphed 3-1. Four days later, Northampton Town were beaten on the opening day of the League season and hopes were high in Doncaster of the club enjoying a successful season. By the end of September, however, just one further league win and a 5-1 thrashing at Exeter City in the League Cup meant much of the optimism had evaporated. The slump in form was a blow to Bremner, though it was nothing compared to the devastation caused by the events of October 4 when Cocker suddenly collapsed and died. Dave Bentley, who had featured in every first team game since Cocker had joined Rovers during the summer, says: "We were on the training pitch at Cantley Park when Les said he was feeling unwell. He said, 'I better get off back to Belle Vue', and drove off. The next thing we knew, the physio was coming up to us and saying, 'Les has had a heart attack at the ground'. We couldn't believe it." Cocker, who the previous evening had driven to Manchester to visit former England coach Bill Taylor in hospital, was rushed to Doncaster Royal Infirmary via ambulance but was pronounced dead on arrival. The news left Bremner devastated. "It came as a shock to us all and it really was a horrible time," remembers Bentley. "Les was only young and as fit as a fiddle. At first, we couldn't take the news in. We also kept thinking that one of us really should have taken Les back, as what would have happened if he had suffered the heart attack at the wheel? I think Les's death hit Billy the hardest of all. They had spent all those years together at Leeds, so it was like losing a member of his family. Billy was devastated."

Just two days later, Rovers were back in action after the decision was taken to play the game at Crewe Alexandra as planned in Cocker's memory. All the players sported black armbands as an own goal and Hugh Dowd's first strike for the club secured a 2-1 win. The two points were immediately dedicated to Cocker, just as was the case after the five straight wins that followed the triumph at Gresty Road. The most impressive was the last of those half dozen victories as leaders Portsmouth were beaten 2-0 in front of

9,801 fans at Belle Vue. It was enough to lift Rovers up to eighth, just three points behind Walsall in the fourth and final promotion place. For Bremner, the run of consecutive wins brought a first personal accolade since finishing his playing career as he was named the Division Four Manager of the Month for October.

By Christmas, Bremner's side had moved up a place to seventh to set up nicely the Boxing Day visit to Fellows Park. Any hopes of putting more pressure on their rivals were dashed, however, as Doncaster conceded twice in the final three minutes to lose 3-1. Not only that, but Bremner became embroiled in a row with referee RA Banks in the tunnel. The Rovers manager was incensed by the Manchester official's handling of the closing stages, which had also seen Alan Little and Billy Russell booked. Banks subsequently reported the incident and Bremner was fined £200 by the Football Association for bringing the game into disrepute.

By the time the fine had been imposed early in the New Year, Doncaster had already begun to lose their way. Having one of the smaller squads in the division was a factor, according to Bremner. So was a lack of training facilities as the Yorkshire winter worsened, the upshot being a slump in form that brought just one win from 15 games. Dave Bentley, who towards the end of 1979 had been asked to take charge of the youth team in the reorganisation of the coaching staff that followed Cocker's death, recalls: "The training ground became a real problem. We had a place that is not far away from where Doncaster use today in Cantley Park, but the weather sometimes meant it was out of bounds. We also used RAF Finningley for a time and I would be lying if I said it wasn't difficult. There were a couple of times when we even had to use the local leisure centre. Billy found it frustrating, as he wanted everything to be as professional as possible. But he also understood the financial limitations the club was working under."

A mounting injury crisis was also not helping, the problems becoming so acute that Bremner was forced to come out of retirement for the visit of Bournemouth on March 29. Without six first-choice players, he also named 16-year-old Ian Snodin on the bench. "I'd had a good first half of the season with the juniors in the Northern Intermediate League and scored a lot of goals," recalls the younger Snodin brother. "Billy had wanted to give me a taste of what it was like to be involved with the first-team and brought me into the squad for a game at Hereford in early January. I was only three months past my 16th birthday. I didn't play and wasn't on the bench, he just wanted me to get the experience because he felt my chance was going to come sooner rather than later." Snodin's debut duly came as a first-half substitute for the injured Bentley against Bournemouth. He recalls: "I came on after half an hour to play alongside Billy in central midfield. He talked me through the rest of the game and I loved every second. Basically, he told me where to go and when. It was a real eye-opener. After that, I was never out of the team."

A goal from Shaun Flanaghan was enough to clinch victory over Bournemouth on Bremner's return, though he was quick to stress afterwards that it had been a one-off. The Rovers manager proved to be as good as his word, watching the remaining nine games from the dugout as his players claimed three wins and four draws to secure a 12th place finish. It was progress, though Bremner admitted to the *Yorkshire Post* after the final day defeat to Port Vale: "The supporters have had a lot to put up with this year and deserve something special to remember." The stage was set for a concerted push for promotion.

Chapter 20

A Special Bond

'Behind every great man is a great woman,' was a phrase popularised by the feminist movement of the 1960s. Later, the Eurythmics would adopt the expression into the lyrics of their iconic top ten hit *Sisters Are Doin' It For Themselves*. Annie Lennox might not approve but, with a tweak, it is also possible for the words to suddenly take on a relevance to the football world. Behind every great manager is a great captain. Certainly, the Don Revie-Billy Bremner axis that drove Leeds United forward for more than a decade was a case of a manager achieving true greatness thanks, in part, to having a great captain. The duo were considered, by family and friends alike, as one, having formed an unbreakable bond when Bremner, as a callow youth, had roomed with senior pro Revie on the eve of his Leeds debut against Chelsea. Later, Bremner, who also babysat his manager's children, would become Revie's on-field lieutenant as United cut a swathe through English football. Revie had chosen wisely when selecting his captain, seeing in Bremner a kindred spirit who possessed an identical desire and will to win.

The bond created during 14 years together at Leeds was something Bremner continued to treasure long after Revie had left Elland Road. Now a manager himself, Bremner knew the importance of having his own on-field lieutenant if anything tangible was to be built at Doncaster Rovers. After 20 months in charge at Belle Vue, he had assembled a squad containing what he considered to be a nice balance of youth and experience. Progress, in terms of league position, had been made but now was the time to really push on. On taking the job, Bremner had set himself the target of winning promotion within three years. Anything less would have to be considered a failure. It meant, in the summer of 1980, the coming season had to end with a place in the top four. And in a teenager with just seven first team appearances under his belt, Bremner felt he had just the player to help make it happen.

Ian Snodin had stood out from the moment Bremner started attending the club's Northern Intermediate League fixtures on Saturday mornings. Then just 15, the young midfielder was clearly still growing but Bremner liked what he saw. Here, the Rovers manager felt, was someone who, with the right tutelage, could command and cajole his colleagues, just as Bremner had done with such distinction in the colours of Leeds and Scotland. A degree of patience would be required, but providing the youngster was given the right guidance there was every chance Rovers would soon have the talismanic figure their manager craved. Snodin junior may have been made to wait until his 16th birthday before signing as an apprentice, unlike his team-mate David Harle who had put pen to paper three weeks earlier despite being born on the same day. But Bremner clearly believed his protégé had what it took to make the grade, even going so far as to administer the dressing down of Ian's life in order to remind him of the sacrifices that had to be made in order to realise his dream of becoming a professional footballer. "Billy was always encouraging me and passing on advice," Ian remembers. "But there was one day when he absolutely ripped me apart. I was 16 and still playing for the youth team, who had a game on the Saturday morning. Despite that, I decided to spend the Friday night at the local youth club. I wasn't drinking, just playing pool. But my Dad was not happy and said, 'You should be staying in the night before a game'. I didn't agree and told him so. The following morning, unbeknown to me, my Dad rang Billy up – they had a close relationship as well – and told him what I had done. Anyway, that morning I scored in a 3-2 win over Hull and Billy asked me if I wanted to travel to the first team game at Bradford City with him. I thought, 'Brilliant, he must be really pleased with how I played'. I couldn't get changed quickly enough so we could set off. Unfortunately, it wasn't praise Billy wanted to give me but a huge telling-off. From the moment I sat down and closed the car door, Billy tore into me. It lasted the full hour it took to drive to Bradford. He really laid it on the line. But, by the time we got to Valley Parade, I had learned my lesson and I never went out again the night before a game."

Happy that the message had got through, Bremner continued to encourage the teenager. By the summer of 1980, he considered it a case of when and not if Snodin would become a mainstay of the side. His debut the previous March against Bournemouth had been followed by eight further appearances before the end of the campaign. Now, however, Ian had to build on that promising start. He recalls: "Division Four was a harsh place to play and I was still only nine stone. But Billy said, 'I believe in you – you're good enough, so that makes you old enough'. We had played together for the reserves a few times before I made my first-team debut and every time was an education. Basically, Billy taught me how to handle myself in a tough environment." Regular pep talks between manager and budding midfielder were something Revie had once done with an appreciative Bremner. Now, he was doing exactly the same. "I think Billy saw a bit of himself in me," says Ian. "It was almost like a fatherly interest that he took in me. To have someone like Billy Bremner doing that was amazing. Don't get me wrong, there were a few times when I didn't agree with what he was saying - most notably during games when I felt he was asking me to do too much. But I had total respect for Billy and would have done anything for him."

When the 1980-81 season began with a League Cup first round first leg tie at home to Mansfield Town, Ian was still a few days short of his 17th birthday. It meant he was watching from the stand as brother Glynn grabbed the headlines with a stunning 20-yard goal that gave Doncaster an early lead, which the Stags subsequently cancelled out. Rovers lost the second leg at Field Mill 2-1 but the consolation was taking a side who had been competing at a higher level the previous season to extra-time. By the end of the first week of the Division Four season, however, there were precious few crumbs of comfort to be had at Belle Vue. First, Port Vale had coasted to a comfortable 3-0 opening day victory in the Potteries. Rovers had then bounced back to beat Darlington 2-0 in midweek only for the following Saturday's meeting with Peterborough United to end in a 4-0 hammering, the club's worst defeat on home soil in four-and-a-half years. A furious Bremner's response was to turn to youth against Hartlepool United as Ian Snodin and Harle were drafted into the side. There was to be no fairytale ending, however, as the home side ran out 1-0 winners at the Victoria Ground. Rovers were second bottom with just two points from a possible eight. Bremner, though, refused to be downhearted as he set about keeping spirits up. "Billy really came into his own when we were up against it," recalls Dave Bentley, who by August, 1980, had been promoted to assistant manager following Cyril Knowles' decision to leave and join the Middlesbrough coaching staff. "His man-management skills were second to none. He had a real ability to get the lads up for games."

Bremner's motivational skills helped Rovers transform their season with a perfect September, winning all six games and scoring 13 goals in the process. A 1-0 triumph over Southend United was particularly enjoyable for Bremner, coming as it did against the early pace-setters who would, by May, be lifting the Fourth Division title. Suddenly, Doncaster were being talked about for all the right reasons. A crowd of 9,623, the club's biggest for a year, watched Lincoln City end the winning run but Rovers refused to be knocked off course. By Christmas, a first promotion in 12 years was on the cards. Belle Vue was a happy place to be, and Glynn Snodin insists the credit belonged to Bremner. "It probably took Billy 18 months to get things running how he wanted them," he says. "By then, the squad had evolved into a nice blend of youth and experience, while off the field the club were going about things much more professionally. Training had also evolved, with the emphasis being put on small-sided games and keeping possession. We were a lot fitter as a result, while probably the biggest transformation was the atmosphere around the club. Billy told me later in life that he had never forgotten what Don Revie had created at Leeds and how he had wanted the same thing for Doncaster. He wanted everyone to get on, to be a unit both on and off the field. Billy very much liked being one of the lads. He loved the banter and regaling all the lads with stories from his own playing career. We would all be sitting in this big communal bath after training, listening intently. No-one wanted to go home. Everyone loved the craic so much that the bath would have to keep being topped up with hot water so we could stay. They were brilliant days. Billy's ability to put a smile on everyone's face was something else. Even after a defeat – and, make no mistake, no-one hated losing more than Billy – he would be there in the dressing room with a smile on his own face, trying to get us going again."

Coping with defeat was something Bremner had to do only once in the first three months of 1981, Hartlepool United claiming a surprise 2-1 win at Belle Vue in early January. Otherwise, Doncaster enjoyed a profitable time with back-to-back draws at promotion rivals Lincoln City and Southend particularly impressive results. By now, Ian Snodin had become a mainstay of the side. "Billy's presence around the club was huge," recalls the midfielder who would make 32 appearances during the 1980-81 season. "When he walked into a room, it went quiet out of respect and his love of football shone through in everything he did. Some days, he would train with the first-team in the morning and then join in with the kids during the afternoon. I was still a young lad but could see how good the blend in the team was, with plenty of experience alongside us younger lads."

Rovers stumbled briefly during the run-in, a 2-0 reverse at Bury being followed by a one-goal defeat to promotion rivals Wimbledon at Plough Lane. The loss to the Dons had seen Bremner return to the side for the first time in five months as sweeper, injury having ruled out five of his key players. It was a rotten way to mark reaching the landmark of 650 League appearances, but the 651st four days later – as a 61st minute substitute -

proved a much happier affair as Stockport County were beaten 2-1. Rovers were almost there and, by now, attracting national interest. For the midweek home game with Bradford City, the cameras from ITV show *World of Sport* descended on Belle Vue to shadow Bremner for the day. Martin Tyler, now famous as the voice of Sky Sports' live football coverage, was the reporter charged with discovering the secret behind the revival of Doncaster Rovers. The cameras were allowed into the dressing room, giving fans a unique insight into an area that is usually off-limits. Those watching at home the following Saturday when Rovers were without a game saw Bremner being calmness personified as his players arrived at 6.30pm. His words as the team prepared to leave almost an hour later were succinct and to the point: "If you want to go up, you will go up. I believe in fate and our name is in the top four."

With Bradford languishing in mid-table, Rovers were strong favourites and they duly took the lead through a 25-yard shot from Steve Lister. At half-time, the cameras were back in the home dressing room. Once again, as the manager entered the room, the players fell silent. Bremner, in a clear attempt to defuse any tension, then wandered over to Glynn Snodin and quipped, 'Have you got your make-up on for the cameras, Snods?' Copying an old trick of Don Revie, Bremner spent the final few minutes of the interval massaging the legs of several players before the team were sent out with the clear message to finish Bradford off. Glynn Snodin duly did just that by netting the second goal of the game, though this was still not enough to prevent the full-back from being criticised post-match for not getting forward enough during the night. The *World of Sport* feature ended with footage of Bremner's wrecked V-reg Datsun, the Rovers manager having been involved in a road accident when travelling along Balby Road after the match. Happily, Tyler reported, the Rovers manager had walked away unscathed after losing control of his car.

The 2-0 win over Bradford meant Rovers needed just two points from their final two games to clinch a place in the top four. That target was subsequently cut in half four days later when their rivals dropped points and Doncaster were without a game. The prize was within touching distance, not that Bremner was going to let anyone think the job was done ahead of the penultimate game of the season at home to Bournemouth. The Cherries, whose last win at Belle Vue had been 22 years earlier, had nothing but pride to play for but Bremner was wary of complacency creeping in. He needn't have worried as a crowd of 11,373 roared Rovers to a 2-1 victory, Alan

Warboys and Ian Nimmo grabbing the all-important goals to get the party underway. Bremner saw promotion as reward for not only his players, but also all those fans who had stuck with the club throughout the lean years. A little over two and a half years earlier, 1,750 hardy souls had turned out in freezing conditions to watch his managerial bow against Rochdale. It represented quite a turnaround, and one that Billy was rightly lauded for bringing about. One man who was delighted by Doncaster's success was long-time friend, John Helm. "People often forget what a good job he did as a manager," says the football commentator. "Billy worked tremendously hard to be a success. In those first few seasons at Doncaster, it was clear to me where he was drawing inspiration from – Don Revie and, to a lesser extent, Jock Stein. Certainly, he saw a strong team spirit as vital. Billy also tried to emulate Don's style of play, making a point of building his defence around two big centre halves as had been the case at Leeds with Jack Charlton and Norman Hunter. Another trait he took from Don was the importance of developing his own players. Don't forget, Billy brought the two Snodin brothers through at Doncaster along with Dave Harle and Daral Pugh. He also seemed to treat Ian Snodin the same way Don had done with Billy 20 or so years earlier. It was almost a father-son relationship."

The scale of Rovers' achievement in finishing third was quickly underlined when Billy's name suddenly began being linked with other clubs. Chelsea, then struggling in the Second Division, were strongly rumoured to be interested after having dispensed with Geoff Hurst's services. Bradford City's name was another put forward in the Press as wanting to discuss their own vacancy but Bremner, showing the loyalty that had characterised his playing career, had no interest in leaving Doncaster. They had given him a chance when no-one else had and that faith deserved to be repaid. Not only that, but there was the challenge of stepping up to the Third Division to tackle head on. Bremner was also happy at the club, though the summer had not been without its worry due to a charge of drink-driving that hung over the Rovers manager. He had been arrested following a crash on the way home from a game towards the end of the season. Eventually, a date was set for the case to be heard at Doncaster Magistrates in November. Bremner, who had been twice the legal limit, admitted the charge and was banned from driving for 15 months. Bremner's remorse was clear, his solicitor Michael Sampson telling the court: 'He is extremely embarrassed to be here today. After the victory for Doncaster Rovers, he was relaxed, happy and unwinding. It went too far."

The charge may have been hanging over Bremner when the 1981-82 season kicked off but he was still excited about what lay ahead. Money would again be tight but the Rovers manager had faith in the players who had won promotion against all the odds. He was determined to give them a chance to impress at a higher level. Colin Douglas was signed from Celtic but, otherwise, there were no more new debutants when the season kicked off.

Some managers may have worried at the apparent lack of strengthening, but not Bremner. Not only were many of his younger players blossoming, but he also took heart from how the four clubs promoted from Division Four in May, 1980, had fared at a higher level with only Walsall finishing in the bottom half. And even then, the Saddlers had stayed up at the expense of Sheffield United. A similar outcome would please Bremner, though preferably without the last day drama that had seen the Blades slide into the basement division for the first time courtesy of Don Given missing a last-minute penalty against Walsall at Bramall Lane. Had he scored, United would have survived at the expense of the Midlands club.

One area Bremner was determined to tackle ahead of the new season was Ian Snodin's tendency to collect needless bookings. Ian recalls: "I had a fiery temper back then, which Billy didn't want me to lose. But he also thought I was talking myself into trouble. I was getting a few bookings for dissent and Billy wanted it to stop. He knew, better than anyone, bookings for a mis-timed tackle came with playing in midfield. But he hated silly bookings and wanted me to channel my competitive spirit better."

Kicking off the season with a 1-0 defeat at home to Reading came as a disappointment. But any fears that Doncaster might struggle on their return to the Third Division after a 10-year absence were soon dispelled. After claiming a battling 2-2 draw at Bristol City on the second Saturday of the League season, Doncaster embarked on a scintillating run of six straight league victories. With the Football League operating under a three points for a win rule for the first time, it meant Rovers were sitting second in the table. The thinking behind the change was that an extra point for a victory would encourage more attacking football, which the League believed would help bring back the legions of fans who were deserting the game. Doncaster may have not quite borne that out with five of those early season wins being by the narrowest of margins. Not that this was of any concern to Bremner, whose side by the end of September had gone 663 minutes without conceding a goal. Unsurprisingly, he was named Manager of the Month for a second time. A 1-0 defeat at Newport County ended both the proud defensive record and the winning run, but Doncaster's response suggested back-to-back promotions might not necessarily be out of the question. Not only were Lincoln City hit for four goals at Belle Vue but, after claiming a point from a 2-2 draw at Swindon Town, Bremner's side went and repeated the trick as Bristol Rovers were thrashed 4-2. It meant October ended with Rovers sitting proudly on top of the Third Division with 26 points from 12 games, a mightily impressive return for a newly-promoted club. Glynn Snodin, by then Doncaster's longest-serving player despite only being 21, recalls: "We absolutely flew out of the blocks in the season after we had been promoted from the Fourth Division. Billy hadn't been able to spend much during the summer but the lads were full of confidence and it showed in how we played. Billy had told us how confident he was that we could do well in the division above but I think even he was surprised by how well we started. For a time, we felt unbeatable."

Unfortunately for Rovers, the adage about pride coming before a fall soon started to ring true at Belle Vue as a 2-0 defeat at Carlisle United on November 3 kick-started a collapse in form. Three further defeats followed during the month and it would be mid-February before Doncaster next won a league game. The nadir came on January 29 when bottom club Wimbledon triumphed 3-1 at Belle Vue. For Glynn Snodin, it was a difficult time. "It was amazing how quickly everything changed," he says. "After such a good start, we simply fell apart. Maybe we got complacent or maybe we just didn't have the strength in depth, I'm not sure. But, either way, to go so long without a win was awful and really rocked the lads, especially the younger ones."

A 2-1 defeat at Exeter City just a week after the demoralising loss to Wimbledon meant Doncaster had claimed a paltry three points from 11 games and slumped to 18th in the table. From being promotion hopefuls, Bremner's side now had all on to avoid relegation. Possible salvation arrived at Belle Vue in the form of Chester, who were rock bottom of the division and enduring a miserable campaign. A 4-3 home win ensued, though not without a few scares along the way with Rovers needing a late scrambled winner by Daral Pugh to secure the points. That first win might have been a nervy affair, but it meant the revival was under way - albeit with a couple of setbacks away from home as the visit to Lincoln City ended in a 5-0 defeat and both Oxford United and Fulham claimed comfortable 3-1 wins at Doncaster's expense. Otherwise, though, the run-in proved rewarding with the unhappy trips to the Manor Ground and Craven Cottage the club's only defeats in the final 14 games. Survival was secured with a game to spare as Walsall were held to a goalless draw at Fellows Park. Rovers eventually finished 19th with 56 points – three clear of Wimbledon in the final relegation place. To many clubs, such a finish after being top at the start of November would have been a disappointment. But to Doncaster, whose resources were dwarfed by nearly all their rivals, sixth bottom and survival represented progress. For the fourth consecutive season under Bremner, Rovers had finished in a higher league position. More pleasingly, however, were the strides being made by his promising band of youngsters. Chief among the manager's reasons for cheer as the summer got under way was how Ian Snodin had adapted to the captaincy. Like Revie with him in the 1960s, Bremner had marked Snodin down as a potential leader very early on. The chance to put his plan into action came courtesy of skipper Alan Warboys being absent from the side through injury, as Ian recalls: "To say it came out of the blue to me would be an understatement. I was still only 18 and just preparing, as normal, for the game. I was actually in the Boot Room when Billy called all the lads together at 1.45pm. That was when he named the team, and right at the start he said, 'Captain today is Ian Snodin'. I couldn't believe I had heard him right, the news really took me back. I knew Alan was out but I never imagined I would be named captain." The elevation to the captaincy had come during a season when the younger Snodin made 33 appearances and scored two goals. He had also won international recognition after being called up to play for the England Youth side in February, something that made his manager immensely proud. "The game was against Scotland at Ibrox and Billy insisted on driving me up to Glasgow," Ian recalls about a game the Scots won 1-0 courtesy of a goal from his future Doncaster team-mate Jim Dobbin. "I ended up having a good game and, by all accounts, Billy was really proud afterwards. He was saying things like, 'Paul McStay is the best Scotland have got and yet my boy from Doncaster played him off the park'. It was a similar story when I first got called up by the Under-21s a couple of years later, especially as most of the other players were from clubs like Everton, Chelsea and Arsenal."

Doncaster had made great strides under Bremner so, as the 1982-83 season got under way, the target was to maintain that progress by finishing higher than 19th. Doing so would not be easy, especially considering the strength of the clubs who had just been promoted from the Fourth Division. Champions Sheffield United's huge potential, for instance, had been underlined by a crowd of almost 24,000 fans for their final home game in May. Bradford City, who had finished as runners-up to the Blades, had also been built into a promising side by Roy McFarland, who had successfully combined the youth and exuberance of Stuart McCall and Peter Jackson with experienced older heads such as Bobby Campbell. Not only that, former England international Trevor Cherry had joined the Bantams from Bremner's old club Leeds earlier in the summer. Throw in ambitious Wigan Athletic, elected to the Football League just five years earlier, and it was clear the new boys would make the Third Division a fiercely competitive competition. Bremner, though, was not one to shirk a challenge and was determined to once again triumph against the odds. Unfortunately, the season turned out to be a nightmare.

A goalless draw at home to Newport County on the opening day was followed by defeats at Bristol Rovers and Oxford United that yielded no goals and saw Rovers goalkeeper Dennis Peacock forced to pick the ball out of his own net five times. Shocking away form would characterise the entire season, Bremner's side not claiming a point from any of their first eight games on the road. At Belle Vue, the fans were initially treated to much more thrilling fare with the four games that followed the Newport stalemate seeing a phenomenal 36 goals scored. First, three goals in the opening six minutes helped Rovers to a 6-1 thrashing of Exeter City as Bremner's side escaped the bottom four. A fortnight later, a truly remarkable game with Reading ended 7-5 in Doncaster's favour. Future Rovers manager Kerry Dixon, who was on the losing side despite netting four goals for the Royals, and Glynn Snodin both hit first-half hat-tricks as the lead changed hands so many times it was difficult for the 3,118 crowd, the club's lowest for two years, to keep track. Rovers briefly rose to 13th following the goalfest against Reading but were soon back in the relegation zone courtesy of a 6-3 hammering at home by Wigan as both Snodin brothers got their names on the scoresheet. Bremner's response when speaking to the *Yorkshire Post* was to liken the amazing sequence of results to a tennis match, adding: 'It's been 6-1, 7-5, 3-6 but we hope to have a few aces left.' With Brentford the next side due to visit Belle Vue, the Doncaster supporters presumed a sense of normality would have to return only to be proved wrong again as the two sides fought out a thrilling 4-4 draw. Yet another defensive horror show had left Bremner frustrated, the only bright spot being that the point was enough to lift Rovers off the foot of the table. Perhaps inevitably, the rest of the campaign was always going to be something of a damp squib in comparison to that crazy run of goals. No-one quite realised, though, as Autumn turned to Winter just how desperate the season would become with Rovers claiming just seven more wins from the remaining 36 games. A 3-0 triumph at Wigan in January, when Glynn Snodin netted twice and Ian once was a rare highlight, while the low point came on the final day when just 1,507 fans turned out to watch Walsall win 3-1 at Belle Vue. A small consolation was that Rovers had, at least, found the net – something that had proved beyond them in six of their previous seven outings. Only Chesterfield finished the campaign with a lower points tally than Doncaster's 38. Relegation was a bitter blow but any thoughts Bremner may walk away were soon dispelled, as Dave Bentley recalls: "Billy was determined to bounce back straight away. He was not one for feeling sorry for himself and he wouldn't let anyone else at the club fall into that trap."

Chapter 21

Bouncing Back

As the people of Doncaster sweltered during the summer heatwave of 1983, few realised the stormy times that lay ahead. In common with the rest of the country, the town had suffered during the recession that eventually saw unemployment peak above 3 million. But Doncaster and its surrounding villages seemed to be suffering no more than anywhere else. There was, though, a concern about how the recession had impacted on the demand for coal. The lifeblood of the local economy, coal had been king in this part of south Yorkshire since the turn of the century. Blessed with being situated above one of England's largest natural seams, Doncaster's economy had benefited from the two national strikes of 1972 and 1974 catapulting the miners up the pay league. More money in miners' wage packets meant more money in the tills of local businesses. The upshot was the area being, largely, protected from the worst of the recession – even allowing for the concerns about the impact a drop in demand for coal may have in the long-term. Life, at least in relation to the rest of the country, was good. Within a year, however, any semblance of normality had been blown away by the start of one of the most brutal and bitter industrial disputes Britain has ever seen.

The miners' strike would bring great hardship and leave a legacy of social devastation that is still being felt today, more than a quarter of a century on. Few businesses would prove to be immune from the fallout, including the local professional sports clubs as a year without pay meant that trips to watch either Doncaster Rovers or the local rugby league team at Tattersfield became a luxury many could no longer afford. Only success on the field would be enough to keep crowds up at a respectable level. For Rovers, this would mean bouncing back at the first attempt after being relegated to the Fourth Division courtesy of a wretched 1982-83 season. By the time the strike had been called on March 12, 1984, Billy Bremner's side were well on their way to doing just that.

The summer following Doncaster's 23rd place finish in the Third Division had been a long one for Bremner. Failure never sat comfortably with one of football's most renowned competitors and he was determined to make amends. Money may have again been in short supply but Bremner had still managed to add five new faces by the time Rovers hosted Wrexham on the opening day of the new Football League season. Thirty-three-year-old striker Ernie Moss had carved out a decent career in the lower leagues, most notably with hometown club, Chesterfield, where his eight seasons had yielded more than 100 goals. Moss was joined at Belle Vue by Andy Kowalski and John Breckin, both 30, and 32-year-old central defender Bill Green. Completing the quintet of summer arrivals was Mark Miller, a 21-year-old capture from Gillingham. Dave Bentley, Bremner's assistant, recalls: "Billy had a good look at the situation during the summer and realised we needed some more experience. Ernie Moss was a big signing, he was exactly what we needed. He'd also had a long career and wanted a new challenge. I also thought Bill Green was an important addition."

Green was the only one of the new signings not to face Wrexham on the opening day, the defender from Chesterfield having to serve a one-game ban. Instead, he watched from the main stand at Belle Vue as Rovers coasted to a 3-0 win. Moss was among the goals on his debut, just as he was in each of Doncaster's opening five games as a creditable draw at Third Division Scunthorpe United in the League Cup was followed by wins over Mansfield Town and Hereford United plus a 3-2 defeat at Reading. The home game against Hereford had been moved to the Sunday to avoid a clash with Doncaster's St Leger race meeting and Rovers' display in a 3-0 win suggested they had the quality to go the distance. Doncaster were top of Division Four on goal difference from York City but, by the time the two White Rose clubs met at Belle Vue towards the end of September, the Minstermen had replaced Rovers at the summit. Goals from Keith Walwyn and John Byrne suggested York's lead would be extended only for Bremner's side to hit back as Moss netted his seventh goal of the season and Colin Douglas clinched a point with a deserved equaliser in front of 4,996 fans. Doncaster slumped to a 4-1 defeat at Torquay United in their next game but any fears the season may go off the rails were swept away by the subsequent run that brought just one further league defeat before the end of the year. That solitary reverse came on December 3 at Swindon Town, the afternoon ending with Bremner venting his frustration over referee Les Burden's handling of the game. The Rovers manager was, along with assistant Dave Bentley, subsequently charged with using foul and abusive language. The pair were found guilty and fined £500 and £100 respectively. That aside, the Rovers management team had every right to be happy come the halfway stage of the season as a thrilling 3-3 draw at Rochdale on January 2 meant their side were sitting second with 41 points, eight behind leaders York. That lead was subsequently cut to five points when Mansfield Town were beaten 3-1 at Belle Vue the following Saturday, in the process making it 12 games unbeaten on home soil – Rovers' best start in 34 years. Bremner was understandably delighted with the form his side were showing, though ever the hard taskmaster, he wanted more. Namely, the Fourth Division championship as the Doncaster players were told the target was to overhaul York at the top of the table. It was a tall order, especially as Denis Smith's side had been at the summit for all but three weeks of the season. Not only that, but, in Walwyn and John Byrne, York boasted a strike-force who had already bagged 32 goals between them.

Undeterred, Doncaster continued the chase with the win over Mansfield that had so pleased Bremner followed by a further six triumphs and three draws from the next nine outings. Unfortunately for Rovers, York's form was proving equally durable. So much so, in fact, that Doncaster still trailed York by a point after beating third placed Bristol City on March 6. Tellingly, however, the gap to the Robins had widened to 11 points. There was also good news off the field for Rovers fans after it was announced that Bremner and Bentley had signed new three-year contracts. It was a sign of faith not only from the club but also the manager, who revealed to the *Yorkshire Post* after agreeing the extension that his initial plan at the start of the season had been to win promotion and then leave. The struggles of the previous two seasons in Division Three had shown Bremner that an injection of cash would be needed to make an impact. With none seemingly on the horizon, he felt the time would be right to go once promotion had been achieved. What changed Bremner's mind was local businessman Peter Wetzel agreeing to join the board. His arrival meant money was now available for team strengthening, something of a novelty for Bremner after five and a half years in charge. The first notable signing came a week before the transfer deadline as John Philliben became the club's record signing after joining from Stirling Albion for £60,000. The defender had, along with the likes of Pat Nevin and Paul McStay, been part of the victorious Scotland side at the 1982 European Under-19 Championship. He had also enjoyed an impressive season at the heart of the Stirling defence in the Scottish Second Division. Twenty four hours later, Bremner again launched a successful raid north of the border as 22-year-old Jim Dobbin agreed to sign from Celtic. Another member of the successful Scottish youth side from two years earlier, he had been earmarked by manager Billy McNeill for good things at Celtic. Unfortunately,

McNeill's departure to Manchester City and replacement by David Hay had seen Dobbin fall out of favour at Parkhead, a short loan switch to Motherwell preceding the move south to Doncaster for £25,000. Bremner was delighted by the two signings, though Dobbin admits to being rather taken aback by his prospective new manager's comments at their initial talks. "Billy was a massive Celtic fan," he recalls, "and his first question to me was, 'Why are you thinking of leaving such a fantastic club?' I was a bit surprised, I thought he should be trying to persuade me to sign for Doncaster not stay at Celtic. But maybe he was just checking me out. I told Billy I was at the age where I wanted to be playing every week and he accepted that. Billy then told me that a money man called Peter Wetzel had joined the board and that the spending would not end with me and John Philliben. Doncaster seemed an ambitious club, so that along with the appeal of playing for one of Scotland's all-time greats in Billy Bremner meant I agreed to sign." An ability to talk prospective signings into joining had paid off again, something Dave Bentley recalls as being a regular occurrence. "Doncaster wasn't an easy sell back then," he says. "Billy was so well respected in the game and his name was often all we had. At times, he had to really work on a signing. But, fair play to him, his words usually did the trick."

Bremner made one more signing before the deadline, Alan Brown coming in from Shrewsbury Town for £35,000. It meant, for an outlay of around £120,000, he had strengthened the defence, midfield and attack ahead of the all-important run-in. The trio featured for the first time together at home to Peterborough United on March 17, five days after National Union of Mineworkers president Arthur Scargill had called the national strike that would have such devastating consequences for south Yorkshire. At that stage, no-one quite knew how long the miners would be out and Dobbin admits he had his own reasons for being uncertain in the wake of the 1-1 draw against Peterborough. He says: "It was a bit of a culture shock after being at Celtic, where I had been playing in Europe. The standard of the Doncaster lads was something that did surprise me, there were some quality players at the club. But a few of the other teams were not the best. Some of those early games were absolutely dire and not much fun to play in." The draw against Peterborough had seen visiting goalkeeper David Seaman produce an outstanding display to frustrate Rovers, who rescued a point in stoppage time through Douglas. There were, however, to be no such excuses in the two games that followed as Burnley triumphed 3-1 in the newly-introduced Associate Members Cup and Aldershot claimed a 2-1 league win at the

Recreation Ground. Doncaster's hopes of lifting the title were fading fast, something that wasn't helped on the first Saturday of April by a flu bug leading to the postponement of the game at home to Reading. York duly claimed a sixth straight win. The gap between Rovers, who through their inactivity had slipped to third, and the leaders now stood at an insurmountable 15 points. Bremner knew any hope of winning the title had all but gone, but was still determined to slow the leaders' progress when Rovers travelled to Bootham Crescent for a contest that attracted a crowd of 11,297 – a figure that would only be beaten in the basement division that season by the 12,786 who saw Bristol City clinch promotion with a home win over Swindon Town in May. The bumper gate witnessed an absorbing contest that could have gone either way as Rovers goalkeeper Dennis Peacock saved a penalty and a strike by Glynn Snodin cancelled out Gary Ford's first half goal in a 1-1 draw. Jim Dobbin recalls: "York were a good side, with John Byrne their real danger man. When I arrived, there were around a dozen games left and York had pulled away from us a little bit. Unfortunately, they finished strongly and really got away from us by the end to be worthy champions. We did play well at York, though."

York's own promotion was duly sealed with an impressive five games to spare when Halifax Town lost 4-1 at Bootham Crescent on Friday April 20. The following day, Rovers were looking to strengthen their own push for Division Three with three points from the trip to Northampton Town. Any hopes the visit to a club sitting 17th in the table would be plain sailing were, however, dispelled around 45 miles short of the County Ground as the team bus broke down. Jim Dobbin recalls: "These were the days before overnight stays became the norm for clubs so we would just travel on the day. We were going along nicely when, suddenly, the bus developed a problem and the driver had to pull over. It soon became clear we wouldn't be going anywhere else on that bus." With the coach filling with fumes, Bremner ushered his players off and then told them to get changed as he looked for an alternative means of transport. In the end, a plan was hatched whereby supporters driving past in their cars would be flagged down and asked to give a couple of players a lift. "It was the only solution," says Dobbin. "Funnily enough, the guy who gave me a lift in his car now works in the press room at Doncaster's new ground. He is called Alan Smith and we still have a laugh about it whenever we meet up."

Making the final leg of the journey by a fleet of private cars meant Rovers arrived late at Northampton, leading to kick-off being delayed by 11 minutes.

Any fears Rovers would be caught cold by the unusual travel plans were, though, swept away as goals from David Harle, Glynn Snodin and Dobbin put the visitors 3-0 ahead inside 28 minutes. Colin Douglas added a fourth after half-time to leave Bremner delighted as the squad made the return trip north on a new coach. Dobbin recalls: "Getting changed on the hard shoulder and travelling in supporters cars wasn't ideal preparation, but it made no difference. Billy even joked afterwards that maybe we should thumb it to games more often."

Rovers were almost there, though much to Bremner's frustration back-to-back defeats against Chester City and Reading saw his side slip to third. What he found particularly hard to stomach was that Chester were bottom of the league and before that 1-0 victory at Sealand Road had won just six games all season. The loss to Reading also brought an end to Doncaster's proud unbeaten home record, leaving the club needing six points from the final four games to guarantee promotion. Three of those came courtesy of a 2-0 home win over Rochdale as results elsewhere saw Rovers' requirement to clinch a place in next season's Division Three reduced to a solitary point. Hundreds of fans headed from Doncaster to Stockport's Edgeley Park two days later in confident mood and their optimism was rewarded as a goal apiece for Moss and Ian Snodin ensured County were beaten 2-0. Runners-up spot was then clinched with a 1-0 win over Crewe Alexandra, meaning a shock defeat to second bottom Hartlepool United at Belle Vue in the final game of the season mattered little. Rovers had finished the season on 85 points, 16 behind champions York but 10 clear of fifth-placed Aldershot. Reading and Bristol City completed the top four. An illustration of the team effort that had brought a second promotion success under Bremner came in the goalscoring charts as Moss and Douglas netted 15 apiece in the league, closely followed by the Snodin brothers as Glynn scored 13 and Ian nine. In contrast, Reading had been so indebted to Trevor Senior's 36 strikes that only one other player, Lawrie Sanchez, reached double figures with ten. Similarly, Keith Walwyn and John Byrne dominated for York with 27 and 25 goals respectively. Assistant manager Dave Bentley recalls: "Those lads were a team in every sense of the word. Ernie Moss's experience was important, while the two Snodins were outstanding. Ian got the headlines but Glynn scored a lot of goals from left-back that year, which is something a lot of people tend to forget. We had tried Glynn further forward in the early days but he wasn't as effective. Billy felt he was better at left-back because from that position he was able to see the whole picture." Glynn, who the following season would go on to be even more prolific from left-back and finish as Doncaster's top scorer, admits to relishing the freedom that came with playing under Bremner. "Billy was great with advice," he says. "But he also used to say to me, 'My brain will be different to you, Snods, because we play in different positions'. He hadn't played out wide so he would say, 'You make the decisions, and if you make the right ones you will be fine – and if you make the wrong decisions then you will know why you are out of the side'. It was simple stuff, but spot on."

Engendering a strong team spirit could not guarantee success. But it could, according to Bremner, go a long way and those involved in the promotion success of 1983-84 are in no doubt as to how vital the atmosphere created by the manager had been. Ian Snodin recalls: "I would have run through walls for Billy Bremner, all the lads would. He had this amazing ability to create a bond between team-mates. I imagine it was a lesson he had learned at Leeds. The team spirit we had at Doncaster was second to none. Billy made sure the blend was right between experience and youth, between the lads from Scotland and those of us from England. It made Doncaster a great club to be part of and why we all looked forward to going to work every morning. The thing with Billy was that all the lads knew he would never ask anyone to do anything he wouldn't do himself. He was always one to muck in and help out." Dave Bentley agrees, adding: "There was one time when it had been snowing heavily and the pitch at Belle Vue was covered. We needed to get the game on, so Billy jumped in his big Toyota Crown car and drove straight on to the pitch to act as a snowplough. It worked, too."

Even those who had only been at Belle Vue a few months by the summer of 1984 could see that Bremner had created something special at the club. Jim Dobbin says: "The team spirit was second to none, so much so we all still turn out today for dinners and reunions. There was nothing fancy about Billy, either as a man or a coach, and he was great to be around. He had been my hero as a boy but there were no airs or graces about him. Kenny Dalglish was the same at Celtic. Billy was also someone who did not bear a grudge. There were some games when he and our goalkeeper Dennis Peacock would have some almighty fall-outs at half-time or after a game. But, because both of them were smokers, the next minute Billy would be offering Dennis a fag and they would be puffing away like nothing had happened. Billy put a lot of effort into getting the right atmosphere. He would have the lads playing bingo on the coach, which is something he had enjoyed at Leeds."

With a return to the Third Division secured, Bremner's thoughts turned to strengthening his squad. Aiden Butterworth was the first to arrive that summer, Bremner tempting him back to football after the former Leeds United striker had grown disillusioned with the game. There was a complication that Butterworth had just started an art course at Leeds Carnegie College and was unable to train with Rovers throughout the week. Bremner, though, was comfortable with the arrangement. He also added Patrick Thistle winger John Buckley to his squad in a £35,000 deal, the Rovers manager's persuasive skills again being a major factor in a transfer target turning down offers from elsewhere. Buckley says: "I already knew Jim Dobbin and John Philliben, who both said it was a good club. But it was Billy who made my mind up within five minutes of meeting him at a Doncaster hotel. His enthusiasm was infectious, while he also said, 'You won't have to worry about defending, I have other people to do that – I want you to attack'. It was music to my ears. What also helped on that initial visit was the fuss Billy made over my Dad, who was basically in awe of this Scottish footballing hero."

Perhaps Bremner's best piece of summer business, however, was keeping hold of Ian Snodin. In Doncaster's promotion success, the midfielder had been watched by scouts from Nottingham Forest, Manchester United and Liverpool. Bremner had admitted to the *Yorkshire Post* shortly after promotion had been clinched that Snodin may be on the move, adding: 'He is probably the best player I have ever seen at his age. I don't want to lose him but he is ambitious and you can't really stand in his way.' By the time the season kicked off almost three months later, though, Snodin was still at Belle Vue and, along with Bremner's two summer signings, part of the side to face Preston North End on the opening day.

The day ended in a disappointing 2-0 defeat but any doubts Rovers may struggle again at a higher level were dispelled by a trio of straight wins. The most notable triumph came at Elm Park where Reading's 33-game unbeaten home run – the longest in the Football League – came to an end courtesy of a 4-1 thrashing. Butterworth missed the win over the Royals but was back in situ a fortnight later to net his first Rovers goal as Bournemouth were beaten 3-1. Two goals from Glynn Snodin then made it five wins from the opening seven games as Bolton Wanderers became the latest side to succumb to the attack-minded newly-promoted club. With Doncaster sitting fourth in the table, excitement was mounting in the town ahead of a first derby meeting with Rotherham United in a decade. Much to Bremner's frustration, however, the club's first five-figure crowd in three years could not inspire his players as the Millers triumphed 1-0. A fortnight later, Buckley's first goal for the club helped seal a 3-2 win over Cambridge United that was followed by a 4-3 win over Plymouth Argyle. Rovers were back up to fifth in the table and harbouring hopes of a second successive promotion success, a feeling further fuelled by a 4-1 thrashing of Swansea City on November 24. Buckley was again on the scoresheet in the victory over the Swans and was relishing every minute in Yorkshire. "Belle Vue might have been a bit of a culture shock after having been at Celtic," he admits. "But playing for Billy was great. He was not a great coach, but he more than made up for it by how he could send us out before a game believing anything was possible. We went out expecting to beat the opposition, it was a knack Billy had of saying the right things. I was definitely not a player who kicked anyone in my career, but if Billy had asked me to then I would have done it. The trust that Billy showed in us all probably made me feel like that. Often, when I went home to Scotland for a couple of days, Billy would lend me his car because I didn't have transport. When someone is willing to show such faith, it makes you want to run that extra mile for him."

One other major attraction for a skilful player such as Buckley was the pitch. Belle Vue may have seen better days as a venue to watch football but the playing surface had always been admired. In the early 1970s, Wembley Stadium's owners had offered the club over £10,000 for the turf. Knowing that the top surface was only so impressive because of the drainage underneath, Rovers refused but it illustrated the reputation the pitch enjoyed. Little had changed a decade or so later, as Buckley discovered during those first few months in Yorkshire. He says: "The pitch was one of the widest around, which was great for me, and also in superb condition. It was lovely to play on."

Despite the quality of the turf suiting the attacking style preferred by Bremner, Rovers were unable to build on the November win over the Swans with the next four games yielding just one point. Buckley says: "On our day, we were as good as anyone. But the problem was we didn't really have the strength in depth to cope with a few injuries. We had been up there in my early days at Doncaster and I really thought promotion might be on but our results suffered as the injuries came along. It was a real shame as that was a very good team." Despite the dip in results during early December, the Doncaster players continued to relish life under their manager. Jim Dobbin recalls: "Football was a very simple game to Billy, so we didn't spend a lot of time looking at the opposition or anything like that. He just wanted us to go out and play our game. Allan Clarke was the same when I played for him at Barnsley. I suppose when you are as good a player as those two were, they didn't feel the need to coach. It was the little things that made Billy special, knowing when to have a laugh with the lads and when to keep us in check. At the right time, he really did enjoy a practical joke, with our kit man Eric Brailsford coming in for a lot of stick. Eric loved it, too, because he knew it was good-natured." Bremner's mischievous sense of fun had been legendary at Leeds, though one Rovers player who may not have found it overly-amusing after one particular trip to the West Country was John Philliben. John Buckley recalls: "There was one game at Bristol Rovers a few months after I joined when we had got a good result. We got back into the dressing room and Billy was already in the giant communal bath with a smile on his face about the result. John Philliben was the first to jump straight in but the water was just too hot. He got out and his skin just started blistering. Billy was killing himself laughing, it turned out he could sit in scalding water and not feel a thing. I suppose we should have known from his own career that Billy had a high pain threshold."

Rising temperatures were not just confined to the dressing room bath for Doncaster as tempers boiled over during the Boxing Day trip to Third Division leaders Bradford City. Stuart McCall, then a young midfielder with the Bantams, recalls: "We had some huge battles with Doncaster. I am not sure why there was a bit of an edge to games, but there definitely was. Ian Snodin and myself would come off the pitch black and blue afterwards. Ian was always fired up, and I put a lot of that down to Billy Bremner being his manager. He was a winner and demanded total commitment from his players." Total commitment was, indeed, what Bremner got at Valley Parade on Boxing Day, 1984, as Rovers overcame having David Harle and Aiden Butterworth sent off in a contest that simmered with violence to win 1-0. Glynn Snodin netted the only goal, though Doncaster were equally indebted to two late saves from Dennis Peacock when reduced to nine men. Bradford, destined to be champions come May, remained four points clear at the top, while Doncaster were down in mid-table but, to Bremner, the win at Valley Parade showed the heights his side were capable of reaching. Inconsistency, brought on by having a small squad, was still a problem but early in the New Year the wider public were given a demonstration as to just how impressive a team Bremner had put together.

The FA Cup had, in recent years, hardly been a successful competition for Doncaster. Just one appearance in the fourth round, achieved under Bremner four seasons earlier, in 29 years told its own miserable story. Even allowing for the improvements Bremner had made to his squad over the past year, few fans were expecting much of an improvement when Rovers were handed a trip to Rochdale in the first round – especially as, in 12 visits since 1966, the Lancashire club had beaten Doncaster nine times and drawn the other three. David Harle's dismissal for what the referee adjudged to be a rugby tackle hardly helped matters but Rovers claimed a 2-1 win to earn a second round trip to Altrincham, the non-League side being beaten 3-1. The reward was a home tie against Queens Park Rangers, who when they arrived at Belle Vue in the second week of January were sitting 14th in the top flight and fresh from beating West Ham at Upton Park. Rovers were 43 places lower in the Football League and few expected an upset, especially after Oldham Athletic had refused Bremner permission to play loanee Derrick Parker. It meant a recall for Butterworth, whose arm had been in a plaster cast until 24 hours before the Cup tie in an attempt to heal a flaked bone. Crucially, however, the view that all the Londoners had to do to progress was to turn up was not one shared by the Rovers dressing room. Glynn Snodin recalls: "Billy was at his best when we were underdogs. He was great at firing us all up, while he also knew how to get the best out of individuals. Some lads would go into their shell if he got in their face, so he treated everyone differently. Billy could also read a game; he knew within the first 10 minutes whether a player was up for it or on top of his game. It was a skill he had."

What Bremner saw in those opening 10 minutes against Rangers delighted him. Not only did his players not let the First Division side settle, they had also caused their defence several problems. At half-time, Bremner repeated the message that QPR could be beaten if Rovers maintained their level of performance. Buoyed by their manager's words, the home team continued to press and the reward came 12 minutes from time when Harle struck a sweet left-foot shot into the net from 20 yards after Terry Fenwick had only partially cleared Ian Snodin's free-kick. Cue bedlam all around Belle Vue with one delighted fan even dancing a celebratory jig on the roof of the visitors' dugout. If Rangers manager Frank Sibley didn't think his world had caved in at that stage, he did when the final whistle blew after an agonising few minutes of stoppage time as thousands of overjoyed Rovers fans poured on to the pitch. John Buckley recalls: "So many came on that it took me a full 40 minutes to get off the pitch. It was a really special moment, and one we fully deserved. We didn't just beat QPR that day, we absolutely annihilated them. They were a good top flight team but we took them apart, there is no other way of describing it. I remember finally getting off the pitch and seeing Billy in the dressing room. He was absolutely made up. He loved it when we played well and we certainly did that day."

As the celebrations continued well into the night, the talk across Doncaster was dominated by who Rovers might draw in the next round. A big club at home was the popular choice, followed by a visit to one of English football's famous old grounds. In the end, it was the latter as Bremner's side were handed a fourth round trip to Everton. The draw was tough, not only were Everton the FA Cup holders but they were also sitting on top of the First Division. To add to the intrigue for Bremner, he had just watched Everton knock his old club Leeds United out in the third round – the game having been moved to the Friday to be shown live on television. Cup fever soon swept Doncaster with 5,000 tickets sold within 24 hours of going on sale. Everyone, it seemed, wanted to be at Goodison Park to see if Rovers could upset the odds once again. Before then, however, Doncaster had a league game at Reading and an Associate Members Cup tie against York City to negotiate. The trip to Elm Park was particularly important in that it would see both Ian Snodin and Butterworth serve the second of a two-game ban, ensuring the pair would be available for the Cup. The game went ahead, though only after an inspection as snow and ice wreaked havoc on the Football League programme. Only 10 matches survived, Reading's reward for beating the weather being a 4-0 victory. Bremner declared himself 'appalled' by his side's display and stressed places in the team to face Everton were by no means secure. The following Tuesday's goalless draw with York, watched by just 1,892 fans, was the ultimate non-event as it seemed both sides had their minds on the Cup – the Minstermen being due to host Arsenal as Rovers travelled to Merseyside.

All thoughts of such a damp squib were soon forgotten, though, as the countdown continued towards the trip to Goodison Park. Almost 10,000 fans were making what promised to be a memorable trip. Bremner, who had enjoyed many tussles with Everton as a player, was determined Rovers would make their mark and sprung something of a surprise by naming Ian Snodin as sweeper. Full-backs Glynn Snodin and Billy Russell were also instructed to get forward as much as possible to try and keep Trevor Steven and Kevin Sheedy busy. The tactics worked well as Everton were given a much sterner test than many in the near 40,000 crowd had been expecting.

In the end, the difference between the two sides was their finishing with Rovers missing several chances but both Trevor Steven and Gary Stevens finding the net during the first half to seal a 2-0 win to keep Everton on course for a second Cup final in as many seasons. Doncaster deservedly drew plenty of plaudits for their performance against a team who would also win the European Cup Winners' Cup later that season. Jim Dobbin recalls: "I had missed the win over QPR so was determined to enjoy the game at Everton. It was a fantastic occasion. Everton were a special team. Because there was no squad rotation in those days, they had all the big guns playing such as Andy Gray up front and Peter Reid in midfield alongside Paul Bracewell. We played really well, especially Ian Snodin at sweeper. I am sure that afternoon helped get Ian his move to Everton a few years later."

After basking in the glow of such an impressive performance, an inevitable sense of anti-climax accompanied the return to League action. Rovers were sitting 14th in the table as the team coach left Merseyside, the position they would still be occupying come the final day of the season ahead of the visit to Gillingham. By now, the miners' strike that had dominated much of 1984 and the early months of 1985 in south Yorkshire had been over for a couple of months. The impact for the mining industry was clear for all to see as pits closed and communities struggled. In contrast, Rovers' prospects looked bright with unmistakeable progress made during the season. Bremner's hope as he headed south towards Kent on the morning of May 11 was that some wise transfer investment during the summer could make promotion a realistic target come the new campaign. Unfortunately, tragic events that were about to unfold 200 miles away meant the priority for Rovers during the summer would instead be keeping Belle Vue open.

Chapter 22

Going Home

The cruel irony of the Bradford fire that claimed 56 lives was lost on no-one, least of all City chairman Stafford Heginbotham. 'Just 90 more minutes,' lamented the shell-shocked Heginbotham in the immediate aftermath of the Valley Parade disaster that claimed 56 lives, 'and that stand would have done its stint.' Less than 48 hours after the final game of the 1984-85 season against Lincoln City, the all-wooden main stand that had stood down one touchline of City's home for 77 years was due to be dismantled. The reason was simple – Bradford had just clinched promotion to the Second Division so Valley Parade would now have to comply with modern safety standards, namely the Safety and Sports Grounds Act (1975). Previously, City, in common with all Third and Fourth Division clubs, had been exempt from the legislation that had been introduced in the wake of the Ibrox disaster of January, 1971, that saw 66 people lose their lives at the end of Glasgow's Old Firm derby between Rangers and Celtic. The reason for this was money, clubs in the lower divisions successfully arguing that the cost would simply be too burdensome. Such short-sighted thinking would lead directly to the then worst disaster to befall English football. Had, for instance, Valley Parade fallen under the auspices of the Act then the tragic events of May 11, 1985, could not have taken place. Either the stand would have been closed or work carried out to eradicate all the hazards that combined to create such a horrendous death trap.

As prime minister, Margaret Thatcher, toured the burnt-out wreckage of the Bradford main stand the following day, it was announced an official inquiry would be launched under Mr Justice Popplewell. Change was on its way, and not before time. A couple of days later, home secretary, Leon Brittan, confirmed the Safety of Sports Grounds Act was to be extended to cover all 92 Football League grounds, plus an additional 22 Rugby League grounds. A figure of £18m was bandied around in the media as to what the total cost would be to bring all stadia up to standard. The effect on the smaller clubs was devastating, as stands and terraces across the country were either closed or demolished. Capacities tumbled, Halifax Town even kicking off the following season with a crowd limit of 1,750 set for The Shay – down from a rarely-tested 16,000.

At Doncaster, the predicament facing the club was not quite as grave. But there were still a mountain of problems to solve. Belle Vue was badly showing its age, the decision not to make any major post-war improvements save for the installation of floodlights having come home to roost. There was so much to do, Rovers officials didn't know where best to start.

By August, the local safety authorities had run out of patience and set Rovers a strict 11-day deadline to carry out the necessary work or face kicking off the season behind closed doors. It was the second consecutive summer that Doncaster had become embroiled in a row with the authorities. Twelve months earlier, it had been an unpaid police bill of £19,800. This, however, was far more serious with no paying spectators for the first home game meaning no income. An inspection by the local authority's safety team earlier in the summer had found a host of problems, from the two stands being wooden structures through to crumbling terracing at the Rossington End that housed visiting supporters. In a damning statement to the *Yorkshire Post*, the South Yorkshire Police committee even went so far as to accuse the club of 'dragging their feet'. Rovers estimated the cost of the improvements would be £265,000, a quarter of which would have to be found from club funds with the balance made up by various grants. Nevertheless, chief executive Les Holloway vowed the work would be done on time. He was as good as his word, the local authority duly granting the necessary safety certificate just in time for the first home game of the season against Bolton Wanderers on August 24. It had been a close run thing, with the upshot of the necessary upgrading of facilities being the demolition of the quaint 700-seater stand that sat behind the North Terrace. Neatly turned out in red and white, the stand was one of several to be lost in the wake of the Bradford fire. The ground capacity also suffered a dramatic cut, halving overnight to 10,500 – of which just 1,050 were seats in the sole remaining wooden stand.

Clearly, the safety work was a cost clubs of Rovers ilk could not have budgeted for. Grants from bodies such as the Football Grounds Improvement Trust helped, but many clubs were still struggling badly. In Rovers' case, the final bill was cushioned by the sale of two players who had given such sterling service – the Snodin brothers. Ian was the first to leave. At 21, he was the younger of the two but had already chalked up 187 league appearances for Doncaster. He was also an England Under-21 international with three caps to his name. A host of scouts had descended on Belle Vue during the previous season and Bremner knew it was time for the midfielder to move on. Assistant manager Dave Bentley recalls: "Billy had played at the very top level so he was not going to stop anyone else doing the same. Basically, he wanted the best for his lads and did not want to hold back anyone he felt good enough. Ian fell into this category. He was an outstanding player for Doncaster and Billy knew he would go on and do really, really well."

As the football world attempted to come to terms with the events at Valley Parade, the younger Snodin brother was a man in demand. His manager wanted to do all he could to help his young protégé make the right choice. Ian recalls: "When the time came to leave Donny, Billy insisted on driving me to whoever wanted to speak to me. In the end, we went to Leeds and West Brom. Billy conducted the negotiations with both Eddie Gray at Leeds and Johnny Giles, who was manager of West Brom. The one thing he never did was tell me who to sign for – that had to be my own decision, he said. I ended up choosing Leeds, and I didn't regret it."

The transfer was agreed on May 16 and the fee was £200,000, a godsend to Doncaster who knew that the fire at Bradford just five days earlier would have huge ramifications for the club's finances. Bremner, though, felt his former club had got themselves a bargain, telling the *Yorkshire Post*: 'He is a better player than I was at his age. He has the ability to become a world class star.' The transfer fee had been funded by Leeds chairman Leslie Silver and director Manny Cussins, while it emerged at the press conference to unveil the new signing that the Elland Road club had watched Ian play no fewer than 11 times during the previous campaign.

Less than a month later, Glynn Snodin was following his brother through the exit door at Belle Vue. Again, Bremner took an almost paternalistic interest in protecting the best interests of a player who had netted no fewer than 45 goals from left-back in the previous three seasons. He also, it seemed, wanted to make sure an old adversary didn't sign one of his star players. Glynn recalls: "Billy didn't want me to go. He was even talking about a testimonial but once I explained I felt it was time to move on he could not have been more supportive. There had been a few offers over the years, including some from Brian Clough at Nottingham Forest. Billy knocked them all back. I am not sure if it was anything to do with the Leeds v Clough stuff from the 1970s, I never asked. But Billy was adamant I would not be going to Forest, even during that summer when I left. In the end, Sheffield Wednesday came in with an offer. Billy, to his credit, kept me informed all the way through and I ended up signing for Wednesday."

In return for the elder Snodin moving across south Yorkshire, Rovers received a fee of £115,000. That and the £200,000 banked for Ian meant Doncaster had funds to bring Belle Vue up to scratch – even if it did take an almighty effort in the end to ensure supporters could watch the first home game against Bolton.

With the Snodin brothers having left, Bremner knew Rovers had to strengthen. Left-back Dave Rushbury arrived in a £10,000 deal from Gillingham as Tony Brown, who'd had two loan spells at Belle Vue the previous season, joined on a free transfer from Leeds United. Perhaps the most important signing, though, was Dave Cusack as player coach. The pair had got to know each other when Cusack had played for Bremner's former team-mate Jack Charlton at Sheffield Wednesday, often sharing a pint during the week or after a game on a Saturday night. Bremner wanted to bring some steel to the Rovers back-line, though wasn't sure he would be able to prise Cusack away from Millwall following the London club's promotion to the Second Division. Cusack recalls: "Billy was the only reason I decided to move. As a youngster, I would jump the train from near my home in south Yorkshire and head up to Leeds to watch Billy and the rest of that great team. It meant having to leap off the train as it slowed down near Elland Road to avoid paying the fare, but it was worth the scramble down the banking to watch Leeds. So, when Billy came in for me, I decided to move. We had been friends for quite a few years by then thanks to Big Jack so I was really looking forward to it."

Cusack's debut came, thanks to Belle Vue being awarded a safety certificate in time, against Bolton in front of 3,414 fans as the sides shared a 1-1 draw. The £60,000 Bremner had paid for Cusack continued to look a sound investment as August turned into September with Rovers still unbeaten. A 3-3 draw at Lincoln followed by hard-fought 1-0 wins over Brentford and Plymouth meant, after seven games, that Rovers were sitting third and one of only two sides still unbeaten in Division Three. Rotherham United, managed by Bremner's former team-mate Norman Hunter, then inflicted a first defeat on Rovers, who suffered further setbacks when losing to Reading and Blackpool. Doncaster were back in mid-table. It was a frustrating turn of events for everyone at Belle Vue. Jim Dobbin says: "Billy had built a really good side, I could see during the summer that the signings he had brought in were good ones. We then started really well and I fancied us to be up there all season." Losing three games in a row had happened just once the previous season, so it came as something of a shock – especially after the encouraging start. The trio of defeats were, however, nothing compared to the bombshell heading Doncaster's way in the wake of Eddie Gray's sacking by Leeds United on Friday, October 11. The Scot had been dismissed three-and-a-quarter years after taking charge at Elland Road following the club's relegation from the First Division. He had been unable to win back a place in the top flight, finishing eighth, tenth and seventh. When the axe fell, ending his 22-year association with the club in the process, United were 14th. Nevertheless, his sacking caused uproar, with the players leading the criticism of the board's decision. Led by captain Peter Lorimer, brought back to Elland Road at the age of 37 by his former team-mate almost two years earlier, the team condemned the timing and handling of the announcement. Furthermore, a statement was released on behalf of the squad to the Press that read: "We are amazed and astonished at the board's decision to terminate the manager's contract. The timing of the announcement, from our point of view, is disturbing and unsettling. But, far more important, is our sympathy for Eddie. He has worked selflessly for the last three years in the interests of the club and has built a team poised to enter the promotion stakes. With three-quarters of the season left and having lost only once in our last eight games, the decision is absolutely demoralising." John Sheridan, then just 21 but already a veteran of 100 games for Leeds, recalls: "Eddie's sacking came as a real shock to the lads because he had been building a good team without much money. He had only been able to pay one decent fee, for Ian Snodin, and yet the board decided to get rid of him. The players were very upset because we felt the team had been starting to blend. On a personal level, I also had a lot of time for Eddie as he had given me my chance."

Supporters were equally unhappy and showed their displeasure the following day during the home game against Middlesbrough. Leeds won 1-0 thanks to a Peter Lorimer penalty but the abiding memory of that day was the demonstrations against the sacking of Gray. The protests continued outside Elland Road after the game, but the board were adamant. A change of approach had been evident in the boardroom since director Leslie Silver had stepped up to replace Manny Cussins in December, 1983. Bill Fotherby, then on the board and a future chairman of the club, recalls: "Manny had been the big money man at Leeds United and used to go round the other directors and ask, 'Am I doing a good job?' They would always reply, 'Yes'. But there was one time when he went round the boardroom table and got to me. I said, 'With the greatest respect, Manny, I think the time has come for you to step down to vice-chairman and for Leslie to take over because we need a change'. Immediately, he said, 'If that's the case then I will do that'. And Leslie became chairman, just like that. It was only then the club could start to change."

Silver, a highly successful businessman who had founded Silver Paint and Lacquer (Holdings) Ltd, had initially become involved with Leeds when asked to provide a loan in return for a seat on the board. Now in full control, he set about the task of tackling the club's two main problems – lack of money and hooliganism – with relish. Initially, he had been supportive of Gray as manager but, less than two years after stepping up to become chairman, Silver believed change was needed. "I was very sad to have to sack Eddie," says the then chairman. "He is such a nice guy and his wife was also expecting a baby at the time. But I felt it had to be done."

The decision to sack Gray had not been a unanimous one, the board split 6-2 in favour of the move. One of those directors who voted against the sacking, Brian Woodward, immediately resigned in protest. Nevertheless, the die was cast and Gray was out – leading to fevered speculation as to who would be his successor. Johnny Giles emerged as the early favourite, just ahead of the Irishman's former team-mates Jack Charlton and Trevor Cherry. Bremner, thanks to his impressive work at Doncaster, was also believed to be in the United board's thoughts.

Bremner was hugely flattered and wanted the job but, ever the professional, maintained his focus ahead of Rovers' impending trip to Wolverhampton Wanderers. The famous old club from the Black Country had suffered more than most from the stricter safety checks that had followed the Bradford fire. Molineux had, because Wolves were then in the top division, been one of the first grounds in the country to be designated under the Safety and Sports Grounds Act (1975). Now, however, with the authorities taking a much harder stance, a ground that had been home to Wolves since 1889 was in trouble. The North Bank, which had all wooden terracing at the back, was closed, as was the Waterloo Stand that also housed the club's dressing rooms. To add to the surreal feel as Doncaster arrived for their first visit to Molineux in almost 62 years, there was a 30-yard patch of bare earth between the touchline and the newly-constructed John Ireland Stand because Wolves had been forced to abandon the grand scheme that would have seen all four sides rebuilt and the pitch moved. Despite the haphazard nature of Molineux, Bremner was still relishing a visit to one of football's more famous venues – even if it had been the scene of one of his most disappointing nights as a player when Leeds were denied the 1972 league title by a 2-1 defeat. As a manager, his first visit ended much more happily with that 2-1 scoreline being reversed in Doncaster's favour as the Yorkshire club moved back into the top ten.

Back in Leeds, Bremner's success on a small budget at Belle Vue had been noted. Just as importantly, his negotiating skills during Ian Snodin's transfer the previous summer had also created a favourable impression on the Elland Road board. He was invited for interview on Friday, October 18. Bremner was one of three prospective managers that the board spoke to, but within 30 minutes of the interview getting under way the decision had been taken to offer the job to the club's former captain. Leslie Silver recalls: "The ambition of every director was to return to the standards of the Revie days. My thinking, which turned out to be illogical in the end, was to bring in someone who had, basically, been brought up working for Don Revie. I hoped Billy had absorbed the touch of magic that Don brought to Leeds United – and if he had, then this would be the way to get Leeds back to where they belonged. So, we took the decision to offer the job to Billy."

Joining Bremner at Elland Road were his assistant at Doncaster, Dave Bentley, and chief scout Dave Blakey. The latter had already worked for Leeds as chief scout when Jimmy Adamson had been manager for two years from 1978. Compensation of £45,000 was agreed with Doncaster to cover the remaining 19 months on Bremner's contract, plus the release of Bentley and Blakey. Rovers chairman Ian Jones told the *Yorkshire Post*: "He is giving up one of the safest jobs in football."

The players at Belle Vue were sad to see their manager leave. John Buckley, who made 52 league appearances for Doncaster under Bremner, said: "It was hard for everyone. I had only been there 15 months but even I could see there would be a big void where Billy had been. He was irreplaceable. It was the little things he did, the nuggets of advice he would pass on. There was one day when we were talking about bravery in players. Billy said, 'There is more than one way of being brave, Bucky. I don't judge you on how hard you tackle or if you tackle at all, but instead how you react to being put on your arse in a game. If you get up and go back for more, that'll do for me'. It sounds a small thing but it made such a big impression on me." Dave Cusack, the £60,000 summer signing from Millwall, was equally sorry to hear about Bremner's departure. He says: "Everyone wanted Billy to stay but we also understood the pull of Leeds United was not something he could turn down. They meant too much to him. Even though we were only together for a few months, I really enjoyed playing for him – even though Billy was someone who never really coached. I realised that very early in pre-season when he pulled me aside to say how we needed to improve the defence. He arranged a five-a-side game and said to me, 'You sort it out'. Billy had been very fortunate to play with players who didn't need coaching so I don't think he knew how. I did say that to him one day. He started to reply with a, 'Yes, but…' but I didn't give him chance to finish as I said, 'Those lads at Leeds didn't need coaching because they were so special'. He accepted my point. But, even though he didn't coach much, we all knew that Billy would be missed when he left. I actually had a chance to go with him to Leeds as a player, but turned it down. I had come north to get some coaching experience so decided to stay at Doncaster and became player-manager. It was a big mistake as I could have joined Leeds, where Billy had money to spend."

Bremner, after almost seven years at Doncaster, was sad to leave and insisted on attending the following day's home game against Bristol Rovers to say his goodbyes. As Leeds fought out a 1-1 draw with Grimsby Town in front of just 11,244 fans, Bremner was sitting in the dugout at Belle Vue as the visitors took advantage of a subdued performance from Rovers to win 2-0. Leaving on a low was a major disappointment for Bremner, though he could at least take satisfaction from Doncaster being just four points off the promotion places as he walked out that Saturday evening. In his absence, Dave Cusack was asked to take temporary charge of the side. It was a task he took to quickly, leading Rovers on a six-game unbeaten run in the league. Cusack was subsequently given the job full-time and Doncaster went on to finish 11th. They slipped to 13th the following season, an admirable showing for a club who until Bremner's arrival had been unable to bridge the gap between the bottom two divisions with any conviction. Even so, a sense had developed in Doncaster that the club had stalled following Bremner's departure. Jim Dobbin, who moved to Barnsley a month or so into the 1986-87 season, says: "Dave Cusack replaced Billy and, with hindsight, it was probably too early for him to go into management. It would have been better for Doncaster if he could have stayed a player for a bit longer. One of the decisions he made was to shorten the pitch, which did us few favours. I know Billy, because of his time as a player, could not turn down Leeds. But I just wish Eddie Gray could have come in as his replacement. He would have continued playing the football we were good at. It was a real missed opportunity for Rovers."

As Bremner prepared for his first day at Elland Road, one member of the squad delighted by his arrival was Ian Snodin. He recalls: "I was gutted when Eddie Gray was sacked. I marched in to see Leslie Silver and said, 'The only reason I am here is because of Eddie'. But then I found out Billy was coming in and it took the disappointment away." Others, though, were more circumspect, as John Sheridan admits: "I didn't know a lot about Billy, apart from what a great playing career he'd had. So, I asked 'Snod' all about Billy and he spoke very highly of him. That put my mind at rest. 'Snod' turned out to be right, as well, because Billy, along with Eddie, was the reason why I became the player I did."

The Leeds United that Bremner walked back into as manager was a very different club to the one he had left a little over nine years earlier. Then, Jimmy Armfield had been in the middle of the re-building job that would see the great Revie team broken up and the likes of Tony Currie, Brian Flynn, Ray Hankin and Arthur Graham gradually assimilated into the team. The season that Bremner moved to Hull had ended with Leeds finishing tenth in the First Division and reaching an FA Cup semi-final. The following season would also see an appearance in the last four, this time of the League Cup, as United moved one place up the table to ninth. By October, 1985, however, years of decline had left their mark. Leeds had just kicked off their fourth consecutive season in the Second Division, while their finances were in such a perilous state that the club had been forced to sell Elland Road to the local council for £2.5m the previous summer. Worse, however, than having to forego ownership of their home to stay alive was the appalling reputation the club's supporters had established for hooliganism and racism. In the Revie years, it had been the team who were more renowned for violence than their followers. Now, all that had changed with United supporters having rioted on the night relegation from the top flight had been all but confirmed at West Brom in 1982. They had done the same just a few months later at Grimsby, while the violence that had marred the 1-0 defeat to Birmingham City on the same day as the Bradford fire had been so bad that the subsequent inquiry described the scenes as 'more clearly resembling the Battle of Agincourt rather than a football match'. One newspaper had even dubbed the hooligans 'Revie's children' – the suggestion being that the fans, like his team, were bad losers. It was amid these less-than-auspicious beginnings that Bremner began his reign as Leeds manager on Monday, October 21. He was determined to make his mark straight away, as *Yorkshire*

Evening Post football correspondent Don Warters duly noted on that afternoon's back page: 'Billy Bremner breezed into Elland Road, told a couple of junior players that the wall of the corridor under the main stand would remain standing without their support – and got down to business.' One of Bremner's first acts was to appoint a new captain with Ian Snodin replacing Peter Lorimer in the role, a move that signalled to the former Scotland international that his second stint as a United player was all but over. Lorimer had been re-signed by Eddie Gray in December, 1983, after two spells in Canada with Toronto Blizzard and Vancouver Whitecaps. At 37, he had been 14 months older than his manager but still gone on to become such a mainstay of the Leeds side that he missed only two of the club's next 83 games. He had also netted another 17 goals, taking his overall tally for the club to 238. Despite that, Lorimer knew his time was up. "I found out through the press that Ian Snodin was the new captain," says the former Scottish international. "Billy never told me face to face. It upset me, if I am honest. Though, it is funny that when Billy got the job, I had a phone call from Johnny Giles who said, 'That's you out then'. He was right."

Lorimer did start in Bremner's first game against Barnsley, the Tykes winning 3-0 as the new Leeds manager branded his side 'naïve'. But that defeat at Oakwell – when Ian Snodin had led the side out – proved to be his one and only appearance under Bremner. Lorimer adds: "I had scored against Middlesbrough in the first game after Eddie had been sacked but, within two weeks, I was dropped and never played again. Whether he just didn't want one of his old team-mates around or if he thought I undermined his authority in the eyes of the younger lads, I don't know. He never told me. I was really disappointed with how it ended. I had been promised a testimonial instead of a signing-on fee when I had come back a couple of years earlier because the club was so skint. I had the choice of three or four clubs at the time and this was Leeds' way of getting me. But when I told Billy about the testimonial, he looked stunned and said he would have to get back to me. He went to see the chairman, who confirmed the arrangement and all Billy could say was, 'Make sure it happens soon'. That suited me and after that I was out." It would be a few more weeks before Lorimer departed, eventually destined for Israel where he had a brief spell coaching Hapoel Haifa. By then, Bremner had started to re-model his squad with, ironically considering the dropping of 38-year-old Lorimer, bringing in some experience considered the priority.

Under Gray, Leeds had blooded a talented batch of youngsters through necessity. The financial problems that led to Elland Road having to be sold dictated such an approach. In time, the likes of Dennis Irwin, Scott Sellars, Terry Phelan, Tommy Wright and Andy Linighan would go on to enjoy successful careers. But Bremner, in common with all managers, needed results in the short-term. So, gradually the juniors that Gray had nurtured during his time in charge were moved on and replaced by older, more experienced players. It was a policy that Gray had no problem with, as the former United manager reveals: "I remember speaking to Billy a few months after he had taken over and he said, 'Eddie, I am going to have to let all of the young lads go because they are tied to you'. A lot of those lads went on to have great careers, but Billy wanted to do it his way. That is only right." Linighan was the first of the promising band of youngsters to leave, a defender destined to score the winner in an FA Cup final for Arsenal being sold to Oldham Athletic for £55,000 in January, 1986. The following summer, Irwin also moved to Boundary Park in a £60,000 deal as Sellars joined Blackburn Rovers for £20,000 and Phelan moved to Swansea City on a free transfer. Wright completed the quintet of youngsters to leave during Bremner's first year in charge when he, too, was signed by Oldham manager Joe Royle for £80,000. Chairman Leslie Silver recalls: "Some of those young lads did go on to have really good careers, but letting them go was Billy's prerogative. It had to be his choice. He wanted to bring in experience. To his credit, Billy was never someone who pressurised the board for money because he felt he could deliver what Don Revie had done for a small amount."

The youngsters would, in time, be replaced by a host of signings Bremner felt were better equipped to help the club back into the top flight. First, though, the club's place in the Second Division had to be retained. At Christmas, Leeds were sitting just above the relegation zone. The New Year then started badly as a 1-0 defeat to Fourth Division Peterborough in the FA Cup was followed by four defeats from the next five league games, meaning that, by the start of March, United were in grave danger of being sucked into the relegation battle. Bremner's side may have been six points clear of third bottom Middlesbrough, but with many of the sides below them having up to five games in hand it was clear results had to improve and fast. Conceding goals had been a major problem since Bremner had taken over, so much so that United had kept just three clean sheets in 18 games by the time Huddersfield Town arrived at Elland Road on March 8. Defeat would, with a trip to Ayresome Park to come, leave Bremner's side in danger of sliding into the bottom three the following Saturday. Bremner moved quickly to plug what he thought was an enormous gap in the centre of defence by signing Brendan Ormsby in a £65,000 deal from Aston Villa. Ormsby had been at Villa Park since his schooldays and played three times during the club's run to the 1982 European Cup final, where they had beaten Bayern Munich 1-0 in Rotterdam. Since then, though, Ormsby had fallen out of favour at Villa so jumped at the chance to join Leeds. He recalls: "Mervyn Day, who I had played with at Villa, was at Leeds and he rang me to say Billy would be coming to watch me play for the reserves. Knowing someone of Billy's ability as a player was coming to watch gave me a real lift and I couldn't sign quick enough when I got the chance. People thought I was stepping down as Leeds were a division below Villa but I never saw it like that and still don't all these years later. I was signing for a big club and Billy Bremner, end of story."

Ormsby enjoyed a scoring debut in a 2-0 win over Huddersfield, which was followed by a 2-2 draw at Middlesbrough. Leeds slipped to fifth bottom as a result, but crucially their advantage over Boro in 20th place now stood at seven points. The corner had been turned as away wins over Portsmouth and Bradford City were followed by a 3-1 victory at home to Millwall. Leeds were safe, destined to finish 14th despite losing three of their final four games. As relieved as Bremner was, however, he still tore into his players after the third of those reverses, a final day trip to champions Norwich City having ended in a 4-0 thrashing. United had taken 2,500 fans to Carrow Road, prompting a fuming Bremner to tell the *Yorkshire Evening Post*: 'With support such as that, I would have been prepared to lose an arm and a leg for the club and still keep battling. My players have to learn to die for Leeds United.'

Chapter 23

So Near...

Ask a Leeds United fan of a certain vintage about the 1980s and chances are the initial response will be a shudder of remembrance. It was a miserable decade for the West Yorkshire club that started amid discontent on the terraces at the job being done by then manager, Jimmy Adamson. With memories of the Revie era still fresh, there was little patience to be found among supporters and Adamson duly paid with his job in September, 1980. Leeds then turned to Allan Clarke, the first of three old boys to try and rediscover the glory days at Elland Road. But the policy failed; relegation in 1982 was followed by a prolonged stint in the Second Division as crowds plummeted and problems mounted. It took the appointment of Howard Wilkinson towards the end of the decade to bring about a change in fortune and promotion back to the top flight in 1990 was the prelude to the club lifting the league title for the third time in their history just two years later.

Until the arrival of the man fans affectionately nicknamed Sgt Wilko in a nod to his reputation as a tough Sergeant Major-type figure, United's story of the 1980s could perhaps best be summed up in one word - mediocrity. Rarely threatening to win promotion, Leeds were equally wretched in the cups with an inability to negotiate more than one hurdle characterising their efforts across the decade. There was, however, one exception to this tale of woe. The 1986-87 season under Bremner.

Ahead of that campaign, United had once again been installed among the favourites for promotion. The more cynical among the Elland Road support may have sagely pointed out how badly the bookmakers had got it wrong in each of the previous four seasons but there was still a tangible sense of optimism as Leeds set off across the Pennines to face Blackburn Rovers on the opening day. Bremner had been busy during the summer, continuing his efforts to bring in the experience he felt was required to launch a promotion challenge. Out had gone youngsters Dennis Irwin, Scott Sellars and Terry Phelan, along with George McCluskey and Gary Hamson. In their place, Bremner spent £125,000 on Keith Edwards, the 29-year-old Sheffield United striker who had been prolific at both Bramall Lane and, in an earlier spell, with Hull City. Jack Ashurst was a surprise addition at the age of 31 from relegated Carlisle United along with Peter Haddock, a Newcastle United defender who had spent a couple of months during the previous season on loan at Fourth Division Burnley. Ashurst and Haddock cost a combined fee of £80,000, while the summer arrivals were completed by East Stirlingshire winger Russell Doig in a £15,000 transfer, Nottingham Forest goalkeeper Ronnie Sinclair on a free and John Buckley as Bremner returned to Doncaster Rovers to snap up the Scot for £35,000. The wheels for the transfer had actually been set in motion the previous October as Bremner left Belle Vue. Buckley recalls: "Billy rang me up as he was leaving Doncaster and said he would be coming back in for me. He wanted to let me know he wanted to sign me once the dust had settled. It made me feel great. Nothing more happened until the summer when Dave Cusack, who had replaced Billy as Doncaster manager, came round one night and said I was the only player who could fetch a fee so would I mind joining Leeds? I didn't let on Billy had spoken to me months earlier."

With Brendan Ormsby, David Rennie, Brian Caswell and Ronnie Robinson having been signed by Bremner during the previous season, the Leeds manager was in confident mood. Dave Bentley, Bremner's assistant at Elland Road, says: "There was not a lot of money available but Billy made good use of it. When we had arrived from Doncaster, there were some good young kids already in the team but Billy's philosophy was that we needed more experience. He worked very hard to bring the players in who he felt would make a difference. He was very successful in that respect. By the start of the 1986-87 season, we really thought the team were capable of kicking on." The coaching staff's optimism was shared by the players, as Ormsby vividly remembers: "I was sitting down with a few of the lads before the season had started and could see everyone felt the same – this could be our year. Billy had made a few signings and there was a real feeling around the club that something special was about to happen."

One player just glad to still be at Elland Road by August, 1986, was John Stiles, son of former World Cup winner Nobby and the nephew of Johnny Giles. Stiles had started his career at Shamrock Rovers, who were managed by Giles, before moving to Leeds 18 months before Bremner's own arrival. He recalls: "The first thing Billy did after taking over was to try to get rid of me. He made it clear very early on that he didn't want me. But, because I had watched a lot of Leeds when Uncle John had played for them, I really wanted to stay so decided to keep my head down and hope for the best. It worked, though I never found out why Billy changed his mind about me.

Knowing I had a future at Leeds meant I was really fired up for the 1986-87 season, which turned out to be probably the best time of my career."

The feel-good factor developing at Elland Road owed, according to those in the dressing room, everything to the manager and his enthusiastic personality. John Sheridan, who would play in all but two of United's 55 league and cup games that season, says: "Billy was great to be around, and to someone like me who played in midfield he was superb in helping to develop my game. His favourite trick was a disguised pass, where he would look one way but then pass it the other. In training, it didn't matter that we all knew it was coming, somehow he pulled it off every time. It was impossible to read. In the end, I started taking the trick into games myself and Billy absolutely loved that."

As anyone who had been at Doncaster during his near seven-year reign knew from experience, Bremner was never happier than when spending time on the training pitch – regardless of whether it was the first team or the juniors. Future Leeds manager Simon Grayson was 16 when the 1986-87 campaign began and an apprentice at Elland Road. "Billy was football mad," he recalls. "There was one day when the first team had finished and he was standing on the touchline watching us train. He had a really nice suit on but, after just a few minutes, he suddenly decided to join in because there was a point he wanted to get across to the lads. It was a really funny sight to see the club's manager, someone we all looked up to, kicking the ball about in the mud, wearing a brand new pair of shoes and a suit. He just loved playing and talking about football. As apprentices, we would have a host of jobs to do such as clean the dressing rooms after the first team had trained. We would just be finishing as Billy wandered in, and he would then start telling us a few stories. An hour or so later, the footballs would come out and we would all go out on to the training pitch and have a kickabout. It meant we had to clean everything all over again and were still there at 7pm. But none of us minded because it was such a great experience."

Bremner's love of football was legendary but those who knew him best could also see there was an extra spring in his step due to being back at Elland Road. Dave Bentley recalls: "Being manager of Leeds, the club where he had spent nearly all his career and enjoyed such wonderful success, made it extra special for Billy. I could see it in his eyes, the pride he had at being Leeds United manager. He had loved being Doncaster Rovers manager but this was something else."

With confidence high, everyone at Elland Road was eagerly looking forward to the opening day trip to Blackburn. On paper, it seemed a decent place to start - Blackburn having finished below Leeds the previous season and just three points clear of the relegation zone. By half-time, all was going well with Andy Ritchie having put the visitors ahead with a well-taken goal. Bremner was happy. By full-time, however, his mood had darkened considerably after seeing Blackburn come from behind to win 2-1 and Ian Snodin sent off following an altercation with Northern Ireland international Jimmy Quinn. United bounced back by beating Stoke City in midweek only for confidence levels to again be jolted as Sheffield United triumphed 1-0 at Elland Road. Three games had brought just three points and Leeds were sitting 11th in the table. Bremner, though, was not unduly worried. Peter Swan, whose Leeds debut had come the previous season, recalls: "Billy was very positive around the lads, but also capable of exploding if he didn't think anyone was putting the effort in. By the start of his first full season as manager, Billy was confident and a couple of poor results early on were not going to change that. He just kept telling the lads it would be our season."

Whether it was the faith of their manager or not, United's results soon started to pick up. Back-to-back derby trips to Barnsley and Huddersfield Town yielded four points and were followed by a thrilling fightback at home to Reading as a two-goal half-time deficit was turned into a memorable 3-2 victory. Leeds were back up to fifth in the table ahead of yet another derby fixture, this time against Bradford City.

With Valley Parade still being rebuilt following the fire disaster of 16 months earlier, Odsal had become the Bantams' temporary base. The home of Bradford Northern Rugby League Club had, though, proved to be an unsuitable venue for football, not least because the pitch was not up to League standard. The vast open terracing that had once hosted a crowd of 102,575 for a Rugby League Challenge Cup final also meant City supporters failed to settle in a ground they felt boasted all the atmosphere of the moon. The previous season, City had played 'home' games at both Elland Road and Huddersfield's Leeds Road before settling on Odsal but a return to Valley Parade could not come soon enough. During the build-up to the ninth meeting of the two West Yorkshire clubs, it was not, however, the state of the pitch that was most concerning Leeds officials. Instead, it was the Football Association's decision to relax the all-ticket restrictions on United away games. Brought in following the riot at Birmingham's St Andrews on the final day of the 1984-85 season, the rule meant both sets of fans had to purchase tickets in advance with no sales on the day. Leeds fans wanting to buy a ticket also had to be an official member of the 'New-U Club' that had been set up in an attempt to weed out the hooligans. In its first season, the scheme had proved a success with few incidents involving United fans. Several Second Division clubs had, though, complained that the restrictions were costing them money because fans were not used to having to buy tickets in advance. The upshot of those protests was, unbelievably, the lifting of the all-ticket rule ahead of United's shortest away trip of the season. Leeds, with good cause as it turned out, feared the worst.

The day of September 20, 1986, started much like any other in Bradford. There were more police on duty in and around the city but, otherwise, life carried on as normal. The same can be said about much of the derby taking place at Odsal, even after Bobby Campbell had given City a first-half lead. Unfortunately, the calm was followed by an almighty storm with Don Goodman netting a second goal for Bradford the catalyst for the carnage that followed. Almost immediately, a section of the 7,000 or so Leeds fans housed on the terrace opposite the main stand started to throw missiles at their Bradford counterparts. Then, the thugs turned their attention to a mobile food van selling fish and chips that was situated at the top of the terrace. The staff who moments earlier had been serving food fled as youths rocked the van in an attempt to push it over. Hot fat spilled on to the floor as a result, causing a severe fire that within seconds had destroyed the van. While this was going on at the back of the terrace, hundreds of other fans had invaded the pitch in an attempt to get the game abandoned. Prompt police action prevented the mob getting into areas reserved for home fans but, with a fire now raging on the terrace, hundreds more poured on to the field to escape the blaze. Referee Neville Ashley immediately took the players back to the dressing rooms as police battled to restore order. In all, 64 arrests were made and £10,000 of damage caused to the food van.

Only when the trouble had abated and Odsal cleared did the referee bring the players back on to play the remaining four minutes as City claimed a 2-0 win. It was a first triumph over Leeds in 54 years but small consolation to a club where memories of the horror that had been the Valley Parade fire were still so fresh. City's Stuart McCall, a lifelong Leeds fan who had been at West Brom when relegation had been all but confirmed in 1982, was disgusted by what he had seen. "I didn't play in the game due to injury," recalls the former Scotland international. "But I was in the stand opposite where all the trouble happened and I could not believe what I was seeing. It was awful, especially for those of us who had been at Valley Parade on the day of the fire. There were people leaving with tears in their eyes that day as all the horrible memories were dredged up. I had followed Leeds all over the country as a youngster but after what happened that day I could never have considered signing for Leeds. No way at all. Billy Bremner had shown a lot of interest in me and I know he approached Bradford about signing me not long after. But after Odsal, there was no way I could have signed. It was nothing against Billy, who as a ginger-haired former Scotland captain had been one of my idols. I gave the same answer to Howard Wilkinson a few years later when he tried to sign me when I left Everton for Rangers."

Bremner, a fierce defender of the Leeds United fans in the past, had also been left numb by the events of Odsal. John Buckley, handed his first start for Leeds in the ill-fated derby, recalls: "Billy was devastated, totally devastated. He couldn't understand why they would want to do something like that. I hate to say it, but I was ashamed of the Leeds fans that day. I was genuinely scared on the pitch. We were told to stick close to a Bradford player as that way the Leeds fans wouldn't attack them. I went and stood with Chris Withe when the invasion happened, and will never forget this one lad coming on with an iron bar wanting to attack someone. It was terrifying."

As the FA launched yet another inquiry into the behaviour of Leeds United supporters, the all-ticket restrictions were reinstated – though not in time to cover the League Cup trip to Oldham Athletic just three days after the Odsal riot. The Leeds players were glad to be back in action so quickly, even if the second round first leg tie at Boundary Park ended in a 3-2 defeat with Andy Linighan, sold by Bremner the previous January, netting the winner. Brendan Ormsby had missed the game with an ankle injury picked up on the opening day at Blackburn. Bremner felt the absence of his main defender had been a major factor in United having conceded eight goals in the last three games, so decided to employ an old trick learned under Don Revie. Ormsby recalls: "We were due to play Hull City at home on the Saturday but I still wasn't over the injury. The Monday after the game at Odsal, I couldn't walk properly so knew there was no way I would make it in time to face Hull. But then, midway through the week, Billy came up to me and said, 'I need you on Saturday – and I would rather have you with one leg than a lot of the other lads with two'. Later, I found out Revie used to say the same to Billy to get him to play when not properly fit but, at the time, I just thought he must really need me. So, I played and even scored as we won 3-0." With Ormsby reunited at the heart of the defence with David Rennie, Leeds' form at home improved but they still continued to struggle on the road. By the turn of the year, the disparity in form had seen Bremner's side claim 28 points from 12 games at Elland Road compared to just six from 10 away from home. The undoubted nadir came on the Sunday before Christmas as United travelled to Stoke City, where the previous season they had crashed to a 6-2 defeat. During the build-up, several players confidently predicted in the local press how there would be no repeat of United being hit for six. They were right, though only because Stoke this time plundered seven goals – including five during the first-half. Ian Baird and John Sheridan netted after the break to ensure the second 45 minutes, at least, ended even at 2-2. That and the sight of 2,000 Leeds fans responding to being 7-1 down by striking up the chant 'next goal wins!' were the only crumbs of comfort to be had from another miserable afternoon at the Victoria Ground. Such a good-natured and peaceful response did not, though, prevent Leeds again hitting the headlines for all the wrong reasons after the draw for the FA Cup third round had been made and the club were paired with Telford United at the non-League club's homely Bucks Head. The local police immediately objected, insisting that the tie could not be played in Telford due to fears over safety. The decision prompted an amazing editorial in the *Yorkshire Evening Post*, which under the headline 'Come on Telford!' read: 'For the first time in its history, the *YEP* today hopes Leeds United will lose a match.' The newspaper then went on to claim moving the game away from Telford represented a victory for the thugs who had sullied the Elland Road club's reputation. It was a stance that infuriated many in Leeds and something that would not be forgotten in the years that followed. Bremner, for his part, was fiercely loyal to the club's supporters. Events such as the fire at Odsal earlier in the season had left him distraught. But, on other occasions when what he considered to be unjustified criticism was levelled at Leeds fans, he was quick to react. Mike Morgan, who still covers Yorkshire football for *The Sun*, recalls: "My relationship with Billy went right back to the 1960s but he did once ban me when manager and it was all to do with a story I wrote about the Leeds fans. There had been some hooliganism at a game and I used the word 'scum' to refer to the Leeds fans who had been involved. It also got used in the headline on the back page. A couple of days later, I went to see Billy and he told me, in no uncertain terms, that I was banned. We had known each other a long time by then but it made no difference. I was out because he didn't like how I had referred to the Leeds fans. There was no talking him round, either. I was banned for a couple of months in the end. It was my first year on *The Sun* so you can imagine the trouble it caused me to be banned from covering the biggest club in Yorkshire."

With staging the FA Cup third round tie at Bucks Head out of the question, United's offer to switch the game to Elland Road was rejected by Telford who eventually settled on West Brom's Hawthorns ground with the kick-off put back to Sunday lunchtime. Fears that the tie could cost the non-League club money due to increased police costs were then allayed by the FA, who promised to cover the £20,000 bill. Bremner, wary of the year when non-League Wimbledon had given Leeds an almighty scare in the FA Cup before being beaten in a replay, made sure his players were under no illusions as to the size of their task. They responded admirably, claiming a 2-1 victory on an icy surface thanks to a late winner by Ian Baird. The draw for the fourth round handed United another away assignment, this time at Third Division Swindon Town and, once again, Baird was on the scoresheet in a 2-1 win.

It was the first time Leeds had negotiated more than one hurdle in the FA Cup since reaching the 1977 semi-final, but any hopes their league form may follow suit were initially wide of the mark as the opening five Second Division games of 1987 brought a defeat and four draws. The pressure was beginning to mount on both Leeds and their manager. John Buckley recalls: "I could see Billy was feeling it. I had been on the periphery of the team since signing in the summer so went to see Billy as I thought he was being unfair to me. Billy said, 'I just can't afford to play you like I did at Doncaster when you had licence to get forward'. I think because it was Leeds, the club where he was such a legendary figure, Billy felt the pressure more than he would have anywhere else. Unfortunately, I paid the price for that and I would say Leeds was probably the unhappiest time of my career."

The need for positive results was also manifesting itself during games, as Brendan Ormsby recalls: "People talk about Sir Alex Ferguson and his hair-dryer treatment of players. Well, he must have taken a leaf out of Billy's book. He could really rip into us if he wasn't happy. I remember one game at Elland Road when we came in at half-time behind. Billy tore into us before some of the lads had even sat down. There was a tray of tea cups in one corner of the dressing room, which Billy just swept his arm through to send them flying. Peter Haddock was sitting closest so he got covered in hot tea, but daren't say anything because Billy was so angry. Poor 'Fish', who is one of the nicest blokes you could hope to meet, just had to sit there as the tea dripped off him. None of us dare look up for fear of catching Billy's eye or seeing 'Fish' and laughing. Billy absolutely hated losing, which is probably why he was such a winner as a player."

Half-time tirades or not, there was a growing sense by the middle of February that the season was approaching a crossroads with United having slipped to ninth in the table. Ian Snodin had also departed in an £840,000 deal to Everton, Bremner accompanying the young midfielder for transfer negotiations with both Howard Kendall and Liverpool manager Kenny Dalglish. Snodin says: "I didn't want to leave because I had such a good rapport with the fans but Leeds needed the money. There wasn't much between Everton and Liverpool, who were first and second in the league at the time. Billy came with me to both but, just as he had when Doncaster manager and I had the choice between Leeds and West Brom, he insisted it had to be my decision. I went to Everton and we went on to win the league title a few months later."

Snodin's departure meant Bremner had some money to spend. The first new arrivals were Micky Adams, a £110,000 capture from Coventry City, and Charlton Athletic striker John Pearson, who joined in a £72,000 deal. A £250,000 bid for Bradford City's John Hendrie was then turned down, while an enquiry about the Scot's team-mate Stuart McCall was also rebuffed. Just a week after the arrival of Pearson and Adams, however, Bremner was again unveiling a pair of new faces as Bobby McDonald signed, initially on loan, from Oxford United and Mark Aizlewood agreed to swap The Valley for Elland Road after a £200,000 fee had been agreed.

Having already played in the FA Cup – McDonald in Oxford's third round defeat to Aldershot and Aizlewood for Charlton in their surprise defeat at home to Walsall – neither could play against QPR in the fifth round. Adams and Pearson were available, though, as Cup fever swept Leeds in the wake of United drawing a top flight side at home. A week after attracting just 14,216 through the turnstiles for a 2-2 draw with Barnsley, United officials were confidently expecting a crowd of around 24,000 for the visit of QPR. In the end, 31,234 turned up with the demand being such that hundreds were locked out and around a dozen clambered on to the roof of the fish and chip shop opposite the stadium on Elland Road. Another few hundred watched the action through a gap in the stands from the Wesley Street car park as a thrilling Cup tie was played out in front of a tremendous atmosphere. The decisive moment came five minutes from time with the scores level at 1-1 as Brendan Ormsby launched himself at a cross to power a header past David Seaman. All the struggles and misery that had been the 1980s for those whose loyalties lay with United were forgotten in an instant as Elland Road celebrated. Ormsby, hotly pursued by his team-mates, ran to the Gelderd End and jumped on to the eight-foot security fence. "It was an amazing feeling," recalls the former defender. "Elland Road was bouncing that day. The gates had been locked long before kick-off so to score the winner was unbelievable. I just ran to the fans. If the fence hadn't been in front of the Kop, I think I'd still be there today! Billy was delighted afterwards and told us we all had to savour the moment and remember what it felt like. He then sent us out on the town. I got the impression he was itching to join us but, as manager, thought better of it because there needed to be a boundary between him and the lads." The crowd had been United's biggest since relegation and brought in record gate receipts of £122,000, beating the previous best of £90,000 when Barcelona had been the visitors for the 1975 European Cup semi-final. More importantly for Bremner, however, was the belief it infused back into his players as United embarked on a run that brought just one defeat from the next ten league games.

Further progress was also made in the Cup, where the memorable win over QPR was followed by a quarter-final trip to Third Division Wigan Athletic. Due to the limited capacity of Springfield Park, tickets were scarce as United were given an allocation of just 2,000. In an attempt to prevent fans turning up without tickets, the tie was beamed back live to Leeds where a further 6,000 watched the game in the Town Hall and Queens Hall. This was enough to satisfy demand, though one fan did try to get in by sleeping overnight at Wigan's ground in a toilet – only to be discovered by a police sniffer dog in the morning. It was about the only thing that failed to go in Leeds' favour as Wigan were beaten 2-0 thanks to goals either side of half-time from Micky Adams and John Stiles. There had been a few scares for Mervyn Day but, on the whole, it had been a nerveless performance – something that Peter Swan puts down solely to Bremner. "I played against Wigan," recalls the Hunslet-born defender who went on to make more than 500 league appearances for seven clubs. "It was a huge game so there were a few nerves around so Billy got us all together in the hotel the night before to play carpet bowls. It was what he had done as a player under Don Revie. He introduced an element of competition by splitting us into pairs and running a book on who would win. It was a great evening that helped us forget the importance of the following day's game for a few hours. I still believe it was a factor in us beating Wigan quite comfortably."

United were now chasing success on two fronts, the draw for the semi-finals pairing Bremner's side with Coventry City as Tottenham Hotspur were handed a tie against Watford. Leeds were the only remaining side from outside the top flight, but that did nothing to dent the belief at Elland Road that it was shaping up to be their year. Bremner, though, was wary of the need to keep his players focused on the league with four important games to be played before the semi-final against Coventry at Hillsbrough on April 12. A defeat at Crystal Palace was a setback, though not one that proved too costly as Leeds hit back to claim seven points from the next three games to ensure they went into the Cup semi-final sitting fifth in the table.

United's first Cup semi-final in ten years had, unsurprisingly, led to a clamour for tickets. An allocation of 21,700 was never going to be satisfy demand, as proved by 18,000 turning up to try and secure a precious ticket when the final batch of 6,000 went on general sale. Six 'Soccer Special' trains were also quickly filled by supporters dreaming of a return to Wembley for the first time since the 1974 Charity Shield that had launched Brian Clough's ill-fated stint in charge. There was a similar sense of excitement among the players, as Brendan Ormsby recalls: "We stayed overnight in Sheffield but, unfortunately, the club booked us into a hotel full of Coventry fans. You can imagine the banter that went on at breakfast and then as we went for a walk before catching the coach to Hillsborough. Billy was at the heart of it." With Bobby McDonald and Mark Aizlewood Cup-tied, all eyes were on Bremner as he named the starting XI. Keith Edwards was just one of several hoping for a recall, only to have to settle for a place on the bench as the manager paired Ian Baird and John Pearson up front. Andy Ritchie, who had been on a week-to-week contract all season due to a dispute with the club, was also in, much to his relief. "It was great to hear I would start," admits Ritchie, who eight years earlier as a Manchester United player had been dropped for the FA Cup final despite having featured in the earlier rounds. "The club would not compromise over my contract that season but Billy never allowed it to become a problem. If I was playing well, that was good enough for him. He was a real players' manager and I appreciated his support. Even so, such a big game meant there were doubts in my mind as to whether this would be the one when I dropped out." Another beneficiary of Bremner's desire to look after his lads in the same way Don Revie had once done with him was Peter Swan, who says: "Billy knew I needed the £750 bonus that came with being in the squad, even if I didn't play. So, he picked me in the squad despite knowing I was injured. That was the sort of bloke he was, always looking after his players."

With the Leeds fans occupying the Leppings Lane terrace that would witness such horror just two years later when 96 Liverpool fans were crushed to death at the FA Cup semi-final, congestion at the turnstiles led to the kick-off being delayed by 15 minutes. The match proved well worth the wait. Coventry may have triumphed at Hillsborough against Sheffield Wednesday in the previous round but it was Leeds who made a blistering start as David Rennie opened the scoring on 14 minutes. The score remained unchanged until midway through the second half when Brendan Ormsby was destined to make a mistake that continues to haunt him to this day. "We were in front and looking quite comfortable," remembers the former United captain. "But then the ball got played through and I went to shepherd it out over the goal-line. Unfortunately, Dave Bennett wrapped his leg round at the last second and kept the ball in. He then leapt up and drilled a cross for Micky Gynn to equalise. I couldn't believe what had happened."

Ten minutes later, Ormsby's agony was compounded when Keith Houchen rounded Mervyn Day to put Coventry ahead. Bremner's response was to bring Keith Edwards on for Pearson, the move paying dividends almost straight away when the substitute equalised with a firm header after being picked out by Andy Ritchie. The pace, which had been unrelenting for the final quarter, understandably dropped in extra-time but there was still plenty to keep the 51,372 crowd gripped. Both sides had chances, but it would be Coventry who clinched a trip to Wembley when Bennett finished from close range on 99 minutes after Day had blocked a Houchen shot. To miss out on a place in the final was heart-breaking, as assistant manager Dave Bentley recalls: "The Cup defeat was horrible, absolutely horrible. Reaching the Cup final was huge back then, much more than it is today. So, to go so close was awful. Everyone was on a real downer." John Stiles, who started all United's Cup ties in 1986-87, vividly remembers the huge disappointment of missing out on reaching the final. Almost a quarter of a century on, though, he is also able to look back philosophically: "When you look at what happened in the final, maybe it was just Coventry's year. We had been every bit as good as Coventry on the day but the way they played to beat Spurs 3-2 in the final tells me maybe it was the right result."

As upset as everyone was to lose to Coventry, there was little doubt as Bremner surveyed the Hillsborough dressing room as to who was feeling it worst. Ormsby recalls: "There were a lot of tears afterwards, most of which were mine. We had been so close to playing in an FA Cup final and I blamed myself. It was an awful experience and one I will never forget. Even now, any Leeds fan that I meet usually wants to discuss one of two things from that season – either my winner against QPR or the equaliser in the semi-final. Often, it depends what stage of the night it is and how much they have had to drink as to which one they bring up first. It is just something I have had to live with."

Seeing how distraught Ormsby was in the dressing room, Bremner waited for the right time to speak to his captain. Ormsby says: "Billy had a quiet word with all the lads and gave us a pep talk, basically reminding us we were playing Shrewsbury two days later in an important league game. Later, though, he pulled me to one side on my own and told me what a good player I was. He also said, 'Don't forget what an important role you played in getting us to the semi-final in the first place'. He had picked his moment brilliantly, as it would not have been right to say that in front of the other lads in the dressing room after the game. I have never forgotten it. In football terms, that was without doubt the worst time of my life. But Billy's words made me feel a lot better about myself."

With their Wembley dreams over, United travelled to Shrewsbury in determined mood. A Cup final appearance would have been wonderful, but the priority all season had been promotion. With eight games remaining, a strong finish might not be enough to force their way into the top three due to the fine form of Derby County, Portsmouth and Oldham Athletic. But, thanks to the introduction of a play-off system at the start of the campaign, a fourth or fifth place finish would be enough to earn a second tilt at promotion. A 2-0 win at Gay Meadow ensured there would be no hangover from the Cup exit, the manner of United's display leading Shrewsbury manager Chic Bates to comment: 'Leeds look like the old Leeds team, which is a credit to Billy Bremner." The words pleased the United manager, just as a 3-2 win over Ipswich Town did four days later. The three points were enough to nudge Leeds back up to fourth, a position they would hold come the end of the regular season. Under the new play-off system, that meant a two-legged tie against the side finishing third – Oldham Athletic. The other semi-final saw fifth-placed Ipswich Town face Charlton, who had finished fourth bottom in the top flight. There was no one-off Wembley showpiece final, that particular initiative still being another three years away. So, instead, the final would again be a two-legged affair with the winners decided on an aggregate score.

Bremner had, initially, not been a fan of the system. He felt it unfair that a side with the third highest tally of points in the division could miss out to a side who finished 10 or even 15 points worse off. With the season now over, he retained the same mis-givings. But, also a realist, he knew that if this was the only chance for Leeds to win promotion then he was not going to turn it down.

With Oldham having finished a place above Leeds, the Latics were to enjoy home advantage for the all-important second leg. That meant Elland Road was the stage for a cagey first leg on May 14, Oldham's game-plan clearly being to stifle Leeds with a well-organised offside trap. The plan almost worked, only for Keith Edwards to again come off the bench to make a decisive impact by netting the only goal with just 85 seconds remaining. With United having won just four times on their travels in the league all season, a one-goal lead was a slender advantage to take across the Pennines. Oldham having been beaten just twice on their plastic pitch meant Bremner knew his side were in for a torrid afternoon. So it proved, as United's advantage was cancelled out after just 18 minutes when Gary Williams latched on to an Ian Ormondroyd flick to beat Mervyn Day. With the aggregate scores now level and so much at stake, the game continued to be a tightly-fought affair that, the longer it wore on, seemed destined for extra-time. That was, however, until the 89th minute when the home side made the breakthrough courtesy of Mike Cecere guiding a cross from Dennis Irwin beyond Day and into the net. Leeds and the 10,000-strong travelling army of fans who had descended on Boundary Park were stunned into silence. All that effort, and yet just like the FA Cup it was all going to end in crushing disappointment. Bremner, sitting on the bench, was distraught, but still managed to find the strength to urge his side forward one last time. Neil Aspin duly heeded his manager's words, the full-back racing forward to join the attack. The ball quickly found Aspin, who swung over a cross for John Pearson to nod back across goal for substitute Edwards. The striker, despite his dramatic winner in the first leg, had almost been left off the bench in favour of Andy Ritchie or Peter Haddock with the decision only taken once the squad had arrived at Boundary Park. It proved an astute move as, for the third big game in a row, Edwards steadied himself before converting the chance. Cue pandemonium on the Rochdale Road End that housed the away supporters. Edwards had sent the tie into extra-time but with no more goals in the additional 30 minutes it was Leeds who went through on the away goals rule. Manager Joe Royle spoke for all of Oldham after the game when he bemoaned how the league had, 'Just become the longest Cup competition in the world, 44 games and we go out on away goals'. Bremner had sympathy for Royle, not least because Leeds had finished seven points adrift of Oldham who also boasted a superior goal difference. Still, he mused as the team coach made its way back along the M62 motorway, they were the rules – meaning Charlton Athletic lay in wait for Leeds in the final.

Lennie Lawrence's side had claimed 10 points from the final five games of the regular First Division to move out of the bottom three, condemning Leicester City to the drop along with Aston Villa and Manchester City. Normally, a fourth bottom finish would have been enough to avoid relegation but the advent of the play-offs had changed all that. Instead, Charlton had been forced to take on Ipswich Town over two legs – triumphing 2-1 on aggregate after the first game at Portman Road had ended goalless. Now, the Londoners had to do the same to Leeds to preserve their top flight status.

The first leg was scheduled for Friday, May 22 at Selhurst Park, Charlton's temporary home since abandoning The Valley two years earlier. Unfortunately, an agreement between Charlton's landlords, Crystal Palace, and the supermarket that now occupied one end of Selhurst Park forbade any football to be played on a Friday so the game was moved to the Saturday. An estimated 10,000 Leeds fans made the trip south, only to return disappointed after Jim Melrose netted the only goal two minutes from time. Bremner refused to be bowed, however, as he told the press after the game: 'Tell Charlton to put their armour on because it is going to be like the Alamo.' It proved a prescient warning as a crowd of 31,395 packed into a noisy Elland Road for the second leg two nights later. The moment the vast majority had been waiting for came eight minutes into the second half when Bob Taylor's shot beat Bob Bolder and Brendan Ormsby made sure from a yard out. If the 1,000 visiting fans packed into a small enclosure on the Lowfields Road terrace had been struggling to make themselves heard before the goal, they had no chance afterwards as United chased the goal that would be enough to clinch promotion. Despite the urgings of their partisan support, the winner never came – meaning a replay at Birmingham's St Andrews would be needed to settle the tie five days later.

For the third consecutive away game, United were backed by a 10,000-plus travelling army of fans who headed to the Midlands believing that promotion was to be their side's destiny. Bremner made two changes, Bob Taylor replaced by John Pearson up front and John Stiles coming in for Andy Ritchie on the right side of midfield. As with the previous two meetings, the replay was a largely cagey affair. The most notable incident of the first half had, in fact, been United captain Ormsby suffering a serious injury. He recalls: "I challenged for the ball and my studs stuck in the turf as my knee went the other way. I was carried off but tried to come back on, only to realise after trying to stand for a few seconds that my night was over. Eventually, it emerged I had done my cartilage, medial ligament and cruciate. It effectively ended my career at Leeds as I only played one more game, almost two years later on the final day of the season. At the time, though, I had no idea it was so bad and I watched the rest of the game from the dugout with my leg strapped up." With their captain shouting encouragement from the bench, United battled in vain to make the breakthrough during normal time. It was the same story at the other end as Charlton struggled to find a way through a determined defence, meaning for the third time in 13 days Leeds would have to play an additional half-hour. During the break ahead of extra-time, Bremner came on to the field to remind his players what was at stake. They responded to his urgings with the opening goal of the night 10 minutes after the restart. John Sheridan, the heartbeat of the midfield, proved to be the man for the big occasion with a beautifully-flighted free-kick that sailed over the defensive wall and past Bolder for his 16th goal of the season. For the watching Ormsby, it proved to be a painful experience. "When Shez scored," he says, "I jumped up out of my seat to celebrate and it was only when I landed that I remembered the injury. It hurt like hell."

Ormsby's pain notwithstanding, it was a sweet moment for Leeds. All they had to do was hold out for the remaining 20 minutes and promotion was theirs. Half-time duly came and went, and still Charlton could find no way through. Sheridan recalls: "I really believed we were going up. Our fans had filled St Andrews that night, while Charlton only had a couple of thousand there, and everywhere we looked our fans were celebrating. We had worked so hard all season and it seemed to have paid off."

The drama that the play-offs have since become renowned for changed all that as a goalmouth scramble ended with Peter Shirtliff neatly side-footing the ball through a crowd of players and past Day from 10 yards out. United's frustration at being pegged back saw Sheridan shoot from the resulting kick-off, his effort sailing harmlessly over the crossbar. Four minutes later, that frustration had turned to despair as Shirtliff netted his second goal of the night with a diving header from Trevor Peake's cross. Bremner made one last effort to rally his troops by reminding them of what had happened at Boundary Park, but this time there was to be no dramatic late fightback as Charlton held on to preserve their First Division status. For Bremner, to end the season with nothing was devastating. His United side had played in 55 games, the most involving the club since the season that culminated in a European Cup final appearance. They had also won plenty of praise, not least for their performance in defeat during the FA Cup semi-final. But, to a man whose autobiography in 1970 had been titled *You Get Nowt For Being Second*, this wasn't enough. He had to be a success, and that meant leading his beloved Leeds United back into the First Division.

Chapter 24

A Boy Named Diego

As the tears flowed in the Leeds United dressing room for the second time in a little under seven weeks, Billy Bremner could empathise with his distraught side. He had been there, particularly at the start of his own playing career when Leeds had continually been left frustrated in their chase for honours. United had finished second in the league, Europe and the FA Cup before the breakthrough finally came by winning the League Cup in 1968. Further success then followed in the form of the Inter Cities' Fairs Cup and the League Championship within 15 months of that Wembley triumph over Arsenal. But, still the disappointments kept coming as Leeds followed their first title success by finishing runners-up three years running. It meant Bremner, standing in the St Andrews dressing room, knew from bitter experience what would be racing through the minds of those sitting in front of him. Words of encouragement were needed because it was paramount that the players understood just how well they had done across the full season. Bremner knew the summer months would be long. So, it was imperative that, before heading off to the beach, the players believed happier days lay ahead. Bremner, for his own part, genuinely felt that would be the case. A slight tweak here and the odd addition there would, he reasoned, be enough to ensure Leeds went one better the following season to reclaim a place in the top flight.

In the boardroom, however, there was a different thought process developing. The directors had enjoyed a season where pride had been restored to the club. They had also been impressed with the job done by their manager, so much so that Bremner had been offered – and accepted – a new three-year contract during the run-in. But there was also the opinion that, following the crushing blow of defeat in the play-off final, a real buzz needed creating around Elland Road. And how better to do that, said managing director Bill Fotherby to the rest of the board, than by signing the biggest name in world football? He explains: "The Cup run and play-off games had generated a spirit and a positive feeling around the club. But I knew, after just having missed out on both fronts, that we needed more. We were in the old Second Division and crowds had fallen to around 15,000 so something spectacular was needed. It was then that it came to me – sign Maradona, who was at the height of his powers having just won the World Cup."

Argentina's success in Mexico the previous year had confirmed Diego Maradona's standing as the world's best player. Not only had he captained his country to victory, but Maradona's own displays had lit up the tournament. A return of five goals and five assists underlined his importance to Argentina's success, while the goal that ultimately knocked England out of the quarter-finals would later be voted the best of all-time by FIFA. By 1987, he had repeated that success on the domestic stage by inspiring unfashionable Napoli to their first Serie A title. His move to southern Italy from Barcelona three years earlier had sparked an instant turnaround in fortunes for a club whose previous success amounted to just two Italian Cups. So, when Napoli clinched their first title on May 10, 1987, Maradona's standing in the footballing outpost went from hero to God. Within a month, Fotherby had launched his publicity drive by telling the *Yorkshire Evening Post* that talks had been opened with the player's representatives over a possible move to West Yorkshire. Under the front page headline 'Maradona! United's sensational bid for Argie soccer superstar', the newspaper's Don Warters revealed how Leeds were hoping to bring Maradona to Elland Road for the 1988-89 season 'due to him having already agreed to play one more season for Napoli'. The front page story went on to claim Spurs were also interested and that a figure of £9m had been suggested as a possible fee but that Leeds believed around £5m would be sufficient. It sounded barely believable to United's supporters even then, less so today knowing what further success Maradona went on to have with Napoli by securing a second Serie A title in 1990 – 12 months after lifting the UEFA Cup. But Fotherby, who went on to become Leeds chairman before leaving Elland Road in 1997 and handing over the reins to his successor Peter Ridsdale, insists: "It was not a gimmick, not at all. We genuinely thought it could happen. I knew Maradona's agent in London at the time, Jon Smith. So, I sidled up to him at a dinner. His initial response was, 'You can't afford Maradona – he'll cost you £5-6m'. I had certain sponsors lined up and told Jon this, so we arranged to meet at Elland Road where we could talk about all the possibilities. We agreed Maradona should come to Elland Road and play in an exhibition game a few days after playing in the Football League Centenary celebrations at Wembley, which were due to take place the following year. I also spoke to the Civic Hall about possibly hiring it out so the great and the good of Leeds could meet Maradona."

With secrecy the order of the day at Leeds, Bremner was at this stage completely in the dark about the fledgling talks. However, Fotherby, who is the first to admit he and the Scot "did not have the easiest of relationships", knew his manager would have to be brought into the loop sooner rather than later. He adds: "By now, I was thinking, 'I'm going to have to tell Billy about this or word is going to get out'. It was in danger of getting out of control. I wasn't sure what response I would get, mainly because of our relationship. I always believed it was vital for the chairman and manager at a club to have a good relationship, as without that closeness it can spell trouble. At Leeds, though, our chairman Leslie Silver did not really socialise with the manager. He preferred to leave the day-to-day contact to me as managing director. I had a fantastic relationship with Billy's successor Howard Wilkinson, who had very much been my appointment after I had been advised by Bobby Robson to go for him. But with Billy, it was not the same. Billy was one of the old school, who didn't want directors interfering in any way. I admit I am a different kind of director to most. I was a footballer and think I have a good instinct for spotting whether a player has ability. But I always got the impression Billy thought I was too influential within the club. Relations became a bit strained so I didn't suggest any players to Billy. Eventually, though, I had to tell him about Maradona. His response? Put it this way, he didn't do any double somersaults. Managers like to pick their own players and if Maradona came he would have to be accompanied by an entourage. I don't think Billy wanted that, so he was sceptical."

Bremner may have been hugely sceptical about the possibility of signing Maradona but, in public, he did at least play the publicity game. The day after the move had first been mooted, he told the *Yorkshire Evening Post*: 'It is a colossal thing to try and bring someone like Maradona to the club but Mr Smith felt we had a feasible proposition. Naturally, I would be delighted for the deal to be pulled off. It is any manager's dream to have a player such as Maradona in the side. If the money can be raised, no-one would be more grateful than me.'

In the days that followed, Leeds continued to maintain the deal was still possible with Maradona's London agent Smith telling the local press in Yorkshire how impressed he was with United's set-up. But, soon, even the ultra-optimistic Fotherby was starting to have doubts. "Everyone tried but, in the end, we just couldn't make the deal happen," he recalls. "Things just petered out, which was a real shame as it would have been amazing for Leeds United. But, even though the deal didn't work out, it still earned us huge publicity. I think it played a part in the re-birth of the club."

The ultimate collapse of the Maradona deal was barely noticed by Bremner, the Scot having been preoccupied with bringing in what he considered to be much more realistic targets. One of those was Glynn Snodin, his former player from Doncaster Rovers having been made available for transfer by Sheffield Wednesday. Bremner duly bid £150,000 and Snodin was unveiled as a Leeds player shortly after the initial Maradona story had broken. Glynn recalls: "I jumped at the chance to work with Billy again. We'd had such good times together at Doncaster and Leeds had come so close to winning promotion the previous season that it seemed the right time to move to Elland Road."

Bremner's only other summer acquisition was Gary Williams, the Aston Villa winger he brought in for £230,000. Williams, a member of the Villa side that had won the European Cup by beating Bayern Munich in Rotterdam five years earlier, joined Snodin as United's two debutants in an opening day 1-1 draw at Barnsley. It was a solid start and one that was followed by two goalless draws and a couple of 1-0 wins. Bremner was pleased with a defence that had only been breached once in those opening five games, though slightly worried that his side had only managed to find the net three times. By the end of September, those concerns had grown with United's goal tally from the opening 11 games standing at a paltry five. Bremner had already been rebuffed by Oxford United when asking after Ray Houghton, while Manchester United had given a similar answer to an enquiry about Peter Davenport. Sporting Lisbon striker Raphael Meade, once of Arsenal, was also the subject of an unsuccessful bid from Bremner, who eventually did make progress in the transfer market when Charlton Athletic's Jim Melrose and Liverpool's Ken De Mange joined. In November, Bobby Davison was brought in from Derby County for £350,000. He scored on his debut as Swindon Town were beaten 4-2 in a game that, over time, has become much more notable as the afternoon a young David Batty made his bow for the club.

Batty was someone Bremner had been watching closely in the youth team and reserves for a couple of seasons. He liked how the youngster exuded fearlessness despite not being the biggest of players, something Bremner recognised as one of his own traits. Dave Bentley recalls: "Funnily enough, the day Billy found out he had got the Leeds job we were both watching a youth team game between Doncaster and Leeds. David Batty was in the Leeds team that morning, and even before we got the news about the job

Billy had said, 'That young lad is a smashing player and could have a decent future'. What we didn't know at the time was Billy would give David his debut a couple of years later." Batty's debut was an impressive affair, the 18-year-old leaving Elland Road with a bottle of champagne after being named man of the match by the sponsors. Batty stayed in the side for the rest of the season, playing his part in a revival that brought five straight wins in December and a Manager of the Month award for Bremner. Typically, the winner wanted everyone to share in his success – as Glynn Snodin recalls: "Billy was presented with the award at the next home game, along with a gallon bottle of Bells whisky. Billy, being Billy, gave us all a bottle each from it, saying the award was down to the players and not him."

Thanks to the winning run, a sense of belief had returned to not only the team but also the city as the New Year's Day visit of Bradford City attracted a crowd of 36,004 – the highest in six years at Elland Road. Goals from Bremner's two signings from the previous summer, Williams and Snodin, duly clinched a 2-0 derby win and the hope among the United management was that 1988 would bring a concerted push for promotion. Instead, the maddening inconsistency that had characterised the opening few months of the season returned and Leeds finished seventh – eight points behind Blackburn Rovers in the final play-off place. Batty's emergence and the winning run of December were rare highlights, though supporters were 'treated' – if that is the right word – to a first Wembley visit in 14 years in a competition held to mark the centenary of the Football League.

The Mercantile Credit Football Festival was designed as a celebration of the League's history with the final scheduled for April 17, 100 years to the day since the competition had been formed at a meeting of the 12 original clubs in Manchester. The League devised a format that would see 16 clubs compete in the Festival - eight from the top flight, four from Division Two and two each from Divisions Three and Four. Qualification was to be decided by the number of points collected between the start of November and the end of February. Any clubs not able to fulfil the required 15 League fixtures would have points allocated on a pro-rata basis. Leeds, thanks in the main to the run of seven wins in eight games that began with the 4-2 triumph over Swindon, collected 30 points, a tally only beaten by Blackburn Rovers and Aston Villa in the second tier.

A Wembley trip would, in the days before play-off and Football League Trophy finals were played at the national stadium, usually have been something to savour. But, in truth, the Festival never came close to capturing the public's imagination. Scare stories in the national press about hooliganism during the build-up didn't help, though the lack of enthusiasm – Wembley was never more than a fifth-full at any one time over the weekend - probably had as much to do with the contrived nature of the tournament. Due to so many teams taking part in the finals weekend, all games in rounds one and two were reduced to just 40 minutes with the semi-finals and final due to last an hour. Because of the limited amount of time, nine of the 15 games had to be settled by a penalty shoot-out – including the final as Nottingham Forest beat Sheffield Wednesday. The previous day, Forest had knocked Leeds out in the first round with a comfortable 3-0 win. It meant the weekend had, just like the season, been a flat one. John Sheridan, who finished the campaign as top scorer with 14 goals, recalls: "We started the season okay but just couldn't repeat the form of the previous year. Things had started to drift. Billy did his best to try and make something happen. He was a real wheeler and dealer in the transfer market. He would spend £30,000 here and £20,000 there, showing he had a knack of putting together a good squad on a small budget. Leeds were not a rich club back then, I think in my eight years the most we ever spent on one player was £250,000."

During those closing weeks of the season, Bremner was as disappointed as anyone that a promotion challenge had not materialised. In front of his players, though, he hid it well in an attempt to keep spirits up. Peter Swan, who during 1987-88 had been switched from defence to attack to contribute some useful goals, says: "Billy was brilliant; a typical red-haired Scotsman who could fly off the handle at you but also treated every one of us like his own sons. On a day-to-day basis, he worked us hard and could be cutting and quite nasty at times. But, he also made sure it was a happy environment. Billy would bring some of his old team-mates down on a Friday morning to take part in games. Norman Hunter was already on the coaching staff but Joe Jordan and Mick Bates would also join in. Billy loved having them around at what was his club. Billy also loved a laugh, he was a real players' manager in that respect and always joining in with the banter. He once tried to stitch me up when it was Children in Need night. The organisers wanted a couple of the lads to take part and one of us was supposed to try and do as many keepy-uppys as possible in a minute. I was hopeless at them, and Billy knew that so he sent me along with Mark Aizlewood. I was dreading it, and certain I would humiliate myself in front of everyone. It was mischievous of Billy, though it back-fired as I only made one mistake. Billy said later his face dropped as he watched me doing an impression of Pele by keeping the ball up loads of times in that minute."

Another group who Bremner remained bright and bubbly with were the Press. Leeds may have been out of the top flight for six years by the end of his second full season in charge, but they were still a newsworthy club. It meant there were considerable demands on the manager's time. Dave Callaghan, who covered United for *BBC Radio Leeds* for seven years from 1987, recalls: "The first meeting I had with Billy was shortly after I had been appointed. I wanted to change things around so I put my ideas to Billy, who was very receptive. The only thing he insisted on was not speaking to the Press straight after games due to being worried about saying something in the heat of the moment. He was such an emotionally involved manager that he was worried about getting himself into trouble. Instead, we had to speak to his assistant, Dave Bentley, which was not ideal as the fans want to hear from the manager. But, that apart, Billy could not have been more helpful to the guys who covered the club. He always kept us informed, even if a lot of it would be off-the-record. Often, after an away game we would get back to Elland Road on the team bus and Billy would invite us all into his office for a drink. Then, he would tell us his thoughts about the game or club matters – under the strict understanding that it was not to be relayed in either the papers or on the radio. It was very informative and gave us all a real insight, meaning we could speak or write with much more authority. This continued throughout Billy's time as manager, even when things had started to go against him in terms of results."

As brave a face as Bremner was putting on things publicly, deep down he knew the clock was ticking. By the summer of 1988, he had been back at Elland Road for almost three years and progress had been made. But a return to the top flight was still proving elusive. The board were getting impatient so the coming season really would be his last chance to get it right. Unfortunately, it started badly with a disappointing 1-1 draw at home to Oxford United followed by a 4-0 thrashing at Portsmouth. The defeat at Fratton Park was made even more damning in the eyes of the board by Bremner having signed Noel Blake and Vince Hilaire from Pompey in the summer. Draws against Manchester City and Bournemouth were then followed by a 2-0 defeat to Chelsea at Elland Road, United's miserable afternoon capped by a return of the club's hooliganism problem as louts put the windows through of a local car showroom after being frustrated in their attempts to confront the visiting fans by the police. Leeds were back in the lower reaches of the Second Division, just where they had been when Bremner succeeded Eddie Gray. The board's mind was made up, the manager had to go. Chairman Leslie Silver recalls: "Billy had been a first-class captain under Don Revie and a wonderful player who was very successful. But he was a poor manager. I had probably realised within about a year of making the appointment that Billy was not the right man. Even as we got to the FA Cup semi-final and went so close to promotion, I had my reservations. A problem was he had no ability in terms of communicating with the directors. We had regular fortnightly meetings in the boardroom and he never came on his own, usually it was his scout Dave Blakey who accompanied him. Billy didn't like speaking in the boardroom, in fact I can't really remember him opening his mouth. If anyone asked a question, Blakey would answer for him. On a personal level, I did like Billy as he was a nice man. But he just wouldn't communicate with the board. Of course, that on its own doesn't have to be a big problem but when performances and results start to suffer then it is. To me, it had become clear it just wasn't working out. The results were not good enough and I also believed the dressing room was not fully behind him. A change was needed. We had a board meeting but the decision had already been made. A few on the board said, 'How can you sack Billy Bremner? He is a legend at the club'. But we had to do something in the best interests of Leeds United."

Silver's belief that Bremner's reign had run its course was shared by managing director Fotherby. "I felt we needed a break from the Revie days," he says. "Three former players had managed the club without it working out so we wanted to move in a new direction. Letting a manager go is never easy, it is probably the most horrible part of the job. But we felt the club needed a bit more than Billy." The decision made, United's board broke the news to Bremner the day after his team had beaten Peterborough United in a League Cup second round first leg tie at London Road. Dave Bentley recalls: "It did come as a shock. We hadn't seen it coming, especially as we had won the night before. Games like Peterborough away can be quite sticky so we were not expecting the sack. Billy was gutted, Leeds were his club. He was also sorry to have to say goodbye to the lads. Billy enjoyed the banter as much as anyone, even in the cards schools on the away trips when if he was losing he would order the bus driver to go round the block until he won again. He loved spending time with such a great group and was really sad to have to say goodbye."

The Leeds players, if not totally surprised by the news bearing in mind recent results, were still upset for Bremner. Glynn Snodin says: "Billy loved being the gaffer at Leeds. Elland Road was his home, Leeds his club. So, it was sad when he was sacked. After being told by the board, Billy called a meeting of the lads to tell us the news. I was filling up all the way through. It was horrible, as Billy was like a second father to me. I was so upset for him because he so wanted to make Leeds United successful again." Peter Swan was another in that emotional last meeting. He says: "It had become clear for a while Billy might be forced out but it was still sad when it happened. Looking back, we probably suffered a hangover from that play-off final defeat that we never really got over." John Sheridan also believes United's chance of promotion under Bremner had been in May, 1987. "Losing to Charlton was what did for Billy," he says. "If we had gone up, Billy could have established us in the First Division. He would have had to strengthen, as quite a few of the lads were coming to the end of their careers. But I am sure Billy would have been given the money to bring in what he felt would have been needed had we gone up by beating Charlton at St Andrews."

Bremner's reign was, after almost three years, over. United had spent £2.25m on transfers and recouped around £1.5m in sales but a return to the top flight had proved beyond the club. It would take the arrival of Howard Wilkinson from Sheffield Wednesday and the release of significant transfer funds to rectify that, as a squad containing Gordon Strachan, Vinnie Jones, Chris Fairclough and Lee Chapman won promotion in 1990. Two years later, United were crowned champions for a third time. Silver adds: "Howard represented a total break from the Revie days in every way imaginable, including the removal of all the old photographs and trophies at Elland Road."

Bremner, in common with all United fans, was delighted to see success return to Elland Road under Wilkinson – even if there was also a touch of envy at the resources afforded his successor. Dave Bentley says: "The thing that stuck in Billy's throat was that he had been asked to cut his budget in the season he left. Yet, when the next manager came in, Leeds suddenly found a money tree at the bottom of the Elland Road car park with millions on it. Howard did a great job. But I know Billy found it a little hard to take. It left a bit of a sour taste. Billy was low for some time afterwards because he had so wanted to achieve big things at Leeds United. With decent cash to spend, I think he could have done that. Who is to say it would not have happened under Billy with the same resources as Howard had?"

Chapter 25

Rovers Return

'Never go back,' is an adage often uttered in football circles. Whether it be a manager considering a return to the scene of former glories or a player hoping to repeat the success of earlier in his career, the advice from their peer group will invariably be, 'Don't do it.' For Billy Bremner, however, the chance to become Doncaster Rovers manager again in the summer of 1989 was one he could not resist. It had been ten months since his sacking by Leeds United and Bremner had tried to keep himself busy. He had been out watching football on a regular basis, noting down players who he felt would be useful signings should an opportunity to return to management arise in the future. He had also kept in touch with his many friends within football, all the while keeping his eye open for any possible openings. But he craved a return to the game that had been his life. Offers had come in, including one to coach abroad, but none really appealed. Then, Doncaster came calling.

Since Bremner's departure in 1985, Rovers had slipped into decline. Initially, the club had appeared to weather the loss of a manager who had been in charge for seven years. Under his successor Dave Cusack, they claimed creditable 11th and 13th place finishes in the Third Division. Soon, though, fortunes were nose diving and Cusack was sacked in December, 1987, with Doncaster in the relegation zone. Dave Mackay's subsequent appointment failed to turn the tide and a 24th place finish meant a return to the basement division. Worse was to follow in the season that saw Bremner lose his job at Leeds as Rovers finished just one place off the bottom of the Football League. Had Darlington not been in even more wretched form, the south Yorkshire club would have been relegated from the League and replaced by Conference champions Maidstone United. It was not just on the field, either, where Rovers had suffered with crowds having dwindled to an average of 2,158 – a little under half what it had been in Bremner's last full season at Belle Vue in 1984-85. Clearly, the club needed a lift and possible salvation came in the form of a new consortium led by Jersey Airline owner, Mike Collett.

Along with fellow board members Peter Wetzel – a director during Bremner's first stint in charge - and Cheshire-based businessman John Ryan,

Collett had big ideas. After a takeover was successfully negotiated, a plan to issue 300,000 new shares in the club was announced as the new board revealed a five-year plan to win a return to the Second Division, a level Doncaster had last played at in 1958. A key factor would be the appointment of a new manager and the three men were unanimous in who it should be. Ryan, who later became Rovers chairman, recalls: "I had supported Rovers since being a boy so when the opportunity arose to get involved in 1989, I jumped at the chance. Peter Wetzel, who had been the main benefactor in the 1980s before becoming disillusioned, was also involved. The proviso was that Billy be brought back as manager. He had been very successful during his first spell and led us to two promotions. Since Billy's departure to Leeds, the club had been in decline and we felt he was the best man to turn it round. Belle Vue was rundown, crowds had dropped to a couple of thousand because there wasn't a lot of money around following the miners' strike and Rovers were, basically, broke. We'd had a couple of years in the Third Division after Billy left but were, by now, back near the foot of the entire Football League. The whole place badly needed a lift, which is why we went for Billy."

An approach was made and, much to their delight, Bremner was interested. One major problem, though, was that Doncaster already had a manager, Joe Kinnear having stepped up from assistant following Dave MacKay's resignation the previous March. Not only that, but the former Tottenham Hotspur defender had just been told by chairman Bernie Boldry that his job was safe. The new board were not, however, ones to hang around and Kinnear was duly sacked on June 30 – a decision that Boldry followed by handing in his resignation. Bremner's appointment was confirmed four days later. At his unveiling, Bremner revealed his delight at being back in football before telling the *Yorkshire Post*: 'I turned down several offers from elsewhere because I believe in the potential of Doncaster Rovers. We were near the top of Division Three and in with a chance of promotion when I left. I believe we can go back up there again.'

To bring about a revival, Bremner knew a squad that had finished the previous season in 91st place needed strengthening. John McGinley, a left winger from Lincoln City, was the first new arrival before Bremner returned to his former club Leeds to sign midfielder John Stiles. He had been an ever-present in United's run to the FA Cup semi-finals under Bremner two years earlier only for injuries to restrict his appearances in the subsequent seasons. Stiles was delighted to be reunited with his former manager, even if their time together at Elland Road had left him with one unwanted distinction. Stiles recalls: "Thanks to Billy, I was the first Leeds United substitute to be substituted. We were playing at Millwall in the Full Members Cup in December, 1987, when Billy brought me on for Peter Haddock. Unfortunately, later in the game I was replaced by John Pearson. You can imagine how happy I was afterwards to be told it had never happened to a Leeds player before. I did ask Billy about it, and he claimed it was tactical. But I think he was just being kind. I was crap that night."

With Stiles and McGinley on board and Bremner having inherited a couple of familiar faces from his Leeds days in Jack Ashurst and Vince Brockie, the new Rovers manager was in hopeful mood ahead of the opening day trip to Exeter City. An unfortunate 1-0 defeat failed to dent his optimism but, soon, the realisation had sunk in that Doncaster had finished in such a lowly position a few months earlier for a reason. By mid-September, they were third bottom and clearly in for a long campaign. There were bright spots, including a 6-0 win at Hartlepool United and an unbeaten run of seven games during the build-up to Christmas. Even then, however, the 19-point haul could only nudge Doncaster up to 17th before a disappointing second half of the campaign saw them fall back three places to 20th.

With their side's league form such a disappointment, Rovers fans were, at least, offered some excitement by the Leyland DAF Cup. By now an established part of the football calendar for clubs in the bottom two divisions, a competition that had started life as the Associate Members' Cup had hardly been a successful one for Rovers. Each of the previous four seasons had, for instance, brought an exit at the first stage. So, when Bremner's side negotiated a preliminary round group containing Huddersfield Town, Grimsby Town and Bury, there was mild surprise at Belle Vue. Subsequent victories over Wigan Athletic and Halifax Town then put Rovers through to the Northern Area final, meaning a trip to Wembley was potentially just 180 minutes away. Just as importantly, the Leyland DAF run had captured the public's imagination with the semi-final win over the Shaymen attracting a crowd of 5,754 – at that stage, the club's highest crowd of the season. That Doncaster would play Tranmere Rovers in the two-legged final was not ideal, John King's side being the Third Division leaders and, therefore, overwhelming favourites. But thanks to having already knocked out three clubs from a higher level, Bremner was in confident enough mood to send his side out to attack in the first leg at Prenton Park. Had Kevin Noteman not missed an open goal after going round Tranmere goalkeeper Eric Nixon, such a bold approach may have paid dividends. Instead, thanks in part to Mark Hughes getting back to clear Noteman's subsequent weak shot off the line, it was the home side who claimed a 2-0 advantage to take into the second leg at Belle Vue. The teams met again a month later but, despite going into the game on the back of three wins in four games, Doncaster could only draw 1-1 in front of 6,670 fans. Bremner was disappointed to miss out on a trip to Wembley, but he felt his side's performances in the competition offered hope for the future. A few key additions and, he felt, Rovers would be set to challenge for promotion.

In came Peterborough United goalkeeper Paul Crichton, Stoke City defender Andy Holmes and Tottenham Hotspur midfielder Eddie Gormley during the summer along with a familiar face from Bremner's time at Leeds. Brendan Ormsby had suffered such a serious injury during the 1987 play-off final replay defeat to Charlton Athletic that he had made just one more appearance for the club in the intervening three years. Despite that, Bremner was desperate to sign a player he felt would become an integral part of what he was trying to build at Doncaster. Ormsby recalls: "I'd been told I could leave Leeds by Howard Wilkinson and Billy invited me down to Belle Vue. The day I went down, it was pouring and it is fair to say I wasn't overly impressed as I pulled into the car park. There were potholes all over and the whole place looked like it was going to fall down. I remember turning to my wife and saying, 'What the hell am I doing here?' Five minutes later, though, and I was ready to sign. Billy had lost none of his infectious enthusiasm and he wanted me as captain, even going so far as to say he was going to build a side capable of winning promotion around me."

With all four summer signings in the starting line-up, Rovers opened the season with a 3-2 win at Carlisle United. After the next four games had also been won, they sat proudly on top of the table. Four straight defeats then tempered expectation only for Bremner's side to respond by losing just one more game before the turn of the year. It meant Doncaster were again back at the summit, a position they held courtesy of a battling goalless draw at third-placed Northampton Town on New Year's Day. Bremner's energy and enthusiasm had, it seemed, once again galvanised the club. John Stiles, who missed just a handful of games in the 1990-91 season, says: "Billy had not changed in the slightest from when we had been together at Leeds. I don't think he could have changed, even if he had wanted to. It didn't matter if it was an FA Cup semi-final or an end-of-season Fourth Division game, he had to win. The passion he had for football was infectious. Just as at Leeds, he joined in with the training and all the banter in the dressing room. His sense of humour was still the same, anyone wearing anything a bit dodgy would be mercilessly given stick. Billy was also great with the young lads at Doncaster, giving them every encouragement."

Unfortunately for Bremner, the New Year's Day draw at Northampton's County Ground proved to be the high point for Doncaster. Defeat at Wrexham a week later may have been followed by back-to-back home wins over Carlisle and Rochdale but, by early March, Rovers were clinging on in the promotion race. The size of the Belle Vue squad had been causing Bremner concern for much of the campaign, so much so that he had been forced to lure Jack Ashurst out of retirement in November to ease an injury crisis. Such were the problems caused by injuries and suspension that, by the end of the campaign, 36-year-old Ashurst had played 29 games. Amid this constant chopping and changing of personnel, results inevitably suffered and Doncaster's season tailed off as a failure to win any of their last eight games led to an 11th place finish. It was a substantial improvement on the previous year, but Bremner was hugely disappointed. To not even claim a play-off place after spending all but six weeks in the top seven had to be deemed a failure. Nevertheless, he remained optimistic that the 1991-92 season would make amends. Alas, it was not to be as a 3-0 opening day home defeat to Carlisle set the tone for what was to follow. By the first Saturday of September, Rovers had lost all four league games and conceded 13 goals. Worse still, Crewe Alexandra had inflicted a 9-4 aggregate drubbing on Bremner's side in the League Cup. A first win of the season briefly raised spirits as Wrexham were beaten 3-1 but, by the end of October, Doncaster were sitting bottom of the League with just six points from 13 games. Bremner had seen enough and resigned on the eve of the trip to Mansfield Town. Ryan, then a director of the club, recalls: "We had given Billy a bit of money but, unfortunately, things had not worked out. I think he realised it just as much as we did and decided to go after two years as manager. It was a shame, but it did nothing to dent Billy's popularity with the fans. The standing he continues to enjoy in the town was why, before Rovers played at Elland Road in 2008, we had a little ceremony at Billy's statue. There was me as chairman, deputy chairman Dick Watson and president Trevor Milton. We laid some flowers and put a Rovers scarf on the statue. There were quite a few Leeds fans present who applauded after the ceremony had finished. It showed how much Doncaster still loves Billy. He spent nine years as our manager in two spells, and while that is not as long as his time at Leeds it still represents a significant part of his career in football."

The Rovers players were just as sad to see Bremner quit. Stiles recalls: "With hindsight, joining Doncaster from Leeds was probably not my wisest move as there were a couple of other clubs from a higher division interested. But I am also glad that I got to play for Billy again. The best way to sum up what playing for Billy was like is that he made what is a dream job even more enjoyable. With the career that my Dad had and also my Uncle John, I was always going to struggle to make a big impression. But I do feel lucky to have played for Billy Bremner – even if he did give me that unwanted distinction of being the first Leeds substitute to be substituted."

Epilogue

Bremner would never work again in football, instead choosing to enjoy semi-retirement surrounded by his beloved family. He did still work, proving to be an accomplished expert summariser on radio as well as a huge success as an after-dinner speaker. His wide array of anecdotes, which much to the surprise of anyone familiar with his forgetful nature were relayed without the need for notes, proved hugely popular. The public speaking also suited Bremner, according to his former assistant Dave Bentley. "He enjoyed the after-dinner circuit as it was a chance to tell all those great stories of his," he says. "The places were always full, because people wanted to hear them. Billy didn't want to do it full-time but it was something that allowed him to talk football – which is what he loved. It also got him away from gardening and hanging around the house, so he enjoyed it even more. Above all, though, what Billy loved to do after leaving football was spend time with his family."

Typically, the tremendous work ethic that had characterised his career in football was very much in evidence. Mike O'Grady, his former team-mate at Leeds, says: "Billy just loved working. I remember seeing him at my old school Corpus Christi, where he was doing an after-dinner speech. He looked tired and I remember thinking, 'I wouldn't be doing this on a Wednesday night, Billy'. But he had such a big appetite for work that he will have never considered winding things down."

As hard as he worked, Bremner's main enjoyment came from his family. The arrival of a first grandchild merely added to his contentment. Tragically, however, this idyll of family life was shattered in the early hours of Sunday, December 7. Bremner had been admitted to Doncaster Royal Infirmary the previous Thursday after feeling unwell at his home near Rotherham. The first indication of the possible severity of the situation was Bremner turning down requests from friends to visit, his reasoning being that he didn't want anyone but close family to see him ill. Even so, the news that Bremner had passed away just two days short of what would have been his 55th birthday still came as a huge shock to the football world. Not only did no-one want to believe the bombshell news, but they couldn't. Bremner had, throughout his career, seemed indestructible. Sadly, the news was correct. Leeds was plunged into mourning and the outpouring of grief was perhaps the strongest since the passing of Don Revie eight-and-a-half years earlier. The gates at Elland Road were immediately covered in shirts, scarves and flags of tribute. One, from United's official supporters club, read: 'We all have to be grateful that Billy chose Leeds United and gave us all so many memories."

Bremner's funeral was held the following Thursday at St Mary's Roman Catholic Church, Edlington, near Doncaster. Bremner's devastated former Leeds team-mates were all present, as was Revie's widow Elsie. Many of the players Bremner had managed at both Leeds and Doncaster were among the congregation along with a host of famous figures from the football world. Manchester United manager Alex Ferguson was so desperate to attend he was there despite only flying back from a Champions League fixture in Turin the previous evening. All were united in tribute to one of the game's greatest players and, just as importantly, a good man. John Buckley, who played under Bremner at two clubs, recalls: "I actually knew Billy had died before most people as a mate of mine's wife worked at Doncaster Royal Infirmary. He rang to tell me the news and I just felt numb. It was awful. Billy had been so good to me. When I suffered a nasty head injury and had to retire from football in the early 1990s, Billy had spoken at a few fundraising dinners and insisted on not being paid. I really appreciated that. The thing I remember most, though, about his funeral is talking to people and realising just how modest Billy had been. No-one could remember him starting a conversation about himself, instead it would always be things like, 'Bucky, you were one of the best I ever had'. I am in no doubt I wasn't, but it was Billy all over to say something like that whenever we met up."

Ian Snodin was another who found it hard to keep his emotions in check during the service at St Mary's. He adds: "At the funeral, his wife Vicky said to me, 'You were always his favourite out of all those who played for him'. That really choked me up and it took me a long time to get over his death. Even now, I doubt a day goes by without me thinking of Billy in some way. He was everything to me and I even once named my house, 'Bremner Lodge' in his memory. It was a lovely, four-bedroom house near Doncaster and I thought, 'Without Billy's influence on my life and career, I would never have been able to own a house like this'. He was everything to me and I looked up to him so much that at every club I joined, I tried to get the number 4 shirt. I had it at Donny, Leeds and Everton. He meant the world to me and, in a way, he was a second father. We were very close and I miss him. There was only one Billy Bremner and I feel very fortunate to have known him."

Perhaps the most fitting tribute, though, came from two men who succeeded Bremner in his treasured role as the on-field lieutenant of Elland Road as the message accompanying a wreath from Gary McAllister and Gordon Strachan. It simply read: "To Leeds United's greatest captain. It was an honour to follow in your footsteps."

Statistics

PLAYER

Leeds United *(December, 1959 to September, 1976)*.
Hull City *(September, 1976 to June, 1978)*.
Doncaster Rovers *(March, 1980 to February, 1982)*.
(All appearances for Doncaster as player-manager)

Honours (all Leeds):
First Division: Champions 1969 & 1974, Runner-up 1965, 1966, 1970, 1971, 1972.
Division Two: Champions 1964.
FA Cup: Winner 1972, Runner-up 1965, 1970, 1973.
League Cup: Winner 1968.
European Cup: Runner-up 1975.
Inter-Cities Fairs Cup: Winner 1968 & 1971, Runner-up 1967.
Footballer of the Year: 1970.

Debut: Chelsea 1 Leeds United 3; January 23, 1960; Division One.
Last game: Doncaster Rovers 0 Newport County 2; February 27, 1982; Division Three.

League appearances

Season	Club	Competition	App	Gls	Pos
1959-60	Leeds United	Div One	11	2	21st (R)
1960-61		Div Two	31	9	14th
1961-62			39	11	19th
1962-63			24	10	5th
1963-64			39	3	1st (P)
1964-65		Div One	40	6	2nd
1965-66			41	8	2nd
1966-67			36(1)	2	4th
1967-68			36	2	4th
1968-69			42	6	1st
1969-70			35	4	2nd

Season	Club	Div	App	Gls	Pos
1970-71			26	3	2nd
1971-72			41	5	2nd
1972-73			38	4	3rd
1973-74			42	10	1st
1974-75			27	1	9th
1975-76			34	5	5th
1976-77			4	0	10th
1976-77	Hull City	Div Two	30	2	14th
1977-78			31	4	22nd (R)
1978-79	Doncaster Rovers	Div Four	-	-	22nd
1979-80			1	-	12th
1980-81			1(2)	0	3rd (P)
1981-82		Div Three	-(1)	0	19th

Domestic Cup competitions

Season	Club	FA Cup			League Cup		
		App	Gls	Rnd	App	Gls	Rnd
1959-60	Leeds United	-	-	3rd	-	-	-
1960-61		1	0	3rd	2	1	4th
1961-62		2	0	3rd	4	1	4th
1962-63		0	0	5th	0	0	3rd
1963-64		3	1	4th	1	0	4th
1964-65		8	1	R/U	1	0	3rd
1965-66		2	0	4th	0	0	3rd
1966-67		6	0	SF	4	0	4th
1967-68		5	0	SF	6	1	Won
1968-69		2	0	4th	2	1	4th
1969-70		9	1	R/U	2	0	3rd
1970-71		2	0	5th	1	0	2nd
1971-72		7	0	Won	4	0	3rd
1972-73		7	1	R/U	5	0	4th
1973-74		5	1	5th	1	0	2nd
1974-75		8	0	6th	2	0	4th
1975-76		2	0	4th	2	0	3rd
1976-77		-	-	-	1	0	2nd
1976-77	Hull City	2	0	3rd	-	-	-
1977-78		1	0	3rd	4	1	4th

Final appearances

1965	FA Cup	Leeds United 1	Liverpool 2 (AET)
1968	League Cup	Leeds United 1	Arsenal 0
1970	FA Cup	Leeds United 2	Chelsea 1 (AET)
	replay	Leeds United 1	Chelsea 2 (AET)
1972	FA Cup	Leeds United 1	Arsenal 0
1973	FA Cup	Leeds United 0	Sunderland 1

European Competition

(all Leeds United)

Season	*Competition*	*App*	*Gls*	*Round*
1965-66	Inter-Cities Fairs Cup	11	2	SF
1966-67	Inter-Cities Fairs Cup	10	1	R/U
1967-68	Inter-Cities Fairs Cup	10	0	Won
1968-69	Inter-Cities Fairs Cup	8	1	4th
1969-70	European Cup	8	3	SF
1970-71	Inter-Cities Fairs Cup	10	3	Won
1971-72	Inter-Cities Fairs Cup	1	0	1st
1972-73	Cup Winners' Cup	7	0	R/U
1973-74	UEFA Cup	4	0	3rd
1974-75	European Cup	6	3	R/U

Final appearances

1967	Inter-Cities Fairs Cup	Dinamo Zagreb	(Leg 1) a	L	0-2
		Dinamo Zagreb	(Leg 2) H	D	0-0
1968	Inter-Cities Fairs Cup	Ferencvaros	(Leg 1) H	W	1-0
		Ferencvaros	(Leg 2) a	D	0-0
1971	Inter-Cities Fairs Cup	Juventus	(Leg 1) a	D	2-2
		Juventus	(Leg 2) H	D	1-1
1975	European Cup	Bayern Munich	(Paris)	L	0-2

(Also played in 1971 Inter-Cities Fairs Cup play-off
against Barcelona, L1-2)

Charity Shield

1969	Leeds United 2	Manchester City 1 (Elland Road)
1974	Leeds United 1	Liverpool 1 (Wembley)

International football

Caps 54, Goals 3.

Debut: Scotland 0 Spain 0; May 8, 1965; Hampden Park.

Last game: Denmark 0 Scotland 1; September 3, 1975; Copenhagen.

Season	App	Goals
1964-65	1	0
1965-66	6	0
1966-67	3	0
1967-68	2	0
1968-69	8	2
1969-70	3	0
1970-71	2	0
1971-72	9	0
1972-73	6(1)	0
1973-74	10	0
1974-75	2	1
1975-76	1	0

Captained Scotland 39 times
(First game against Denmark in October, 1968).

Goals scored versus:

Austria	H	W 2-1	(WCQ, Nov 1968);
Wales	a	W 5-3	(HI, May 1969);
Spain	H	L 1-2	(ECQ, Nov 1974).

(WCQ – World Cup qualifier, ECQ – European Championship qualifier, HI – Home International).

MANAGER

Doncaster Rovers *(November, 1978 to October , 1985).*
Leeds United *(October, 1985 to September 1988).*
Doncaster Rovers *(July 1989 to November, 1991).*

Honours

Division Four: Promoted 1981 & 1984 (both Doncaster).
FA Cup: semi-finalists 1987 (Leeds).
Second Division: Play-off finalists 1987 (Leeds).
Manager of the Month: Div Four – Oct 1979, Sept 1980, Sept 1981.
(Doncaster). Division Two – Dec 1987 (Leeds).

First game: Doncaster Rovers 1 Rochdale 0;
December 2, 1978, Division Four.
Last game: Cardiff City 2 Doncaster Rovers 1;
October 26, 1991; Division Four.

Season	Club	Competition	Pos
1978-79	Doncaster Rovers	Division Four	22nd
1979-80			12th
1980-81			3rd (P)
1981-82		Division Three	19th
1982-83			23rd (R)
1983-84		Division Four	2nd (P)
1984-85		Division Three	11th
1985-86			11th
			(finished 13th)
1985-86	Leeds United	Division Two	14th
1986-87			4th
1987-88			7th
1988-89			19th
			(finished 10th)
1989-90	Doncaster Rovers	Division Four	20th
1990-91			11th
1991-92			22nd
			(finished 21st)

Acknowledgments

First, I must thank the many dozens of Billy's friends, former team-mates, former players, officials and journalists who gave up their time so freely during my research for this book. There are far too many to list here but what I would like to say is I enjoyed tremendously hearing you reminisce and tell your stories about a man who clearly touched so many lives. I hope you all feel this book is an accurate portrayal of one of football's most enduring characters.

I am grateful to Barry Cox and his team at Great Northern Books. Not only do they make the job of author a pleasant one but the attention to detail and care shown a book once written really does make all those hours spent slaving over a hot keyboard worthwhile. Special thanks must also go to Andrew Collomosse, who, as a Huddersfield Town fan, once again overcame his natural antipathy towards Leeds United to do a fine job on the final draft. Similarly, the help of David Clay in scouring the *Yorkshire Post* photographic archive has been invaluable. Over the years, the library at the *YP* has been plundered with many images whipped off to God-knows where. It is only thanks to David's painstaking work in going through the original negatives that the *YP's* archive is being restored digitally. Many of the images in this book have not been seen for thirty or, in some cases, forty years and it is thanks to David that they have been unearthed. While on the subject of the *YP*, I would also like to thank my bosses and colleagues for their support during the writing of not only this book but also *Revie: Revered and Reviled*.

Finally, I would like to thank my ever-patient wife Anne for her love, encouragement and support throughout the writing of this book. Having the dining room colonised for months on end by ever-expanding research work cannot have been easy. Nor, in fact, can it have been much fun to get home after a busy and tiring day at work to find hubby, who had been on a day off from the *Yorkshire Post*, nowhere to be seen and the washing-up still not having been done due to me having spent the day travelling up and down the country to conduct interviews and research. Thank you, my darling.

Richard Sutcliffe
September 2011

Bibliography

Behind The Dream, Joe Jordan (Hodder & Stoughton, 2004).

Bremner!, Bernard Bale (Andre Deutsch, 1998).

Cup Final Story 1946-1965, David Prole (Robert Hale, 1966).

Don Revie – Portrait of a Footballing Enigma, Andrew Mourant (Mainstream Publishing, 1990).

English Football – Rough Guide, Dan Goldstein (Rough Guides, 1999).

International Football Book – Tenth Edition (Souvenir Press, 1968).

Jack Charlton – The Autobiography, Jack Charlton with Peter Byrne (Partridge Press, 1996).

Jimmy Armfield – The Autobiography, Jimmy Armfield (Headline, 2004).

Keep Fighting, Paul Harrison (Black & White Publishing, 2010).

Leeds United and a Life in the Press Box, John Wray (Vertical Editions, 2008).

Leeds United and Don Revie, Eric Thornton (Rober Hale & Company, 1970).

Leeds United – A Complete Record, Martin Jarred and Malcolm Macdonald (Breedon Books, 1996).

Leeds United in Europe, Richard Sutcliffe, John Wray & Richard Coomber (Leeds United Publishing, 2000).

Leeds United Book of Football No 1 (Souvenir Press, 1969).

Leeds United Book of Football No 2 (Souvenir Press, 1970).

Leeds United Book of Football No 3 (Souvenir Press, 1971).

Leeds United Internationals, Martin Jarred (Breedon Books, 2009).

Leeds United – The Complete European Record, Martin Jarred and Malcolm Macdonald (Breedon Books, 2003).

Look Back In Amber, David Goodman (Parrs Wood Press, 2005).

Marching On Together – My Life With Leeds United, by Eddie Gray & Jason Tomas (Headline, 2001).

Peter Lorimer – Leeds and Scotland Hero, Peter Lorimer and Phil Rostron (Mainstream Publishing, 2005).

Revie: Revered & Reviled, Richard Sutcliffe (Great Northern, 2010).

Rothmans Football Year Book, Jack Rollin & Leslie Vernon or Jack Rollin (Queen Anne Press & Headline, various years).

The Boys of '72, David Saffer (Tempus, 2005).

The FA Cup Final – A Post-War History, Ivan Ponting (Tony Williams Productions, 1993).

The Football Grounds of Great Britain, Simon Inglis (Willow Books, 1987).

The Last Fancy Dan, Duncan McKenzie with David Saffer (Vertical Editions, 2009).

The Leeds United Story, Martin Jarred and Malcolm Macdonald (Breedon Books, 2002).

The Second Most Important Job in the Country (Virgin Publishing, 2000).

The Unforgiven, Rob Bagchi & Paul Rogerson (Aurum Press, 2002).

LUCAS

From the Streets of Soweto to Soccer Superstar
The Authorised Biography of Lucas Radebe
by Richard Coomber

The South African international so captured the hearts of Leeds fans that they still chant his name years after he retired and the Kaiser Chiefs band took their name from his first club. In his native land he is an iconic figure, who led his country to two World Cups as they emerged from the sporting wilderness and whose reputation as a player and a man helped convince the rest of the world that the World Cup finals should go to South Africa.

This is the story of how Lucas overcame a tough childhood, survived a shooting, and refused to be diverted from his destiny by injury, homesickness, freezing English winters and terrible English food to become not only a football superstar but acknowledged as one of the nicest people in the game. Lucas Radebe's story is much more than just another biography of a footballer. It is inspiring and heart-warming, tinged with tragedy yet marked throughout by his trademark smile that has lit up two continents and touched thousands of lives.

The story of a man whom Nelson Mandela called "my hero".

★★★★★ Four Four Two Magazine

"A compelling insight into a Leeds Legend."
Henry Winter, Daily Telegraph

"This book is an absorbing and compelling account of Lucas'
inspirational story."
Anthony Clavane, Sunday Mirror

www.greatnorthernbooks.co.uk

Also available from Great Northern Books:

REVIE
Revered and Reviled
The Authorised Biography
by Richard Sutcliffe

Don Revie remains, more than two decades on from his untimely death at the age of just 61, one of football's most controversial and complex characters. After a playing career that brought plaudits and the prestigious Footballer of the Year award, Revie moved into management with Leeds United in 1961. By the time he left Elland Road to take charge of the England national team 13 years later, he had built one of the best teams English football had ever seen. Hailed as one of the most innovative managers of his generation, Revie was named England Manager of the Year in 1969, 70 and 72.

Yet despite winning two league titles, an FA Cup, two European trophies and a League Cup, Leeds were hated outside their own city. Later, he would be banned for 10 years by the FA for walking out on England to accept a lucrative job in the Middle East before tragically dying from motor neurone disease.

Through the eyes of those who knew him best - family, friends, team-mates, players, colleagues and even a member of the Royal Family - Revie....Revered and Reviled tells how a child born in Middlesbrough in the depression-hit 1920s rose to the very top as both a player and manager.

"Superb new book [that] benefits immensely from access to Revie's family, bringing colour to a figure often depicted in black and white. The best football biography of 2010"
Henry Winter, Daily Telegraph

"A brilliant book."
Daily Mirror

www.greatnorthernbooks.co.uk

MATTEO
In my Defence
The Autography of Dominic Matteo
written with Richard Sutcliffe

Dominic Matteo has played alongside some of English football's biggest names. He has also played at some of Europe's finest stadia, while he remains one of the few internationals to have appeared for both England and Scotland.

Here, Matteo charts the ups and downs of a career that began when he was spotted as a 10-year-old playing for his local boys' team by then Liverpool manager Kenny Dalglish. He went on to spend 15 years at Anfield, six of which were in the first-team where his team-mates included Ian Rush, Robbie Fowler, Steven Gerrard, Jamie Redknapp, Jamie Carragher, David James and Michael Owen.

Matteo then moved to Leeds United, a club who then seemed to be on the cusp of great things as David O'Leary's swashbuckling young side cut a swathe through the cream of Europe. Eighteen months after Matteo had been signed, Leeds had risen to the top of the Premier League only for the dream to quickly turn sour. Matteo was at Elland Road throughout the rise and fall that culminated in relegation, so has a unique insight into one of the most spectacular collapses in English football. He was the club captain as Leeds slid out of the Premier League and has strong views on just where it all went so badly wrong. Matteo went on to join Blackburn Rovers and then Stoke City before a serious back injury, which still troubles him today, brought a premature end to his career.

"Great player. Great book."
Robbie Fowler

www.greatnorthernbooks.co.uk